AMERICA IN LITERATURE

The Midwest

AMERICA IN LITERATURE

General Editor, Max Bogart

The Northeast, James Lape, editor
The South, Sara Marshall, editor
The West, Peter Monahan, editor
The Midwest, Ronald Szymanski, editor
The Small Town, Flory Jones Schultheiss, editor
The City, Adele Stern, editor

AMERICA IN LITERATURE

The Midwest

EDITED BY

Ronald Szymanski

Supervisor of English
Department of Elementary and Secondary Education
Milwaukee Public Schools

CHARLES SCRIBNER'S SONS • NEW YORK

Library of Congress Cataloging in Publication Data
Main entry under title:
America in literature: the Midwest
Includes index.
1. American literature—Middle West.
2. Middle West—Literary collections.
I. Szymanski, Ronald.
PS563.M49 810'.8'0977 79-4078
ISBN 0-684-16137-0

1 3 5 7 9 11 13 15 17 19 V/P 20 18 16 14 12 10 8 6 4 2

Printed in the United States of America

Cover Illustration: *Grey and Gold* by John Rogers Cox. Courtesy of the Cleveland Museum of Art, Mr. and Mrs. William H. Marlett Fund.

Picture Research: Yvonne Freund

ACKNOWLEDGMENTS

RUTH SUCKOW, "A Start in Life." From *Iowa Interiors* by Ruth Suckow. Copyright 1926 by Alfred A. Knopf, Inc. Copyright 1954 by Ruth Suckow Nuhn. Reprinted by permission of Holt, Rinehart and Winston, Publishers.

EDGAR LEE MASTERS, "Seth Compton," "William And Emily," "George Gray," and "Mrs. Charles Bliss." From *Spoon River Anthology*, 1931, Macmillan Publishing Co., Inc. Reprinted by permission of Ellen C. Masters.

SHERWOOD ANDERSON, "Sophistication." From *Winesburg, Ohio* by Sherwood Anderson.

Acknowledgments continue on page 233, an extension of the copyright page.

CONTENTS

AMERICA IN LITERATURE

The Midwest

Introduction

The Middle West is nowhere; an abstract nowhere. However earnestly writers proud of being natives of it may endeavor to give it form and character, it remains out of focus, amorphous, and a mystery. . . . What seems local is national, what seems national is universal, what seems Middle Western is in the commonest way human.—GLENWAY WESTCOTT, "GOOD-BYE, WISCONSIN"

The literary insights and outlooks of the American Midwest present a regional mosaic created by native writers from Ohio, Indiana, Illinois, Michigan, Wisconsin, Minnesota, Iowa, Nebraska, North Dakota, South Dakota, Missouri, and Kansas. Midwestern literature offers glimpses of a multi-landscaped environment: wilderness, agricultural, rural, industrial, urban. It reflects the region's vague sense of itself and points out the factors that make it so difficult to characterize: territorial vastness, mid-continental position, cultural diversity, nationalistic outlook. Midwestern writing exemplifies traits of character that have come to be identified particularly with this region: conservatism, conventionality, a competitive spirit, and a firm belief in democracy.

All of these factors and characteristics together produce a region of striking diversity—so much so that one wonders how the pioneers ever managed to establish permanent villages and towns with an identity and a sense of present and future. Two qualities customarily identified with the region undoubtedly played a great role. The first is the strong sense of egalitarianism, which came about as a result of economic parity, commonly shared living standards, and the frontier's absense of traditional aristocratic values. In other words, everyone was in the same boat, and knew it; it might almost be said that everyone liked it.

And the second cohesive element in the development of the Midwest is the strong sense of individualism for which the region is justly famous. In settling the vast midwestern expanse, the early pioneers exercised individ-

Fur Traders Descending the Missouri, George Caleb Bingham

ual judgment, initiative, and self-reliance—traits that in turn were fostered by the geography of the region. Later immigrants and settlers followed that tradition, choosing to work their own homesteads and cultivate their own lands, rather than join in any collective effort. During the territorial expansion of the later nineteenth century and the tremendous increase in the emigrant population (as recorded by Ole Rölvaag in *Giants in the Earth*), midwestern towns and cities grew apace. Industrial centers gradually became part of the landscape. The spirit of individualism was greatly influenced by the spread of urbanism and all that attended it: specialization, conformity, and de-personalization. The region thus entered the modern age.

Midwestern literature presents characters of mobility and a great sense of restlessness—and not without reason. Novels and short stories about the pioneer experience recorded feelings of uprootedness and uncertainty among migrants and immigrants on the frontier. The restlessness was inevitable. The pioneers realized that in the movement westward they had severed ties with established ways and traditions—they knew, too, that such constant change and uncertainty were necessary preconditions for the fashioning of their new, secure lives. Fictional accounts of country and small-town life at the turn of the century portrayed central characters departing for the city, sometimes only to discover the corrupting effects of a materialistic and moralistic society—Dreiser's *Sister Carrie* is a fine example. During the 1920s, writers of expatriate fiction such as Ernest Hemingway and F. Scott Fitzgerald suggested the rootlessness as well as the insecurity and moral chaos which occurred as the aftermath of World War I. In addition, the migration of cultural minorities toward the central midwest, cityward, and to the great industrial centers, was described in ethnic literature by writers like Harry Mark Petrakis and James T. Farrell.

Midwestern writers of the late nineteenth and early twentieth centuries helped usher in a whole new era in American literature. They rejected the established literary *romanticism* of the day, turning instead toward a new *realism*. In so doing they developed a new literary perspective based not on the imaginative and the ideal but on the real, the actual. They strove to create vivid images and characters, but took them from their perceptions of reality and the world around them, not from the imagination and the operations of fantasy. Wanting to represent truth, realists like Hamlin Garland, Willa Cather, Edgar Lee Masters, Sherwood Anderson, Carl Sandburg, Sinclair Lewis, and Ruth Suckow concentrated on normative human experience. They maintained an objective view of human nature, a view that allowed for the fullest examination of motivation and psychological makeup. Their objectivity, however, did not prevent them from taking a stand; as moralists, they wrote of and for ordinary people in language dominated by acute social consciousness. Many, like Hamlin Garland and Ruth Suckow, were authentic regionalists who showed their loyalty to the distinctive local patterns of life most familiar to them. They used the informal, colloquial speech of the people, and attempted an artistic but accurate rendering of mid-American speech.

There were also such writers as Theodore Dreiser, James T. Farrell and Richard Wright, for whom the recording of the commonplace involved the discovery of the extraordinary and excessive in the routine of daily existence. With clinical objectivity, these literary naturalists wrote of poverty and misery, of the "survival of the fittest," and of the uneducated or unsophisticated—characters victimized by hereditary and environmental forces. Their fiction was essentially realism infused with a measured pessimism. Contemporary authors including Harry Mark Petrakis and Gwendolyn Brooks have continued in the realistic tradition, producing literature close to life and reflecting their immediate social milieu.

The realistic tradition in midwestern literature has produced unique and gifted writers. Willa Cather was particularly distinguished as a stylist known for her selection of the exact word, her succinctness, and her success in creating scenes drawn from the rural Midwest. In the rhythmic free verse of his famous *Chicago Poems,* Carl Sandburg expressed his commitment to the vernacular of the laboring class in his concrete descriptions of the urban landscape. Ernest Hemingway created novels and short fiction in a terse and repetitive style noted for its objectivity, colloquial language, and extensive use of dialogue. More recently, Kurt Vonnegut, Jr., has used elements like black humor and stream of consciousness to convey with critical realism a new environ or kind of character.

The midwestern literary tradition is largely a realistic one. The writers represented in this volume have taken the commonplace and have made it durable, provocative literary material. This is the real achievement of midwestern literature, and its main accomplishment: it verified and authenticated the American experience not through fantasy and the romanticized re-creation of great people and events, but by examining the patterns and motions of everyday human lives. The result is fiction as rich and varied as the human imagination.

Environments and Attitudes

Writers native to the Midwest captured the physical appearance of various environments and used these images to evoke a mood or reveal an attitude. Theme and motif also emerged from the relationship between character and setting.

Regionalists of farm literature represented country life by writing about the pioneer venture, the adjustment to seasonal changes and the sense of fulfillment experienced in working the land. Most important, they attempted to record beliefs and sentiments associated with agricultural midwesterners, namely: conservatism, individualism, anti-intellectualism, and primitivism. Some of these literary ruralists described people who appeared to adjust positively to the farm environment. Others, like Ruth Suckow in the fictional collection *Iowa Interiors,* recreated with lyric quality a rural America from which pioneer zest had long since vanished, leaving a vacuum of endless chores, loneliness and fear. In "A Start in Life," for example, Suckow used natural conditions to provide a metaphor for the cold, unsympathetic world, and the interiors of homes to symbolize the interiors of the human heart.

Small towns, too, were one of the environments revealed by regionalists from the Midwest. Prior to the twentieth century, writers tended to idealize these villages as communities of neighborliness, economic well-being, unspoiled innocence and purest democracy. By the second decade of the twentieth century, however, realists identified with the "revolt from the village" movement began to treat socially and intellectually limiting aspects of small-town life, including mediocrity, meanness, hypocrisy, narrow prejudice and self-righteous morality. Written as a series of free-verse

July Hay, Thomas Hart Benton

monologues spoken by those buried in the local cemetery, Edgar Lee Masters' *Spoon River Anthology* characterized a community of inhabitants whose confessions revealed vital, frustrated, or defeated lives. The psychic realism with which Sherwood Anderson dramatized village life in the short-story collection *Winesburg, Ohio* produced an atmosphere of alienation, of emotional and spiritual poverty. He evolved the concept of the "grotesque" in order to portray maladjusted and repressed townspeople longing for release from their own timidity and from the stifling conventions of their time and place. Because these grotesques were unable to communicate with one another, they moved toward, or were driven toward, George Willard—the young newspaper reporter who appeared normal. "Sophistication," the climactic narrative of Anderson's masterpiece, described George and Helen White drawn together by a shared awareness of growing maturity and by a need to be understood and to love and be loved. The story illustrated George's victory over self-consciousness and self-pity through the recognition of time and death.

Several midwestern writers also made significant attempts to reflect their cultural and emotional ties with the city and to chronicle the impact of industrialism. Cityscape novelists and short-story writers depicted the urban environment's influence upon the protagonist's character and destiny, or revealed the social milieu and distinct urban types within a specific city block or neighborhood. Theodore Dreiser in the novel *Sister Carrie*, for example, presented his principal character caught up in a confusing maze of distorted aims and values. To urban poets, too, the city was seen in opposing ways. Carl Sandburg affirmed a democratic metropolis bearing the character of robustness, technology and discipline, whereas Philip Levine documented signs of industrial ugliness and blight, and Theodore Roethke expressed the frightening implications of its impersonal, mechanical society.

To still other literary figures reared in the Midwest, land in its natural state was viewed as inspirational or spiritually renewing.

Through "Moss-Gathering" and "A Blessing," poets Theodore Roethke and James Wright conveyed man's relationship with flora and fauna as part of his attitude toward nature. For Ernest Hemingway, the Michigan woods and lake country provided a place of restoration from some of the less pleasant realities of existence, including the complexities of human relationships. The region served as the background for several episodes in the fictional life of Nick Adams, Hemingway's semi-autobiographical hero. In "The Three-Day Blow," which appeared in the short-story volume *In Our Time*, the author used the image of an autumnal wind storm to illuminate the human disharmony in Nick caused by the end of his romance with a girl named Marjorie. A story of initiation into young adulthood, it explored the theme of loss and resultant melancholy. The narrative's psychological penetration and its skillful representation of conversation made it one of Hemingway's richest and most artistic.

A Start in Life

RUTH SUCKOW

The Switzers were scurrying around to get Daisy ready by the time that Elmer Kruse should get through in town. They had known all week that Elmer might be in for her any day. But they hadn't done a thing until he appeared. "Oh, it was so rainy today, the roads were so muddy, they hadn't thought he'd get in until maybe next week." It would have been the same any other day.

Mrs. Switzer was trying now at the last moment to get all of Daisy's things into the battered telescope that lay open on the bed. The bed had not "got made"; and just as soon as Daisy was gone, Mrs. Switzer would have to hurry off to the Woodworths' where she was to wash today. Daisy's things were scattered over the dark brown quilt and the rumpled sheet that were dingy and clammy in this damp weather. So was the whole bedroom, with its sloping ceiling and old-fashioned square-paned windows, the commode that they used for a dresser, littered with pin tray, curlers, broken comb, ribbons, smoky lamp, all mixed up together; the door of the closet open, showing the confusion of clothes and shabby shoes. . . . They all slept in this room—Mrs. Switzer and Dwight in the bed, the two girls in the cot against the wall.

"Mamma, I can't find the belt to that plaid dress."

"Oh, ain't it somewheres around? Well, I guess you'll have to let it go. If I come across it I can send it out to you. Someone'll be going past there."

She had meant to get Daisy all mended and "fixed up" before she went out to the country. But somehow . . . oh, there was always so much to see to when she came home. Gone all day, washing and cleaning for other people; it didn't leave her much time for her own house.

She was late now. The Woodworths liked to have her get the washing out early so that she could do some cleaning too before she left. But she couldn't help it. She would have to get Daisy off first. She had already had on her wraps ready to go, when Elmer came—her cleaning cap, of a blue faded almost into gray, and the ancient black coat with gathered sleeves that she wore over her work dress when she went out to wash.

"What's become of all your underclothes? They ain't all dirty, are they?"

"They are, too. You didn't wash for us last week, mamma."

"Well, you'll just have to take along what you've got. Maybe there'll be some way of getting the rest to you."

"Elmers come in every week, don't they?" Daisy demanded.

"Yes, but maybe they won't always be bringing you in."

She jammed what she could into the telescope, thinking with her helpless, anxious fatalism that it would have to do somehow.

"Daisy, you get yourself ready now."

"I am ready. Mamma, I want to put on my other ribbon."

"Oh, that's way down in the telescope somewhere. You needn't be so anxious to fix yourself up. This ain't like going visiting."

Daisy stood at the little mirror preening herself—such a homely child, "all Switzer," skinny, with pale sharp eyes set close together and thin, stringy, reddish hair. But she had never really learned yet how homely she was. She was the oldest, and she got the pick of what clothes were given to the Switzers. Goldie and Dwight envied her. She was important in her small world. She was proud of her blue coat that had belonged to Alice Brooker, the town lawyer's daughter. It hung unevenly about her bony little knees, and the buttons came down too far. Her mother had tried to make it over for her.

Mrs. Switzer looked at her, troubled, but not knowing how she could tell her all the things she ought to be told. Daisy had never been away before except to go to her Uncle Fred's at Lehigh. She seemed to think that this would be the same. She had so many things to learn. Well, she would find them out soon enough—only too soon. Working for other people—she would learn what that meant. Elmer and Edna Kruse were nice young people. They would mean well enough by Daisy. It was a good chance for her to start in. But it wasn't the same.

Daisy was so proud. She thought it was quite a thing to be "starting in to earn." She thought she could buy herself so much with that dollar and a half a week. The other children stood back watching her, round-eyed and impressed. They wished that they were going away, like Daisy.

They heard a car come splashing through the mud in low.

"There he is back! Have you got your things on? Goldie—go out and tell him she's coming."

"No, me tell him, me!" Dwight shouted jealously.

"Well—both of you tell him. Land! . . ."

She tried hastily to put on the cover of the bulging telescope and to fasten the straps. One of them broke.

"Well, you'll have to take it the way it is."

It was an old thing, hadn't been used since her husband, Mert, had "left off canvassing" before he died. And he had worn it all to pieces.

"Well, I guess you'll have to go now. He won't want to wait. I'll try and send you out what you ain't got with you." She turned to Daisy. Her face was working. There was nothing else to do, as everyone said. Daisy would have to help, and she might as well learn it now. Only, she hated to see Daisy go off, to have her starting in. She knew what it meant. "Well—you try and work good this summer, so they'll want you to stay. I hope they'll bring you in sometimes."

Daisy's homely little face grew pale with awe, suddenly, at the sight of her mother crying, at something that she dimly sensed in the pressure of her mother's thin strong arms. Her vanity in her new importance was somehow shamed and dampened.

Elmer's big new Buick, mud-splashed but imposing, stood tilted on the uneven road. Mud was thick on the wheels. It was a bad day for driving, with the roads a yellow mass, water lying in all the wheel ruts. This little road that led past these few houses on the outskirts of town, and up over the hill, had a cold rainy loneliness. Elmer sat in the front seat of the Buick, and in the back was a big box of groceries.

"Got room to sit in there?" he asked genially. "I didn't get out, it's so muddy here!"

"No, don't get out," Mrs. Switzer said hastily. "She can put this right on the floor there in the back." She added, with a timid attempt at courtesy, "Ain't the roads pretty bad out that way?"

"Yes, but farmers get so they don't think so much about the roads."

"I s'pose that's so."

He saw the signs of tears on Mrs. Switzer's face, and they made him anxious to get away. She embraced Daisy hastily again. Daisy climbed over the grocery box and scrunched herself into the seat.

"I guess you'll bring her in with you some time when you're coming," Mrs. Switzer hinted.

"Sure. We'll bring her."

He started the engine. It roared, half died down as the wheels of the car spun in the thick wet mud.

In that moment, Daisy had a startled view of home—the small house standing on a rough rise of land, weathered to a dim color that showed dark streaks from the rain; the narrow sloping front porch whose edge had a soaked gnawed look; the chickens, greyish-black, pecking at the wet ground; their playthings, stones, a wagon, some old pail covers littered about; a soaked discolored piece of underwear hanging on the line in the back yard. The yard was tussocky and overhung the road with shaggy long grass where the yellow bank was caved in under it. Goldie and Dwight were gazing at her solemnly. She saw her mother's face—a thin, weak, loving face, drawn with neglected weeping, with its reddened eyes and poor teeth . . . in the old coat and heavy shoes and cleaning cap, her work-worn hand with its big knuckles clutching at her coat. She saw the playthings they had used yesterday, and the old swing that hung from one of the trees, the ropes sodden, the seat in crooked. . . .

The car went off, slipping on the wet clay. She waved frantically, suddenly understanding that she was leaving them. They waved at her.

Mrs. Switzer stood there a little while. Then came the harsh rasp of the old black iron pump that stood out under the box-elder tree. She was pumping water to leave for the children before she went off to work.

II

Daisy held on as the car skidded going down the short clay hill. Elmer didn't bother with chains. He was too used to the roads. But her eyes brightened with scared excitement. When they were down, and Elmer slowed up going along the tracks in the deep wet grass that led to the main road, she looked back, holding on her hat with her small scrawny hand.

Just down this little hill—and home was gone. The big car, the feel of her telescope under her feet, the fact that she was going out to the country, changed the looks of everything. She saw it all now.

Dunkels' house stood on one side of the road. A closed-up white house. The windows stared blank and cold between the old shutters. There was a chair with a broken straw seat under the fruit trees. The Dunkels were old

Catholic people who seldom went anywhere. In the front yard was a clump of tall pines, the rough brown trunks wet, the green branches, dark and shining, heavy with rain, the ground underneath mournfully sodden and black.

The pasture on the other side. The green grass, lush, wet and cold, and the outcroppings of limestone that held little pools of rainwater in all the tiny holes. Beyond, the low hills gloomy with timber against the lowering sky.

They slid out on to the main road. They bumped over the small wooden bridge above the swollen creek that came from the pasture. Daisy looked down. She saw the little swirls of foam, the long grass that swished with the water, the old rusted tin cans lodged between the rocks.

She sat up straight and important, her thin, homely little face strained with excitement, her sharp eyes taking in everything. The watery mudholes in the road, the little thickets of plum-trees, low and wet, in dark interlacings. She held on fiercely, but made no sound when the car skidded.

She felt the grandeur of having a ride. One wet Sunday, Mr. Brooker had driven them all home from church, she and Goldie and Dwight packed tightly into the back seat of the car, shut in by the side curtains against which the rain lashed, catching the muddy scent of the roads. Sometimes they could plan to go to town just when Mr. Pattey was going to work in his Ford. Then they would run out and shout eagerly, "Mr. Pattey! Are you going through town?" Sometimes he didn't hear them. Sometimes he said, with curt good nature, "Well, pile in"; and they all hopped into the truck back. "He says we can go along with him."

She looked at the black wet fields through which little leaves of bright green corn grew in rows, at showery bushes of sumac along the roadside. A gasoline engine pumping water made a loud desolate sound. There were somber-looking cattle in the wet grass, and lonely, thick-foliaged trees growing here and there in the pastures. She felt her telescope on the floor of the car, the box of groceries beside her. She eyed these with a sharp curiosity. There was a fresh pineapple—something the Switzers didn't often get at home. She wondered if Edna would have it for dinner. Maybe she could hint a little to Edna.

She was out in the country. She could no longer see her house even if she wanted to—standing dingy, streaked with rain, in its rough grass on the little hill. A lump came into her throat. She had looked forward to playing with Edna's children. But Goldie and Dwight would play all morning without her. She was still proud of her being the oldest, of going out with Elmer and Edna; but now there was a forlornness in the pride.

She wished she were in the front seat with Elmer. She didn't see why he hadn't put her there. She would have liked to know who all the people were who lived on these farms; how old Elmer's babies were; and if he and Edna always went to the movies when they went into town on Saturday nights. Elmer must have lots of money to buy a car like this. He had a new house on his farm, too, and Mrs. Metzinger had said that it had plumbing. Maybe they would take her to the movies, too. She might hint about that.

When she had gone to visit Uncle Fred, she had had to go on the train. She liked this better. She hoped they had a long way to go. She called out to Elmer:

"Say, how much farther is your place?"

"What's that?" He turned around. "Oh, just down the road a ways. Scared to drive in the mud?"

"No, I ain't scared. I like to drive most any way."

She looked at Elmer's back, the old felt hat crammed down carelessly on his head, the back of his neck with the golden hair on the sunburned skin above the blue of his shirt collar. Strong and easy and slouched a little over the steering wheel that he handled so masterfully. Elmer and Edna were just young folks; but Mrs. Metzinger said that they had more to start with than most young farmers did, and that they were hustlers. Daisy felt that the pride of this belonged to her too, now.

"Here we are!"

"Oh, is this where you folks live?" Daisy cried eagerly.

The house stood back from the road beyond a space of bare yard with a little scattering of grass just starting—small, modern, painted a bright new white and yellow. The barn was new too, a big splendid barn of frescoed brick, with a silo of the same. There were no trees. A raw desolate wind blew across the back yard as they drove up beside the back door.

Edna had come out on the step. Elmer grinned at her as he took out the box of groceries, and she slightly raised her eyebrows. She said kindly enough:

"Well, you brought Daisy. Hello, Daisy, are you going to stay with us this summer?"

"I guess so," Daisy said importantly. But she suddenly felt a little shy and forlorn as she got out of the car and stood on the bare ground in the chilly wind.

"Yes, I brought her along," Elmer said.

"Are the roads very bad?"

"Kind of bad. Why?"

"Well, I'd like to get over to mamma's some time today."

"Oh, I guess they aren't too bad for that."

Daisy pricked up her sharp little ears. Another ride. That cheered her.

"Look in the door," Edna said in a low fond voice, motioning with her head.

Two little round, blond heads were pressed tightly against the screen door. There was a clamor of "Daddy, daddy!" Elmer grinned with a half bashful pride as he stood with the box of groceries, raising his eyebrows with mock surprise and demanding: "Who's this? What you shoutin' 'daddy' for? You don't think daddy's got anything for you, do you?" He and Edna were going into the kitchen together until Edna remembered and called back hastily:

"Oh, come in, Daisy!"

Daisy stood, a little left out and solitary, there in the kitchen, as Billy, the older of the babies, climbed frantically over Elmer, demanding candy, and the little one toddled smilingly about. Her eyes took in all of it. She was impressed by the shining blue-and-white linoleum, the range with its nickel and enamel, the bright new woodwork. Edna was laughing and scolding at Elmer and the baby. Billy had made his father produce the candy. Daisy's sharp little eyes looked hungrily at the lemon drops until Edna remembered her.

"Give Daisy a piece of your candy," she said.

He would not go up to Daisy. She had to come forward and take one of the lemon drops herself. She saw where Edna put the sack, in a dish high in the cupboard. She hoped they would get some more before long.

"My telescope's out there in the car," she reminded them.

"Oh! Elmer, you go and get it and take it up for her," Edna said.

"What?"

"Her valise—or whatever it is—out in the car."

"Oh, sure," Elmer said with a cheerful grin.

"It's kind of an old telescope," Daisy said conversationally. "I guess it's been used a lot. My papa used to have it. The strap broke when mamma was fastening it this morning. We ain't got any suitcase. I had to take this because it was all there was in the house, and mamma didn't want to get me a new one."

Edna raised her eyebrows politely. She leaned over and pretended to spat the baby as he came toddling up to her, then rubbed her cheek against his round head with its funny fuzz of hair.

Daisy watched solemnly. "I didn't know both of your children was boys. I thought one of 'em was a girl. That's what there is at home now—one boy and one girl."

"Um-hm," Edna replied absently. "You can go up with Elmer and take off your things, Daisy," she said. "You can stop and unpack your valise now, I guess, if you'd like to. Then you can come down and help me in the kitchen. You know we got you to help me," she reminded.

Daisy, subdued, followed Elmer up the bright new stairs. In the upper hall, two strips of very clean rag rug were laid over the shining yellow of the floor. Elmer had put her telescope in one of the bedrooms.

"There you are!"

She heard him go clattering down the stairs, and then a kind of murmuring and laughing in the kitchen. The back door slammed. She hurried to the window in time to see Elmer go striding off toward the barn.

She looked about her room with intense curiosity. It too had a bright varnished floor. She had a bed all of her own—a small, old-fashioned bed, left from some old furnishings, that had been put in this room that had the pipes and the hot-water tank. She had to see everything, but she had a stealthy look as she tiptoed about, started to open drawers of the dresser, looked out of her window. She put her coat and hat on the bed. She would rather be down in the kitchen with Edna than unpack her telescope now.

She guessed she would go down where the rest of them were.

III

Elmer came into the house for dinner. He brought in a cold, muddy, outdoor breath with him. The range was going, but the bright little kitchen seemed chilly, with the white oilcloth on the table, the baby's varnished high chair and his little fat, mottled hands.

Edna made a significant little face at Elmer. Daisy did not see. She was standing back from the stove, where Edna was at work, looking at the baby.

"He can talk pretty good, can't he? Dwight couldn't say anything but 'mamma' when he was that little."

Edna's back was turned. She said meaningly:

"Now, Elmer's come in to dinner, Daisy, we'll have to hurry. You must help me get on the dinner. You can cut bread and get things on the table. You must help, you know. That's what you are supposed to do."

Daisy looked startled, a little scared and resentful. "Well, I don't know where you keep your bread."

"Don't you remember where I told you to put it this morning? Right over in the cabinet, in that big box. You must watch, Daisy, and learn where things are."

Elmer, a little embarrassed at the look that Edna gave him, whistled as he began to wash his hands at the sink.

"How's daddy's old boy?" he said loudly, giving a poke at the baby's chin.

As Edna passed him, she shook her head, and her lips just formed: "Been like that all morning!"

He grinned comprehendingly. Then both their faces became expressionless.

Daisy had not exactly heard, but she looked from one to the other, silent and dimly wondering. The queer ache that had kept starting all through the morning, under her interest in Edna's things and doings, came over her again. She sensed something different in the atmosphere than she had ever known before—some queer difference between the position of herself and of the two babies, a faint notion of what mamma had meant when she had said that this would not be visiting.

"I guess I'm going to have the toothache again," she said faintly.

No one seemed to hear her.

Edna whisked off the potatoes, drained the water. . . . "You might bring me a dish, Daisy." Daisy searched a long time while Edna turned impatiently and pointed. Edna put the rest of the things on the table herself. Her young, fresh, capable mouth was tightly closed, and she was making certain resolutions.

Daisy stood hesitating in the middle of the room, a scrawny, unappealing figure. Billy—fat, blond, in funny, dark blue union-alls—was trotting busily about the kitchen. Daisy swooped down upon him and tried to bring him to the table. He set up a howl. Edna turned, looked astonished, severe.

"I was trying to make him come to the table," Daisy explained weakly.

"You scared him. He isn't used to you. He doesn't like it. Don't cry, Billy. The girl didn't mean anything."

"Here, daddy'll put him in his place," Elmer said hastily.

Billy looked over his father's shoulder at Daisy with suffused, resentful blue eyes. She did not understand it, and felt strangely at a loss. She had been left with Goldie and Dwight so often. She had always made Dwight go to the table. She had been the boss.

Edna said in a cool, held-in voice, "Put these things on the table, Daisy."

They sat down. Daisy and the other children had always felt it a great treat to eat away from home instead of at their own scanty, hastily set table. They had hung around Mrs. Metzinger's house at noon, hoping to be asked to stay, not offended when told that "it was time for them to run off now." Her pinched little face had a hungry look as she stared at the potatoes and fried ham and pie. But they did not watch and urge her to have more, as Mrs. Metzinger did, and Mrs. Brooker when she took pity on the Switzers and had them there. Daisy wanted more pie. But none of them seemed to be taking more, and so she said nothing. She remembered what her mother had said, with now a faint comprehension: "You must remember you're out working for other folks, and it won't be like it is at home."

After dinner, Edna said: "Now you can wash the dishes, Daisy."

She went into the next room with the children. Daisy, as she went hesitatingly about the kitchen alone, could hear Edna's low contented humming as she sat in there rocking, the baby in her lap. The bright kitchen was empty and lonely now. Through the window, Daisy could see the great barn looming up against the rainy sky. She hoped that they would drive to Edna's mother's soon.

She finished as soon as she could, and went into the dining room, where Edna was sewing on the baby's rompers. Edna went on sewing. Daisy sat down disconsolately. That queer low ache went all through her. She said in a small dismal voice:

"I guess I got the toothache again."

Edna bit off a thread.

"I had it awful hard a while ago. Mamma come pretty near taking me to the dentist."

"That's too bad," Edna murmured politely. But she offered no other condolence. She gave a secret little smile at the baby asleep on a blanket and a pillow in one corner of the shiny leather davenport.

"Is Elmer going to drive into town tomorrow?"

"Tomorrow? I don't suppose so."

"Mamma couldn't find the belt of my plaid dress and I thought if he was, maybe I could go along and get it. I'd like to have it."

Daisy's homely mouth drooped at the corners. Her toothache did not seem to matter to anyone. Edna did not seem to want to see that anything was wrong with her. She had expected Edna to be concerned, to mention remedies. But it wasn't a toothache, that strange lonesome ache all over her. Maybe she was going to be terribly sick. Mamma wouldn't come home for supper to be told about it.

She saw mamma's face as in that last glimpse of it—drawn with crying, and yet trying to smile, under the old cleaning cap, her hand holding her coat together. . . .

Edna glanced quickly at her. The child was so mortally unattractive, unappealing even in her forlornness. Edna frowned a little, but said kindly:

"Now, you might take Billy into the kitchen out of my way, Daisy, and amuse him."

"Well, he cries when I pick him up," Daisy said faintly.

"He won't cry this time. Take him out and help him play with his blocks. You must help me with the children, you know."

"Well, if he'll go with me."

"He'll go with you, won't he, Billy boy? Won't you go with Daisy, sweetheart?"

Billy stared and then nodded. Daisy felt a thrill of comfort as Billy put his little fat hand in hers and trotted into the kitchen beside her. He had the fattest hands, she thought. Edna brought the blocks and put the box down on the floor beside Daisy.

"Now, see if you can amuse him so that I can get my sewing done."

"Shall you and me play blocks, Billy?" Daisy murmured.

He nodded. Then he got hold of the box with one hand, tipped out all the blocks on the floor with a bang and a rattle, and looked at her with a pleased proud smile.

"Oh, no, Billy, You mustn't spill out the blocks. Look, you're too little to play with them. No, now—now wait! Let Daisy show you. Daisy'll build something real nice—shall she?"

He gave a solemn nod of consent.

Daisy set out the blocks on the bright linoleum. She had never had such blocks as these to handle before. Dwight's were only a few old, unmatched, broken ones. Her spirit of leadership came back, and she firmly put away that fat hand of Billy's whenever he meddled with her building. She could make something really wonderful with these blocks.

"No, Billy, you mustn't. See, when Daisy's got it all done, then you can see what the lovely building is."

She put the blocks together with great interest.

She knew what she was going to make—it was going to be a new house; now, a new church. Just as she got the walls up, in came that little hand again, and then with a delighted grunt Billy swept the blocks pell-mell about the floor. At the clatter, he sat back, pursing up his mouth to give an ecstatic "Ooh!"

"Oh, Billy—you musn't, the building wasn't done! Look, you've spoiled it. Now you've got to sit 'way off here while I try to build it over again."

Bill's look of triumph turned to surprise and then to vociferous protest as Daisy picked him up and firmly transplanted him to another corner of the room. He set up a tremendous howl. He had never been set aside like that before. Edna came hurrying out. Daisy looked at Edna for justification, but instinctively on the defensive.

"Billy knocked over the blocks. He spoiled the building."

"Wah! Wah!" Billy gave loud heartbroken sobs. The tears ran down his fat cheeks and he held out his arms piteously toward his mother.

"I didn't hurt him," Daisy said, scared.

"Never mind, lover," Edna was crooning. "Of course he can play with his blocks. They're Billy's blocks, Daisy," she said. "He doesn't like to sit and see you put up buildings. He wants to play, too. See, you've made him cry now."

"Do' wanna stay here," Billy wailed.

"Well, come in with mother then." She picked him up, wiping his tears.

"I didn't hurt him," Daisy protested.

"Well, never mind now. You can pick up the blocks and then sweep the floor, Daisy. You didn't do that when you finished the dishes. Never mind," she was saying to Billy. "Pretty soon daddy'll come in and we'll have a nice ride."

Daisy soberly picked up the blocks and got the broom. What had she done to Billy? He had tried to spoil her building. She always made Dwight keep back until she had finished. Of course it was Daisy, the oldest, who should lead and manage. There had been no one to hear her side. Everything was different. She winked back tears as she swept, poorly and carelessly.

Then she brightened up as Elmer came tramping up on the back porch and then through the kitchen.

"Edna!"

"She's in there," Daisy offered.

"Want to go now? What! Is the baby asleep?" he asked blankly.

Edna gave him a warning look and the door was closed.

Daisy listened hard. She swept very softly. She could catch only a little of what they said—"Kind of hate to go off . . . I know, but if we once start . . . not a thing all day . . . what we got her for . . ." She had no real comprehension of it. She hurried and put away the broom. She wanted to be sure and be ready to go.

Elmer tramped out, straight past her. She saw from the window that he was backing the car out from the shed. She could hear Edna and Billy upstairs, could hear the baby cry a little as he was wakened. Maybe she ought to go out and get on her wraps, too.

Elmer honked the horn. A moment later Edna came hurrying downstairs, in her hat and coat, and Billy in a knitted cap and red sweater crammed over his union-alls, so that he looked like a little brownie. The baby had his little coat, too.

Edna called out: "Come in and get this boy, daddy." She did not look at Daisy, but said hurriedly: "We're going for a little ride, Daisy. Have you finished the sweeping? Well, then, you can pick up those pieces in the dining room. We won't be gone so very long. When it's a quarter past five, you start the fire, like I showed you this noon, and slice the potatoes that were left, and the meat. And set the table."

The horn was honked again.

"Yes! Well, we'll be back, Daisy. Come, lover, daddy's in a hurry."

Daisy stood looking after them. Billy clamored to sit beside his daddy. Edna took the baby from Elmer and put him beside her on the back seat. There was room—half of the big back seat. There wasn't anything, really to be done at home. That was the worst of it. They just didn't want to take her. They all belonged together. They didn't want to take anyone else along. She was an outsider. They all—even the baby—had a freshened look of expectancy.

The engine roared—they had started; slipping on the mud of the drive, then forging straight ahead, around the turn, out of sight.

IV

She went forlornly into the dining room. The light from the windows was dim now in the rainy, late afternoon. The pink pieces from the baby's rompers were scattered over the gay rug. She got down on her hands and knees, slowly picking them up, sniffing a little. She heard the Big Ben clock in the kitchen ticking loudly.

That dreadful ache submerged her. No one would ask about it, no one would try to comfort her. Before, there had always been mamma coming home, anxious, scolding sometimes, but worried over them if they didn't feel right, caring about them. Mamma and Goldie and Dwight cared about her—but she was away out in the country, and they were at home. She didn't want to stay here, where she didn't belong. But mamma had told her that she must begin helping this summer.

Her ugly little mouth contorted into a grimace of weeping. But silent weeping, without any tears; because she already had the cold knowledge that no one would notice or comfort it.

FROM *Spoon River Anthology*

EDGAR LEE MASTERS

SETH COMPTON

When I died, the circulating library
Which I built up for Spoon River,
And managed for the good of inquiring minds,
Was sold at auction on the public square,
As if to destroy the last vestige
Of my memory and influence.
For those of you who could not see the virtue
Of knowing Volney's "Ruins" as well as Butler's "Analogy"
And "Faust" as well as "Evangeline,"
Were really the power in the village,
And often you asked me,
"What is the use of knowing the evil in the world?"
I am out of your way now, Spoon River,
Choose your own good and call it good.
For I could never make you see
That no one knows what is good
Who knows not what is evil;
And no one knows what is true
Who knows not what is false.

WILLIAM AND EMILY

There is something about Death
Like love itself!
If with some one with whom you have known passion,
And the glow of youthful love,
You also, after years of life
Together, feel the sinking of the fire,
And thus fade away together,
Gradually, faintly, delicately,
As it were in each other's arms,
Passing from the familiar room—
That is a power of unison between souls
Like love itself!

IN
ELIZABETH
OF
JOSHUA FLEET

GEORGE GRAY

I have studied many times
The marble which was chiseled for me—
A boat with a furled sail at rest in a harbor.
In truth it pictures not my destination
But my life.
For love was offered me and I shrank from its disillusionment;
Sorrow knocked at my door, but I was afraid;
Ambition called to me, but I dreaded the chances.
Yet all the while I hungered for meaning in my life.
And now I know that we must lift the sail
And catch the winds of destiny
Wherever they drive the boat.
To put meaning in one's life may end in madness,
But life without meaning is the torture
Of restlessness and vague desire—
It is a boat longing for the sea and yet afraid.

MRS. CHARLES BLISS

Reverend Wiley advised me not to divorce him
For the sake of the children,
And Judge Somers advised him the same.
So we stuck to the end of the path.
But two of the children thought he was right,
And two of the children thought I was right.
And the two who sided with him blamed me,
And the two who sided with me blamed him,
And they grieved for the one they sided with.
And all were torn with the guilt of judging,
And tortured in soul because they could not admire
Equally him and me.
Now every gardener knows that plants grown in cellars
Or under stones are twisted and yellow and weak.
And no mother would let her baby suck
Diseased milk from her breast.
Yet preachers and judges advise the raising of souls
Where there is no sunlight, but only twilight,
No warmth, but only dampness and cold—
Preachers and judges!

Sophistication

SHERWOOD ANDERSON

It was early evening of a day in the late fall and the Winesburg County Fair had brought crowds of country people into town. The day had been clear, and the night came on warm and pleasant. On the Trunion Pike, where the road after it left town stretched away between berry fields now covered with dry brown leaves, the dust from passing wagons arose in clouds. Children, curled into little balls, slept on the straw scattered on wagon beds. Their hair was full of dust and their fingers black and sticky. The dust rolled away over the fields and the departing sun set it ablaze with colors.

In the main street of Winesburg crowds filled the stores and the sidewalks. Night came on, horses whinnied, the clerks in the stores ran madly about, children became lost and cried lustily, an American town worked terribly at the task of amusing itself.

Pushing his way through the crowds in Main Street, young George Willard concealed himself in the stairway leading to Doctor Reefy's office and looked at the people. With feverish eyes he watched the faces drifting past under the store lights. Thoughts kept coming into his head and he did not want to think. He stamped impatiently on the wooden steps and looked sharply about. "Well, is she going to stay with him all day? Have I done all this waiting for nothing?" he muttered.

George Willard, the Ohio village boy, was fast growing into manhood and new thoughts had been coming into his mind. All that day, amid the jam of people at the Fair, he had gone about feeling lonely. He was about to leave Winesburg to go away to some city where he hoped to get work on a city newspaper, and he felt grown up. The mood that had taken possession of him was a thing known to men and unknown to boys. He felt old and a little tired. Memories awoke in him. To his mind his new sense of maturity set him apart, made of him a half-tragic figure. He wanted someone to un-

derstand the feeling that had taken possession of him after his mother's death.

There is a time in the life of every boy when he for the first time takes the backward view of life. Perhaps that is the moment when he crosses the line into manhood. The boy is walking through the street of his town. He is thinking of the future and of the figure he will cut in the world. Ambitions and regrets awake within him. Suddenly something happens; he stops under a tree and waits as for a voice calling his name. Ghosts of old things creep into his consciousness; the voices outside of himself whisper a message concerning the limitations of life. From being quite sure of himself and his future he becomes not at all sure. If he be an imaginative boy a door is torn open and for the first time he looks out upon the world, seeing, as though they marched in procession before him, the countless figures of men who before his time have come out of nothingness into the world, lived their lives and again disappeared into nothingness. The sadness of sophistication has come to the boy. With a little gasp he sees himself as merely a leaf blown by the wind through the streets of his village. He knows that in spite of all the stout talk of his fellows he must live and die in uncertainty, a thing blown by the winds, a thing destined like corn to wilt in the sun. He shivers and looks eagerly about. The eighteen years he has lived seem but a moment, a breathing space in the long march of humanity. Already he hears death calling. With all his heart he wants to come close to some other human, touch someone with his hands, be touched by the hand of another. If he prefers that the other be a woman, that is because he believes that a woman will be gentle, that she will understand. He wants, most of all, understanding.

When the moment of sophistication came to George Willard his mind turned to Helen White, the Winesburg banker's daughter. Always he had been conscious of the girl growing into womanhood as he grew into manhood. Once on a summer night when he was eighteen, he had walked with her on a country road and in her presence had given way to an impulse to boast, to make himself appear big and significant in her eyes. Now he wanted to see her for another purpose. He wanted to tell her of the new impulses that had come to him. He had tried to make her think of him as a man when he knew nothing of manhood and now he wanted to be with her and to try to make her feel the change he believed had taken place in his nature.

As for Helen White, she also had come to a period of change. What George felt, she in her young woman's way felt also. She was no longer a girl and hungered to reach into the grace and beauty of womanhood. She had come home from Cleveland, where she was attending college, to spend a day at the Fair. She also had begun to have memories. During the day she sat in the grandstand with a young man, one of the instructors from the college, who was a guest of her mother's. The young man was of a pedantic turn of mind and she felt at once he would not do for her purpose. At the Fair she was glad to be seen in his company as he was well dressed and a stranger. She knew that the fact of his presence would create an impression. During the day she was happy, but when night came on she began to grow restless. She wanted to drive the instructor away, to get out of his presence. While they sat together in the grandstand and while the eyes of former schoolmates were upon them, she paid so much attention to her escort that he grew interested. "A scholar needs money. I should marry a woman with money," he mused.

Helen White was thinking of George Willard even as he wandered gloomily through the crowds thinking of her. She remembered the summer evening when they had walked together and wanted to walk with him again. She thought that the months she had spent in the city, the going to theaters and the seeing of great crowds wandering in lighted thoroughfares, had changed her profoundly. She wanted him to feel and be conscious of the change in her nature.

The summer evening together that had left its mark on the memory of both the young man and woman had, when looked at quite sensibly, been rather stupidly spent. They had walked out of town along a country road. Then they had stopped by a fence near a field of young corn and George had taken off his coat and let it hang on his arm. "Well, I've stayed here in Winesburg—yes—I've not yet gone away but I'm growing up," he had said. "I've been reading books and I've been thinking. I'm going to try to amount to something in life.

"Well," he explained, "that isn't the point. Perhaps I'd better quit talking."

The confused boy put his hand on the girl's arm. His voice trembled. The two started to walk back along the road toward town. In his desperation George boasted, "I'm going to be a big man, the biggest that ever lived here in Winesburg," he declared. "I want you to do something, I don't know what. Perhaps it is none of my business. I want you to try to be different from other women. You see the point. It's none of my business I tell you. I want you to be a beautiful woman. You see what I want."

The boy's voice failed and in silence the two came back into town and went along the street to Helen White's house. At the gate he tried to say something impressive. Speeches he had thought out came into his head, but they seemed utterly pointless. "I thought—I used to think—I had it in my mind you would marry Seth Richmond. Now I know you won't," was all he could find to say as she went through the gate and toward the door of her house.

On the warm fall evening as he stood in the stairway and looked at the crowd drifting through Main Street, George thought of the talk beside the field of young corn and was ashamed of the figure he had made of himself. In the street the people surged up and down like cattle confined in a pen. Buggies and wagons almost filled the narrow thoroughfare. A band played and small boys raced along the sidewalk, diving between the legs of men. Young men with shining red faces walked awkwardly about with girls on their arms. In a room above one of the stores, where a dance was to be held, the fiddlers tuned their instruments. The broken sounds floated down through an open window and out across the murmur of voices and the loud blare of the horns of the band. The medley of sounds got on young Willard's nerves. Everywhere, on all sides, the sense of crowding, moving life closed in about him. He wanted to run away by himself and think. "If she wants to stay with that fellow, she may. Why should I care? What difference does it make to me?" he growled and went along Main Street and through Hern's grocery into a side street.

George felt so utterly lonely and dejected that he wanted to weep, but pride made him walk rapidly along, swinging his arms. He came to Westley Moyer's livery barn and stopped in the shadows to listen to a group of men who talked of a race Westley's stallion, Tony Tip, had won at the Fair during the afternoon. A crowd had gathered in front of the barn and before the crowd walked Westley, prancing up and down and boasting. He held a whip in his hand and kept tapping the ground. Little puffs of dust arose in the lamplight. "Hell, quit your talking," Westley exclaimed. "I wasn't afraid, I knew I had 'em beat all the time. I wasn't afraid."

Ordinarily George Willard would have been intensely interested in the boasting of Moyer, the horseman. Now it made him angry. He turned and hurried away along the street. "Old wind bag," he sputtered. "Why does he want to be bragging? Why don't he shut up?"

George went into a vacant lot and as he hurried along, fell over a pile of rubbish. A nail protruding from an empty barrel tore his trousers. He sat down on the ground and swore. With a pin he mended the torn place and then arose and went on. "I'll go to Helen White's house, that's what I'll do. I'll walk right in. I'll say that I want to see her. I'll walk right in and sit down, that's what I'll do," he declared, climbing over a fence and beginning to run.

On the veranda of Banker White's house Helen was restless and distraught. The instructor sat between the mother and daughter. His talk wearied the girl. Although he had also been raised in an Ohio town, the instructor began to put on the airs of the city. He wanted to appear cosmopolitan. "I like the chance you have given me to study the background out of which most of our girls come," he declared. "It was good of you, Mrs. White, to have me down for the day." He turned to Helen and laughed. "Your life is still bound up with the life of this town?" he asked. "There are people here in whom you are interested?" To the girl his voice sounded pompous and heavy.

Helen arose and went into the house. At the door leading to a garden at the back she stopped and stood listening. Her mother began to talk. "There is no one here fit to associate with a girl of Helen's breeding," she said.

Helen ran down a flight of stairs at the back of the house and into the garden. In the darkness she stopped and stood trembling. It seemed to her that the world was full of meaningless people saying words. Afire with eagerness she ran through a garden gate and turning a corner by the banker's barn, went into a little side street. "George! Where are you, George?" she cried, filled with nervous excitement. She stopped running, and leaned against a tree to laugh hysterically. Along the dark little street came George Willard, still saying words. "I'm going to walk right into her house. I'll go right in and sit down," he declared as he came up to her. He stopped and stared stupidly. "Come on," he said and took hold of her hand. With hanging heads they walked away along the street under the trees. Dry leaves rustled under foot. Now that he had found her George wondered what he had better do and say.

At the upper end of the fairground in Winesburg, there is a half decayed old grandstand. It has never been painted and the boards are all warped out of shape. The fairground stands on top of a low hill rising out of the valley of Wine Creek and from the grandstand one can see at night, over a cornfield, the lights of the town reflected against the sky.

George and Helen climbed the hill to the fairground, coming by the path past Waterworks Pond. The feeling of loneliness and isolation that had come to the young man in the crowded streets of his town was both broken and intensified by the presence of Helen. What he felt was reflected in her.

In youth there are always two forces fighting in people. The warm unthinking little animal struggles against the thing that reflects and remembers, and the older, the more sophisticated thing had possession of George Willard. Sensing his mood, Helen walked beside him filled with respect. When they got to the grandstand they climbed up under the roof and sat down on one of the long benchlike seats.

There is something memorable in the experience to be had by going into a fairground that stands at the edge of a Middle Western town on a night after the annual fair has been held. The sensation is one never to be forgotten. On all sides are ghosts, not of the dead, but of living people. Here, during the day just passed, have come the people pouring in from the town and the country around. Farmers with their wives and children and all the people from the hundreds of little frame houses have gathered within these board walls. Young girls have laughed and men with beards have talked of the affairs of their lives. The place has been filled to overflowing with life. It has itched and squirmed with life and now it is night and the life has all gone away. The silence is almost terrifying. One conceals oneself standing silently beside the trunk of a tree and what there is of a reflective tendency in his nature is intensified. One shudders at the thought of the meaninglessness of life while at the same instant, and if the people of the town are his people, one loves life so intensely that tears come into the eyes.

In the darkness under the roof of the grandstand, George Willard sat beside Helen White and felt very keenly his own significance in the scheme of existence. Now that he had come out of town where the presence of the people stirring about, busy with a multitude of affairs, had been so irritating, the irritation was all gone. The presence of Helen renewed and refreshed him. It was as though her woman's hand was assisting him to make some minute readjustment of the machinery of his life. He began to think of the people in the town where he had always lived with something like reverence. He had reverence for Helen. He wanted to love and to be loved by her, but he did not want at the moment to be confused by her womanhood. In the darkness he took hold of her hand and when she crept close put a hand on her shoulder. A wind began to blow and he shivered. With all his strength he tried to hold and to understand the mood that had come upon him. In that high place in the darkness the two oddly sensitive human atoms held each other tightly and waited. In the mind of each was the same thought. "I have come to this lonely place and here is this other," was the substance of the thing felt.

In Winesburg the crowded day had run itself out into the long night of the late fall. Farm horses jogged away along lonely country roads pulling their portion of weary people. Clerks began to bring samples of goods in off the sidewalks and lock the doors of stores. In the Opera House a crowd had gathered to see a show and further down Main Street the fiddlers, their instruments tuned, sweated and worked to keep the feet of youth flying over a dance floor.

In the darkness in the grandstand Helen White and George Willard remained silent. Now and then the spell that held them was broken and they turned and tried in the dim light to see into each other's eyes. They kissed but that impulse did not last. At the upper end of the fairground a half dozen men worked over horses that had raced during the afternoon. The men had built a fire and were heating kettles of water. Only their legs could be seen as they passed back and forth in the light. When the wind blew, the little flames of the fire danced crazily about.

George and Helen arose and walked away into the darkness. They went along a path past a field of corn that had not yet been cut. The wind whispered among the dry corn blades. For a moment during the walk back into town the spell that held them was broken. When they had come to the crest of Waterworks Hill they stopped by a tree and George again put his hands on the girl's shoulders. She embraced him eagerly and then again they drew quickly back from that impulse. They stopped kissing and stood a little apart. Mutual respect grew big in them. They were both embarrassed and to relieve their embarrassment dropped into the animalism of youth. They laughed and began to pull and haul at each other. In some way chastened and purified by the mood they had been in they became, not man and woman, not boy and girl, but excited little animals.

It was so they went down the hill. In the darkness they played like two splendid young things in a young world. Once, running swiftly forward, Helen tripped George and he fell. He squirmed and shouted. Shaking with laughter, he rolled down the hill. Helen ran after him. For just a moment she stopped in the darkness. There is no way of knowing what woman's thoughts went through her mind but, when the bottom of the hill was reached and she came up to the boy, she took his arm and walked beside him in dignified silence. For some reason they could not have explained they had both got from their silent evening together the thing needed. Man or boy, woman or girl, they had for a moment taken hold of the thing that makes the mature life of men and women in the modern world possible.

Chicago

CARL SANDBURG

Hog Butcher for the World,
Tool Maker, Stacker of Wheat,
Player with Railroads and the Nation's Freight
Handler;
Stormy, husky, brawling,
City of the Big Shoulders:

They tell me you are wicked and I believe them, for I have
seen your painted women under the gas lamps luring
the farm boys.
And they tell me you are crooked and I answer: Yes, it is true I
have seen the gunman kill and go free to kill again.
And they tell me you are brutal and my reply is: On the faces
of women and children I have seen the marks of
wanton hunger.
And having answered so I turn once more to those who sneer
at this my city, and I give them back the sneer and say
to them:
Come and show me another city with lifted head singing so
proud to be alive and coarse and strong and cunning.
Flinging magnetic curses amid the toil of piling job on job,
here is a tall bold slugger set vivid against the little
soft cities;
Fierce as a dog with tongue lapping for action, cunning as a
savage pitted against the wilderness,
Bareheaded,
Shoveling,

Wrecking,
Planning,
Building, breaking, rebuilding.
Under the smoke, dust all over his mouth, laughing with white teeth,
Under the terrible burden of destiny laughing as a young man laughs,
Laughing even as an ignorant fighter laughs who has never lost a battle,
Bragging and laughing that under his wrist is the pulse, and under his ribs the heart of the people,
Laughing!
Laughing the stormy, husky, brawling laughter of Youth, half-naked sweating, proud to be Hog Butcher, Tool Maker, Stacker of Wheat, Player with Railroads and Freight Handler to the Nation.

Prayers of Steel

CARL SANDBURG

Lay me on an anvil, O God.
Beat me and hammer me into a crowbar.
Let me pry loose old walls.
Let me lift and loosen old foundations.

Lay me on an anvil, O God.
Beat me and hammer me into a steel spike.
Drive me into the girders that hold a skyscraper together.

Take red-hot rivets and fasten me into the central girders.
Let me be the great nail holding a skyscraper through blue
nights into white stars.

Coming Home

PHILIP LEVINE

A winter Tuesday, the city pouring fire,
Ford Rouge sulfurs the sun, Cadillac, Lincoln,
Chevy gray. The fat stacks
of breweries hold their tongues. Rags,
papers, hands, the stems of birches
dirtied with words.
                                        Near the freeway
you stop and wonder what came off,
recall the snowstorm where you lost it all,
the wolverine, the northern bear, the wolf
caught out, ice and steel raining
from the foundries in a shower
of human breath. On sleds in the false sun
the new material rests. One brown child
stares and stares into your frozen eyes
until the lights change and you go
forward to work. The charred faces, the eyes
boarded up, the rubble of innards, the cry
of wet smoke hanging in your throat,
the twisted river stopped at the color of iron.
We burn this city every day.

Winter Twilight, Charles Burchfield

Highway: Michigan

THEODORE ROETHKE

Here from the field's edge we survey
The progress of the jaded. Mile
On mile of traffic from the town
Rides by, for at the end of day
The time of workers is their own.

They jockey for position on
The strip reserved for passing only.
The drivers from production lines
Hold to advantage dearly won.
They toy with death and traffic fines.

Acceleration is their need:
A mania keeps them on the move
Until the toughest nerves are frayed.
They are the prisoners of speed
Who flee in what their hands have made.

The pavement smokes when two cars meet
And steel rips through conflicting steel.
We shiver at the siren's blast.
One driver, pinned beneath the seat,
Escapes from the machine at last.

Dolor

THEODORE ROETHKE

I have known the inexorable sadness of pencils,
Neat in their boxes, dolor of pad and paper-weight,
All the misery of manilla folders and mucilage,
Desolation in immaculate public places,
Lonely reception room, lavatory, switchboard,
The unalterable pathos of basin and pitcher,
Ritual of multigraph, paper-clip, comma,
Endless duplication of lives and objects.
And I have seen dust from the walls of institutions,
Finer than flour, alive, more dangerous than silica,
Sift, almost invisible, through long afternoons of tedium,
Dropping a fine film on nails and delicate eyebrows,
Glazing the pale hair, the duplicate grey standard faces.

*The Magnet Attracting: A Waif Amid Forces**

THEODORE DREISER

When Caroline Meeber boarded the afternoon train for Chicago, her total outfit consisted of a small trunk, a cheap imitation alligator-skin satchel, a small lunch in a paper box, and a yellow leather snap purse, containing her ticket, a scrap of paper with her sister's address in Van Buren Street, and four dollars in money. It was in August, 1889. She was eighteen years of age, bright, timid, and full of the illusions of ignorance and youth. Whatever touch of regret at parting characterized her thoughts, it was certainly not for advantages now being given up. A gush of tears at her mother's farewell kiss, a touch in her throat when the cars clacked by the flour mill where her father worked by the day, a pathetic sigh as the familiar green environs of the village passed in review, and the threads which bound her so lightly to girlhood and home were irretrievably broken.

To be sure there was always the next station, where one might descend and return. There was the great city, bound more closely by these very trains which came up daily. Columbia City was not so very far away, even once she was in Chicago. What, pray, is a few hours—a few hundred miles? She looked at the little slip bearing her sister's address and wondered. She gazed at the green landscape, now passing in swift review, until her swifter thoughts replaced its impression with vague conjectures of what Chicago might be.

When a girl leaves her home at eighteen, she does one of two things. Either she falls into saving hands and becomes better, or she rapidly assumes the cosmopolitan standard of virtue and becomes worse. Of an intermediate balance, under the circumstances, there is no possibility. The city has its cunning wiles, no less than the infinitely smaller and more human tempter. There are large forces which allure with all the soulfulness of ex-

* Selection from *Sister Carrie*.

pression possible in the most cultured human. The gleam of a thousand lights is often as effective as the persuasive light in a wooing and fascinating eye. Half the undoing of the unsophisticated and natural mind is accomplished by forces wholly superhuman. A blare of sound, a roar of life, a vast array of human hives, appeal to the astonished senses in equivocal terms. Without a counselor at hand to whisper cautious interpretations, what falsehoods may not these things breathe into the unguarded ear! Unrecognized for what they are, their beauty, like music, too often relaxes, then weakens, then perverts the simpler human perceptions.

Caroline, or Sister Carrie, as she had been half affectionately termed by the family, was possessed of a mind rudimentary in its power of observations and analysis. Self-interest with her was high, but not strong. It was, nevertheless, her guiding characteristic. Warm with the fancies of youth, pretty with the insipid prettiness of the formative period, possessed of a figure promising eventual shapeliness and an eye alight with certain native intelligence, she was a fair example of the middle American class—two generations removed from the emigrant. Books were beyond her interest—knowledge a sealed book. In the intuitive graces she was still crude. She could scarcely toss her head gracefully. Her hands were almost ineffectual. The feet, though small, were set flatly. And yet she was interested in her charms, quick to understand the keener pleasures of life, ambitious to gain in material things. A half-equipped little knight she was, venturing to reconnoiter the mysterious city and dreaming wild dreams of some vague, far-off supremacy, which should make it prey and subject—the proper penitent, groveling at a woman's slipper.

"That," said a voice in her ear, "is one of the prettiest little resorts in Wisconsin."

"Is it?" she answered nervously.

The train was just pulling out of Waukesha. For some time she had been conscious of a man behind. She felt him observing her mass of hair. He had been fidgeting, and with natural intuition she felt a certain interest growing in that quarter. Her maidenly reserve, and a certain sense of what was conventional under the circumstances, called her to forestall and deny this familiarity, but the daring and magnetism of the individual, born of past experiences and triumphs, prevailed. She answered.

He leaned forward to put his elbows upon the back of her seat and proceeded to make himself volubly agreeable.

"Yes, that is a great resort for Chicago people. The hotels are swell. You are not familiar with this part of the country, are you?"

"Oh, yes, I am," answered Carrie. "That is, I live at Columbia City. I have never been through here, though."

"And so this is your first visit to Chicago," he observed.

All the time she was conscious of certain features out of the side of her eye. Flush, colorful cheeks, a light mustache, a gray fedora hat. She now turned and looked upon him in full, the instinct of self-protection and coquetry mingling confusedly in her brain.

"I didn't say that," she said.

"Oh," he answered, in a very pleasing way and with an assumed air of mistake, "I thought you did."

Here was a type of the traveling canvasser for a manufacturing house—a class which at the time was first being dubbed by the slang of the day "drummers." He came within the meaning of a still newer term, which had sprung into general use among Americans in 1880, and which concisely expressed the thought of one whose dress or manners are calculated to elicit the admiration of susceptible young women—a "masher." His suit was of a striped and crossed pattern of brown wool, new at the time, but since become familiar as a business suit. The low crotch of the vest revealed a stiff shirt bosom of white and pink stripes. From his coat sleeves protruded a pair of linen cuffs of the same pattern, fastened with large, gold-plate buttons, set with the common yellow agates known as "cat's-eyes." His fingers bore several rings—one, the ever-enduring heavy seal—and from his vest dangled a neat gold watch chain, from which was suspended the secret insignia of the Order of Elks. The whole suit was rather tight-fitting, and was finished off with heavy-soled tan shoes, highly polished, and the gray fedora hat. He was, for the order of intellect represented, attractive, and whatever he had to recommend him, you may be sure was not lost upon Carrie, in this, her first glance.

Lest this order of individual should permanently pass, let me put down some of the most striking characteristics of his most successful manner and method. Good clothes, of course, were the first essential, the things without which he was nothing. A strong physical nature, actuated by a keen desire for the feminine, was the next. A mind free of any consideration of the problems or forces of the world and actuated not by greed, but an insatiable love of variable pleasure. His method was always simple. Its principal element was daring, backed, of course, by an intense desire and admiration for the sex. Let him meet with a young woman twice and he would straighten her necktie for her and perhaps address her by her first name. In the great department stores he was at his ease. If he caught the attention of some young woman while waiting for the cash boy to come back with his change, he would find out her name, her favorite flower, where a note would reach her, and perhaps pursue the delicate task of friendship until it proved unpromising, when it would be relinquished. He would do very well with more pretentious women, though the burden of expense was a slight deterrent. Upon entering a parlor car, for instance, he would select a chair next to the most promising bit of femininity and soon inquire if she cared to have the shade lowered. Before the train cleared the yards he would have the porter bring her a footstool. At the next lull in his conversational progress he would find her something to read, and from then on, by dint of compliment gently insinuated, personal narrative, exaggeration and service, he would win her tolerance, and, mayhap, regard.

A woman should some day write the complete philosophy of clothes. No matter how young, it is one of the things she wholly comprehends. There is an indescribably faint line in the matter of man's apparel which somehow divides for her those who are worth glancing at and those who are not. Once an individual has passed this faint line on the way downward he will get no glance from her. There is another line at which the dress of a man will cause her to study her own. This line the individual at her elbow now marked for Carrie. She became conscious of an inequality. Her own plain blue dress, with its black cotton tape trimmings, now seemed to her shabby. She felt the worn state of her shoes.

"Let's see," he went on, "I know quite a number of people in your town. Morgenroth the clothier and Gibson the dry goods man."

"Oh, do you?" she interrupted, aroused by memories of longings their show windows had cost her.

At last he had a clue to her interest, and followed it deftly. In a few minutes he had come about into her seat. He talked of sales of clothing, his travels, Chicago, and the amusements of that city.

"If you are going there, you will enjoy it immensely. Have you relatives?"

"I am going to visit my sister," she explained.

"You want to see Lincoln Park," he said, "and Michigan Boulevard.

They are putting up great buildings there. It's a second New York—great. So much to see—theaters, crowds, fine houses—oh, you'll like that."

There was a little ache in her fancy of all he described. Her insignificance in the presence of so much magnificence faintly affected her. She realized that hers was not to be a round of pleasure, and yet there was something promising in all the material prospect he set forth. There was something satisfactory in the attention of this individual with his good clothes. She could not help smiling as he told her of some popular actress of whom she reminded him. She was not silly, and yet attention of this sort had its weight.

"You will be in Chicago some little time, won't you?" he observed at one turn of the now easy conversation.

"I don't know," said Carrie vaguely—a flash vision of the possibility of her not securing employment rising in her mind.

"Several weeks, anyhow," he said, looking steadily into her eyes.

There was much more passing now than the mere words indicated. He recognized the indescribable thing that made up for fascination and beauty in her. She realized that she was of interest to him from the one standpoint which a woman both delights in and fears. Her manner was simple, though for the very reason that she had not yet learned the many little affectations with which women conceal their true feelings. Some things she did appeared bold. A clever companion—had she ever had one—would have warned her never to look a man in the eyes so steadily.

"Why do you ask?" she said.

"Well, I'm going to be there several weeks. I'm going to study stock at our place and get new samples. I might show you 'round.

"I don't know whether you can or not. I mean I don't know whether I can. I shall be living with my sister, and—"

"Well, if she minds, we'll fix that." He took out his pencil and a little pocket notebook as if it were all settled. "What is your address there?"

She fumbled her purse which contained the address slip.

He reached down in his hip pocket and took out a fat purse. It was filled with slips of paper, some mileage books, a roll of greenbacks. It impressed her deeply. Such a purse had never been carried by any one attentive to her. Indeed, an experienced traveler, a brisk man of the world, had never come within such close range before. The purse, the shiny tan shoes, the smart new suit, and the *air* with which he did things, built up for her a dim world of fortune, of which he was the center. It disposed her pleasantly toward all he might do.

He took out a neat business card, on which was engraved Bartlett, Caryoe & Company, and down in the left-hand corner, Chas. H. Drouet.

"That's me," he said, putting the card in her hand and touching his name. "It's pronounced Drew-eh. Our family was French, on my father's side."

She looked at it while he put up his purse. Then he got out a letter from a bunch in his coat pocket. "This is the house I travel for," he went on, pointing to a picture on it, "corner of State and Lake." There was pride in his voice. He felt that it was something to be connected with such a place, and he made her feel that way.

"What is your address?" he began again, fixing his pencil to write.

She looked at his hand.

"Carrie Meeber," she said slowly. "Three hundred and fifty-four West Van Buren Street, care S. C. Hanson."

He wrote it carefully down and got out the purse again. "You'll be at home if I come around Monday night?" he said.

"I think so," she answered.

How true it is that words are but the vague shadows of the volumes we mean. Little audible links, they are, chaining together great inaudible feelings and purposes. Here were these two, bandying little phrases, drawing purses, looking at cards, and both unconscious of how inarticulate all their real feelings were. Neither was wise enough to be sure of the working of the mind of the other. He could not tell how his luring succeeded. She could not realize that she was drifting, until he secured her address. Now she felt that she had yielded something—he, that he had gained a victory. Already they felt that they were somehow associated. Already he took control in directing the conversation. His words were easy. Her manner was relaxed.

They were nearing Chicago. Signs were everywhere numerous. Trains flashed by them. Across wide stretches of flat, open prairie they could see lines of telegraph poles stalking across the fields toward the great city. Far away were indications of suburban towns, some big smokestacks towering high in the air.

Frequently there were two-story frame houses standing out in the open fields, without fence or trees, lone outposts of the approaching army of homes.

To the child, the genius with imagination, or the wholly untraveled the approach to a great city for the first time is a wonderful thing. Particularly if it be evening—that mystic period between the glare and gloom of the world when life is changing from one sphere or condition to another. Ah, the promise of the night. What does it not hold for the weary! What old illusion of hope is not here forever repeated! Says the soul of the toiler to itself, "I shall soon be free. I shall be in the ways and the hosts of the merry. The streets, the lamps, the lighted chamber set for dining are for me. The theater, the halls, the parties, the ways of rest and the paths of song—these are mine in the night." Though all humanity be still enclosed in the shops, the thrill runs abroad. It is in the air. The dullest feel something which they may not always express or describe. It is the lifting of the burden of toil.

Sister Carrie gazed out of the window. Her companion, affected by her wonder, so contagious are all things, felt anew some interest in the city and pointed out its marvels.

"This is northwest Chicago," said Drouet. "This is the Chicago River," and he pointed to a little muddy creek, crowded with the huge masted wanderers from far-off waters nosing the black-posted banks. With a puff, a clang, and a clatter of rails it was gone. "Chicago is getting to be a great town," he went on. "It's a wonder. You'll find lots to see here."

She did not hear this very well. Her heart was troubled by a kind of terror. The fact that she was alone, away from home, rushing into a great sea of life and endeavor, began to tell. She could not help but feel a little choked for breath—a little sick as her heart beat so fast. She half closed her eyes and tried to think it was nothing, that Columbia City was only a little way off.

"Chicago! Chicago!" called the brakeman, slamming open the door. They were rushing into a more crowded yard, alive with the clatter and clang of life. She began to gather up her poor little grip and closed her hand firmly upon her purse. Drouet arose, kicked his legs to straighten his trousers, and seized his clean yellow grip.

"I suppose your people will be here to meet you?" he said. "Let me carry your grip."

"Oh, no," she said, "I'd rather you wouldn't. I'd rather you wouldn't be with me when I meet my sister."

"All right," he said in all kindness. "I'll be near, though, in case she isn't here, and take you out there safely."

"You're so kind," said Carrie, feeling the goodness of such attention in her strange situation.

"Chicago!" called the brakeman, drawing the word out long. They were under a great shadowy train shed, where the lamps were already beginning to shine out, with passenger cars all about and the train moving at a snail's pace. The people in the car were all up and crowding about the door.

"Well, here we are," said Drouet, leading the way to the door. "Good-bye, till I see you Monday."

"Good-bye," she answered, taking his proffered hand.

"Remember, I'll be looking till you find your sister."

She smiled into his eyes.

They filed out, and he affected to take no notice of her. A lean-faced, rather commonplace woman recognized Carrie on the platform and hurried forward.

"Why, Sister Carrie!" she began, and there was a perfunctory embrace of welcome.

Carrie realized the change of affectional atmosphere at once. Amid all the maze, uproar, and novelty she felt cold reality taking her by the hand. No world of light and merriment. No round of amusement. Her sister carried with her most of the grimness of shift and toil.

"Why, how are all the folks at home?" she began. "How is Father, and Mother?"

Carried answered, but was looking away. Down the aisle, toward the gate leading into the waiting room and the street, stood Drouet. He was looking back. When he saw that she saw him and was safe with her sister he turned to go, sending back the shadow of a smile. Only Carrie saw it. She felt something lost to her when he moved away. When he disappeared she felt his absence thoroughly. With her sister she was much alone, a lone figure in a tossing, thoughtless sea.

A Blessing

JAMES WRIGHT

Just off the highway to Rochester, Minnesota,
Twilight bounds softly forth on the grass.
And the eyes of those two Indian ponies
Darken with kindness.
They have come gladly out of the willows
To welcome my friend and me.
We step over the barbed wire into the pasture
Where they have been grazing all day, alone.
They ripple tensely, they can hardly contain their happiness
That we have come.
They bow shyly as wet swans. They love each other.
There is no loneliness like theirs.
At home once more,
They begin munching the young tufts of spring in the darkness.
I would like to hold the slenderer one in my arms,
For she has walked over to me
And nuzzled my left hand.
She is black and white,
Her mane falls wild on her forehead,
And the light breeze moves me to caress her long ear
That is delicate as the skin over a girl's wrist.
Suddenly I realize
That if I stepped out of my body I would break
Into blossom.

Moss-Gathering

THEODORE ROETHKE

To loosen with all ten fingers held wide and limber
And lift up a patch, dark-green, the kind for lining cemetery
baskets,
Thick and cushiony, like an old-fashioned doormat,
The crumbling small hollow sticks on the underside mixed with
roots,
And wintergreen berries and leaves still stuck to the top,—
That was moss-gathering.
But something always went out of me when I dug loose those
carpets
Of green, or plunged to my elbows in the spongy yellowish
moss of the marshes:
And afterward I always felt mean, jogging back over the
logging road,
As if I had broken the natural order of things in that
swampland;
Disturbed some rhythm, old and of vast importance,
By pulling off flesh from the living planet;
As if I had committed, against the whole scheme of life, a
desecration.

The Three-Day Blow

ERNEST HEMINGWAY

The rain stopped as Nick turned into the road that went up through the orchard. The fruit had been picked and the fall wind blew through the bare trees. Nick stopped and picked up a Wagner apple from beside the road, shiny in the brown grass from the rain. He put the apple in the pocket of his Mackinaw coat.

The road came out of the orchard on to the top of the hill. There was the cottage, the porch bare, smoke coming from the chimney. In back was the garage, the chicken coop and the second-growth timber like a hedge against the woods behind. The big trees swayed far over in the wind as he watched. It was the first of the autumn storms.

As Nick crossed the open field above the orchard the door of the cottage opened and Bill came out. He stood on the porch looking out.

"Well, Wemedge," he said.

"Hey, Bill," Nick said, coming up the steps.

They stood together, looking out across the country, down over the orchard, beyond the road, across the lower fields and the woods of the point to the lake. The wind was blowing straight down the lake. They could see the surf along Ten Mile point.

"She's blowing," Nick said.

"She'll blow like that for three days," Bill said.

"Is your dad in?" Nick said.

"No. He's out with the gun. Come on in."

Nick went inside the cottage. There was a big fire in the fireplace. The wind made it roar. Bill shut the door.

"Have a drink?" he said.

He went out to the kitchen and came back with two glasses and a pitcher of water. Nick reached the whisky bottle from the shelf above the fireplace.

"All right?" he said.

"Good," said Bill.

They sat in front of the fire and drank the Irish whisky and water.

"It's got a swell, smoky taste," Nick said, and looked at the fire through the glass.

"That's the peat," Bill said.

"You can't get peat into liquor," Nick said.

"That doesn't make any difference," Bill said.

"You ever seen any peat?" Nick asked.

"No," said Bill.

"Neither have I," Nick said.

His shoes, stretched out on the hearth, began to steam in front of the fire.

"Better take your shoes off," Bill said.

"I haven't got any socks on."

"Take them off and dry them and I'll get you some," Bill said. He went upstairs into the loft and Nick heard him walking about overhead. Upstairs was open under the roof and was where Bill and his father and he, Nick, sometimes slept. In back was a dressing room. They moved the cots back out of the rain and covered them with rubber blankets.

Bill came down with a pair of heavy wool socks.

"It's getting too late to go around without socks," he said.

"I hate to start them again," Nick said. He pulled the socks on and slumped back in the chair, putting his feet up on the screen in front of the fire.

"You'll dent in the screen," Bill said. Nick swung his feet over to the side of the fireplace.

"Got anything to read?" he asked.

"Only the paper."

"What did the Cards do?"

"Dropped a double header to the Giants."

"That ought to cinch it for them."

"It's a gift," Bill said. "As long as McGraw can buy every good ball player in the league there's nothing to it."

"He can't buy them all," Nick said.

"He buys all the ones he wants," Bill said. "Or he makes them discontented so they have to trade them to him."

"Like Heinie Zim," Nick agreed.

"That bonehead will do him a lot of good."

Bill stood up.

"He can hit," Nick offered. The heat from the fire was baking his legs.

"He's a sweet fielder, too," Bill said. "But he loses ball games."

"Maybe that's what McGraw wants him for," Nick suggested.

"Maybe," Bill agreed.

"There's always more to it than we know about," Nick said.

"Of course. But we've got pretty good dope for being so far away."

"Like how much better you can pick them if you don't see the horses."

"That's it."

Bill reached down the whisky bottle. His big hand went all the way around it. He poured the whisky into the glass Nick held out.

"How much water?"

"Just the same."

He sat down on the floor beside Nick's chair.

"It's good when the fall storms come, isn't it?" Nick said.

"It's swell."

"It's the best time of year," Nick said.

"Wouldn't it be hell to be in town?" Bill said.

"I'd like to see the World Series," Nick said.

"Well, they're always in New York or Philadelphia now," Bill said. "That doesn't do us any good."

"I wonder if the Cards will ever win a pennant?"

"Not in our lifetime," Bill said.

"Gee, they'd go crazy," Nick said.

"Do you remember when they got going that once before they had the train wreck?"

"Boy!" Nick said, remembering.

Bill reached over to the table under the window for the book that lay there, face down, where he had put it when he went to the door. He held his glass in one hand and the book in the other, leaning back against Nick's chair.

"What are you reading?"

"*Richard Feverel.*"

"I couldn't get into it."

"It's all right," Bill said. "It ain't a bad book, Wemedge."

"What else have you got I haven't read?" Nick asked.

"Did you read the *Forest Lovers?*"

"Yup. That's the one where they go to bed every night with the naked sword between them."

"That's a good book, Wemedge."

"It's a swell book. What I couldn't ever understand was what good the sword would do. It would have to stay edge up all the time because if it went over flat you could roll right over it and it wouldn't make any trouble."

"It's a symbol," Bill said.

"Sure," said Nick, "but it isn't practical."

"Did you ever read *Fortitude?*"

"It's fine," Nick said. "That's a real book. That's where his old man is after him all the time. Have you got any more by Walpole?"

"*The Dark Forest,*" Bill said. "It's about Russia."

"What does he know about Russia?" Nick asked.

"I don't know. You can't ever tell about those guys. Maybe he was there when he was a boy. He's got a lot of dope on it."

"I'd like to meet him," Nick said.

"I'd like to meet Chesterton," Bill said.

"I wish he was here now," Nick said. "we'd take him fishing to the 'Voix tomorrow."

"I wonder if he'd like to go fishing," Bill said.

"Sure," said Nick,. "He must be about the best guy there is. Do you remember the *Flying Inn?*"

> " 'If an angel out of heaven
> Gives you something else to drink,
> Thank him for his kind intentions;
> Go and pour them down the sink.' "

"That's right," said Nick. "I guess he's a better guy than Walpole."

"Oh, he's a better guy, all right," Bill said.

"But Walpole's a better writer."

"I don't know," Nick said. "Chesterton's a classic."

"Walpole's a classic, too," Bill insisted.

"I wish we had them both here," Nick said. "We'd take them both fishing to the 'Voix tomorrow."

"Let's get drunk," Bill said.

"All right," Nick agreed.

"My old man won't care," Bill said.

"Are you sure?" said Nick.

"I know it," Bill said.

"I'm a little drunk now," Nick said.

"You aren't drunk," Bill said.

He got up from the floor and reached for the whisky bottle. Nick held out his glass. His eyes fixed on it while Bill poured.

Bill poured the glass half full of whisky.

"Put in your own water," he said. "There's just one more shot."

"Got any more?" Nick asked.

"There's plenty more but dad only likes me to drink what's open."

"Sure," said Nick.

"He says opening bottles is what makes drunkards," Bill explained.

"That's right," said Nick. He was impressed. He had never thought of that before. He had always thought it was solitary drinking that made drunkards.

"How is your dad?" he asked respectfully.

"He's all right," Bill said. "He gets a little wild sometimes."

"He's a swell guy," Nick said. He poured water into his glass out of the pitcher. It mixed slowly with the whisky. There was more whisky than water.

"You bet your life he is," Bill said.

"My old man's all right," Nick said.

"You're damn right he is," said Bill.

"He claims he's never taken a drink in his life," Nick said, as though announcing a scientific fact.

"Well, he's a doctor. My old man's a painter. That's different."

"He's missed a lot," Nick said sadly.

"You can't tell," Bill said. "Everything's got its compensations."

"He says he's missed a lot himself," Nick confessed.

"Well, dad's had a tough time," Bill said.

"It all evens up," Nick said.

They sat looking into the fire and thinking of this profound truth.

"I'll get a chunk from the back porch," Nick said. He had noticed while looking into the fire that the fire was dying down. Also he wished to show he could hold his liquor and be practical. Even if his father had never touched a drop Bill was not going to get him drunk before he himself was drunk.

"Bring one of the big beech chunks," Bill said. He was also being consciously practical.

Nick came in with the log through the kitchen and in passing knocked a pan off the kitchen table. He laid the log down and picked up the pan. It had contained dried apricots, soaking in water. He carefully picked up all the apricots off the floor, some of them had gone under the stove, and put them back in the pan. He dipped some more water onto them from the pail by the table. He felt quite proud of himself. He had been thoroughly practical.

He came in carrying the log and Bill got up from the chair and helped him put it on the fire.

"That's a swell log," Nick said.

"I'd been saving it for the bad weather," Bill said. "A log like that will burn all night."

"There'll be coals left to start the fire in the morning," Nick said.

"That's right," Bill agreed. They were conducting the conversation on a high plane.

"Let's have another drink," Nick said.

"I think there's another bottle open in the locker," Bill said.

He kneeled down in the corner in front of the locker and brought out a square-faced bottle.

"It's Scotch," he said.

"I'll get some more water," Nick said. He went out into the kitchen again. He filled the pitcher with the dipper dipping cold spring water from the pail. On his way back to the living room he passed a mirror in the dining room and looked in it. His face looked strange. He smiled at the face in the mirror and it grinned back at him. He winked at it and went on. It was not his face but it didn't make any difference.

Bill had poured out the drinks.

"That's an awfully big shot," Nick said.

"Not for us, Wemedge," Bill said.

"What'll we drink to?" Nick asked, holding up the glass.

"Let's drink to fishing," Bill said.

"All right," Nick said. "Gentlemen, I give you fishing."

"All fishing," Bill said. "Everywhere."

"Fishing," Nick said. "That's what we drink to."

"It's better than baseball," Bill said.

"There isn't any comparison," said Nick. "How did we ever get talking about baseball?"

"It was a mistake," Bill said. "Baseball is a game for louts."

They drank all that was in their glasses.

"Now let's drink to Chesterton."

"And Walpole," Nick interposed.

Nick poured out the liquor. Bill poured in the water. They looked at each other. They felt very fine.

"Gentlemen," Bill said, "I give you Chesterton and Walpole."

"Exactly, gentlemen," Nick said.

They drank. Bill filled up the glasses. They sat down in the big chairs in front of the fire.

"You were very wise, Wemedge," Bill said.

"What do you mean?" asked Nick.

"To bust off that Marge business," Bill said.

"I guess so," said Nick.

"It was the only thing to do. If you hadn't, by now you'd be back home working trying to get enough money to get married."

Nick said nothing.

"Once a man's married he's absolutely bitched," Bill went on. "He hasn't got anything more. Nothing. Not a damn thing. He's done for. You've seen the guys that get married."

Nick said nothing.

"You can tell them," Bill said. "They get this sort of fat married look. They're done for."

"Sure," said Nick.

"It was probably bad busting it off," Bill said. "But you always fall for somebody else and then it's all right. Fall for them but don't let them ruin you."

"Yes," said Nick.

"If you'd have married her you would have had to marry the whole family. Remember her mother and that guy she married."

Nick nodded.

"Imagine having them around the house all the time and going to Sunday dinners at their house, and having them over to dinner and her telling Marge all the time what to do and how to act."

Nick sat quiet.

"You came out of it damned well," Bill said. "Now she can marry somebody of her own sort and settle down and be happy. You can't mix oil and water and you can't mix that sort of thing any more than if I'd marry Ida that works for Strattons. She'd probably like it, too."

Nick said nothing. The liquor had all died out of him and left him alone. Bill wasn't there. He wasn't sitting in front of the fire or going fishing tomorrow with Bill and his dad or anything. He wasn't drunk. It was all gone. All he knew was that he had once had Marjorie and that he had lost her. She was gone and he had sent her away. That was all that mattered. He might never see her again. Probably he never would. It was all gone, finished.

"Let's have another drink," Nick said.

Bill poured it out. Nick splashed in a little water.

"If you'd gone on that way we wouldn't be here now," Bill said.

That was true. His original plan had been to go down home and get a job. Then he had planned to stay in Charlevoix all winter so he could be near Marge. Now he did not know what he was going to do.

"Probably we wouldn't even be going fishing tomorrow," Bill said. "You had the right dope, all right."

"I couldn't help it," Nick said.

"I know. That's the way it works out," Bill said.

"All of a sudden everything was over," Nick said. "I don't know why it was. I couldn't help it. Just like when the three-day blows come now and rip all the leaves off the trees."

"Well, it's over. That's the point," Bill said.

"It was my fault," Nick said.

"It doesn't make any difference whose fault it was," Bill said.

"No, I suppose not," Nick said.

The big thing was that Marjorie was gone and that probably he would never see her again. He had talked to her about how they would go to Italy together and the fun they would have. Places they would be together. It was all gone now.

"So long as it's over that's all that matters," Bill said. "I tell you, Wemedge, I was worried while it was going on. You played it right. I understand her mother is sore as hell. She told a lot of people you were engaged."

"We weren't engaged," Nick said.

"It was all around that you were."

"I can't help it," Nick said. "We weren't."

"Weren't you going to get married?" Bill asked.

"Yes. But we weren't engaged," Nick said.

"What's the difference?" Bill asked judicially.

"I don't know. There's a difference."

"I don't see it," said Bill.

"All right," said Nick. "Let's get drunk."

"All right," Bill said. "Let's get really drunk."

"Let's get drunk and then go swimming," Nick said.

He drank off his glass.

"I'm sorry as hell about her but what could I do?" he said. "You know what her mother was like!"

"She was terrible," Bill said.

"All of a sudden it was over," Nick said. "I oughtn't to talk about it."

"You aren't," Bill said. "I talked about it and now I'm through. We won't ever speak about it again. You don't want to think about it. You might get back into it again."

Nick had not thought about that. It had seemed so absolute. That was a thought. That made him feel better.

"Sure," he said. "There's always that danger."

He felt happy now. There was not anything that was irrevocable. He might go into town Saturday night. Today was Thursday.

"There's always a chance," he said.

"You'll have to watch yourself," Bill said.

"I'll watch myself," he said.

He felt happy. Nothing was finished. Nothing was ever lost. He would go into town on Saturday. He felt lighter, as he had felt before Bill started to talk about it. There was always a way out.

"Let's take the guns and go down to the point and look for your dad," Nick said.

"All right."

Bill took down the two shotguns from the rack on the wall. He opened a box of shells. Nick put on his Mackinaw coat and his shoes. His shoes were stiff from the drying. He was still quite drunk but his head was clear.

"How do you feel?" Nick asked.

"Swell. I've just got a good edge on." Bill was buttoning up his sweater.

"There's no use getting drunk."

"No. We ought to get outdoors."

They stepped out the door. The wind was blowing a gale.

"The birds will lie right down in the grass with this," Nick said.

They struck down toward the orchard.

"I saw a woodcock this morning," Bill said.

"Maybe we'll jump him," Nick said.

"You can't shoot in this wind," Bill said.

Outside now the Marge business was no longer so tragic. It was not even very important. The wind blew everything like that away.

"It's coming right off the big lake," Nick said.

Against the wind they heard the thud of a shotgun.

"That's dad," Bill said. "He's down in the swamp."

"Let's cut down that way," Nick said.

"Let's cut across the lower meadow and see if we jump anything," Bill said.

"All right," Nick said.

None of it was important now. The wind blew it out of his head. Still he could always go into town Saturday night. It was a good thing to have in reserve.

Ethnic Identity and Anonymity

The ethnic diversity currently found in the American Middle West was achieved gradually and not without a certain degree of conflict, compromise and loss—especially for the Native Americans whose plight was given sensitive expression by Marnie Walsh in the poem "Thomas Iron-Eyes."

Pioneer immigrants from Europe shared an experience common to many of their generation on the midwestern frontier. They suffered a separation from the continuing cultural influences of the Old World. Literary accounts representing Norwegian, Swedish, Czech, Bohemian, French, Russian, and German groups expressed these hardships of physical and emotional transplanting. Ole Rölvaag in the novel *Giants in the Earth,* for example, embraced both the theme of the pioneer venture and that of the immigrant's adjustment to the new environment, describing a group of Norwegians who settled in the Dakotas during the last quarter of the nineteenth century. The chapter "Home-founding" illuminated two fundamental attitudes toward the frontier experience in the characterizations of Per Hansa and Beret. He typified the natural pioneer: optimistic, resourceful, inventive, a man of action determined to establish a homestead in virgin territory. His wife, on the other hand, exemplified the pioneer more shaped by than shaper of the wilderness environ. Sensitive and timid, she brooded over its loneliness and desolation, and longed for the certainty of her homeland. Since the author kept Beret at the narrative's center, he seemed to suggest that the tragic view of the pioneering process was a realistic one. Equally important, Rölvaag demonstrated that the existence of open farmlands allowed those immigrants who wished to maintain

Barn raising on the Rainy River

their own language, customs and traditions to do so without experiencing a feeling of strangeness and unwelcomeness.

In contrast, many immigrants, first-generation Americans, and migrant blacks coming to the urban Midwest were forced to settle in poorer communities, sometimes near or in slums. Hoping to retain a sense of national, racial or religious identity, they located as groups, thus creating ethnic districts within large cities like Chicago. Chicagoan Harry Mark Petrakis in his short fiction and novels, for example, reflected a thorough familiarity with the city's Greek-American section. At times, as in "Pericles on 31st Street," ethnic humor and the device of stereotyping were used by him to characterize ethnic differences. Other literature by and about these minorities reflected the bittersweet nature of their poverty, the aspects of provincialism arising from their unconventional attitudes and traditions and the cultural gap which frequently developed between them and their children. Novels and short stories like those by James T. Farrell also exposed the jealous hostilities among individuals or groups with different ethnic backgrounds. His story "The Fastest Runner on Sixty-first Street," for instance, was a fictionalized account of a street fight which occurred in August 1919.

Several leading black writers, either native midwesterners or migrants from the South, produced a significant body of literature concerning black identity and anonymity. Paul Laurence Dunbar, the first nationally recognized black poet, treated subjects and themes related to the nature of black separateness. Richard Wright's novel *Native Son* revealed a naturalistic recording of protest and despair in the midst of a kind of regional devotion. In "Jazz, Jive, and Jam," one of numerous Simple sketches originally prepared for his column in the *Chicago Defender*, Langston Hughes identified with the uneducated, laboring-class blacks who lived in Chicago's negro district, and who did not care about adopting the white culture. "These common people," said Hughes, "are not afraid of spirituals, as for a long time their more intelligent brethren were, and jazz is their child." Poems such as "I, Too, Sing America" also expressed his implicit dream of a decisive moral encounter that would bring brotherhood to America. Gwendolyn Brooks shared with Hughes the achievement of being responsive to the black community's vision of itself and of the changing forms of its vibrations during decades of rapid change. The life of women, usually black women, and the life of blacks in general, particularly those who had grown up since the Second World War in the Midwest, figured prominently in her poetry. With much the same confidence, Robert Hayden explored themes about black heritage and black consciousness in poems like "Frederick Douglass" and "Runagate Runagate."

Thomas Iron-Eyes

Born Circa 1840, Died 1919
Rosebud Agency, So. Dak.

MARNIE WALSH

I

I woke before the day, when the night bird
Knocked three times upon my door
To warn the Other Sleep was coming.
By candlelight I painted the two broad stripes
Of white across my forehead, the three scarlet spots
Upon my cheek. I greased well my braids
With sour fat from the cooking pan, then tied them
With a bit of bright string
Saved for this occasion.
From the trunk I took the dress of ceremony:
The breechclout and the elkskin shirt,
The smoke of their breath strong in my nose;
The smoke not of this time, this life or place
But of my youth, of many lodges I dwelt within,
The pony raids, the counting coup,
The chase and kill of buffalo;
The smell of grass when it was green,
The smell of coming snows
When food was plentiful within the camp
And ice crept over the rivers.
I put on the dress; then the leggings with scalps,
Now thin and colorless as the hair
Of sickly animals, sinew tied along the seams;
And on my feet the red-beaded moccasins
Worn by none but the bravest of warriors.
I lie here, my dry bones and ancient skin
Holding my old heart.
The daystar finds me ready for the journey.

II

Another time, another life, another place,
My people would have wrapped me
In deerskin, sewed me in the finest hides;
Borne me in honor to the cottonwood bier,
Laying at my right hand the sacred pipe
And at my left the arrows and bow, the lance
I bound with thongs and hung
With the feathers from the eagle's breast.
Below the scaffold of the dead
My pony of the speckled skin and fierce heart
Would be led, and with a blow of the stone axe
Lie down to wait my needs.
Far above in the sacred hoop of the sky
Long-sighted hawks hanging on silent wings
Would mark my passing.

III

When the Life-Giver hid from the night
The dark wind would speak to my spirit
And I would arise, taking up my weapons.
Mounting my horse I would follow
The great path over the earth, beyond the stars.
I would see the glow of cooking fires
As bright as arrow tips across the northern sky;
Waiting for me, old friends would dance and feast
And play the games of gambling.
Behind me drums would beat and willow whistles cry
Like the doves of spring who nested
In the berry bushes near the river of my village.
I would pause to hear my sons in council,
Speaking of my deeds in war, my strength and wisdom.
My woman in her sorrow would tear her clothing,
Bloody her face marked with ashes,
And with a knife cut off her plaited hair.

IV

But I am Thomas, here, where no grass grows,
Where no clear rivers run;
Where dirt and despair abound,
Where heat and rain alike rust out
The souls of my people, the roofs of tin;
Where disease like a serpent slips from house to house
And hunger sits in the dooryard.
I am Thomas. I wait for the wagon
To bring the government box of pine;
I wait for the journey to the burying ground
Below the sandy butte where rattlesnakes
Stink in burrows, and the white man's wooden trinities
Stand in crooked rows.
There I will be put beneath the earth.
They will seal in my spirit.
I will not hear the dark wind's cry
To come and take the starry road
Across the circle of the sky.

*Home-Founding**

OLE RÖLVAAG

Early the next morning Per Hansa and one of the Solum boys set out on the fifty-two-mile journey to Sioux Falls, where Per Hansa filed an application for the quarter-section of land which lay to the north of Hans Olsa's. To confirm the application, he received a temporary deed to the land. The deed was made out in the name of *Peder Benjamin Hansen;* it contained a description of the land, the conditions which he agreed to fulfil in order to become the owner, and the date, *June 6, 1873.*

Sörine wanted Beret and the children to stay with her during the two days that her husband would be away; but she refused the offer with thanks. If they were to get ready a home for the summer, she said, she would have to take hold of matters right away.

. . . "For the summer?" exclaimed the other woman, showing her astonishment. "What about the winter, then?"

Beret saw that she had uttered a thought which she ought to have kept to herself; she evaded the question as best she could.

During the first day, both she and the boys found so much to do that they hardly took time to eat. They unloaded both the wagons, set up the stove, and carried out the table. Then Beret arranged their bedroom in the larger wagon. With all the things taken out it was quite roomy in there; it made a tidy bedroom when everything had been put in order. The boys thought this work great fun, and she herself found some relief in it for her troubled mind. But something vague and intangible hovering in the air would not allow her to be wholly at ease; she had to stop often and look about, or stand erect and listen. . . . Was that a sound she heard? . . . All the while, the thought that had struck her yesterday when she had first got down from the wagon, stood vividly before her mind: here there was nothing even to hide behind! . . . When the room was finished, and a blanket

* Selection from chapter two of *Giants in the Earth.*

Mr. Jerns, Dry Valley, Custer County, Nebraska, 1886

had been hung up to serve as a door, she seemed a little less conscious of this feeling. But back in the recesses of her mind it still was there. . . .

After they had milked the cow, eaten their evening porridge, and talked awhile to the oxen, she took the boys and And-Ongen and strolled away from camp. With a common impulse, they went toward the hill; when they had reached the summit, Beret sat down and let her gaze wander aimlessly around. . . . In a certain sense, she had to admit to herself, it was lovely up here. The broad expanse stretching away endlessly in every direction, seemed almost like the ocean—especially now, when darkness was falling. It reminded her strongly of the sea, and yet it was very different . . . This formless prairie had no heart that beat, no waves that sang, no soul that could be touched . . . or cared. . . .

The infinitude surrounding her on every hand might not have been so oppressive, might even have brought her a measure of peace, if it had not been for the deep silence, which lay heavier here than in a church. Indeed, what was there to break it? She had passed beyond the outposts of civilization; the nearest dwelling places of men were far away. Here no warbling of birds rose on the air, no buzzing of insects sounded;* even the wind had died away; the waving blades of grass that trembled to the faintest breath now stood erect and quiet, as if listening, in the great hush of the evening. . . . All along the way, coming out, she had noticed this strange thing: the stillness had grown deeper, the silence more depressing, the farther west they journeyed; it must have been over two weeks now since she had heard a bird sing! Had they travelled into some nameless, abandoned region? Could no living thing exist out here, in the empty, desolate, endless wastes of green and blue? . . . How *could* existence go on, she thought, desperately? If life is to thrive and endure, it must at least have something to hide behind! . . .

The children were playing boisterously a little way off. What a terrible noise they made! But she had better let them keep on with their play, as long as they were happy. . . . She sat perfectly quiet, thinking of the long, oh, so interminably long march that they would have to make, back to the place where human beings dwelt. It would be small hardship for her, of course, sitting in the wagon; but she pitied Per Hansa and the boys—and then the poor oxen! . . . He certainly would soon find out for himself that a

* Original settlers are agreed that there was neither bird nor insect life on the prairie, with the exception of mosquitoes, the first year that they came.

home for men and women and children could never be established in this wilderness. . . . And how could she bring new life into the world out here! . . .

Slowly her thoughts began to centre on her husband; they grew warm and tender as they dwelt on him. She trembled as they came. . . .

But only for a brief while. As her eyes darted nervously here and there, flitting from object to object and trying to pierce the purple dimness that was steadily closing in, a sense of desolation so profound settled upon her that she seemed unable to think at all. It would not do to gaze any longer at the terror out there, where everything was turning to grim and awful darkness. . . . She threw herself back in the grass and looked up into the heavens. But darkness and infinitude lay there, also—the sense of utter desolation still remained. . . . Suddenly, for the first time, she realized the full extent of her loneliness, the dreadful nature of the fate that had overtaken her. Lying there on her back, and staring up into the quiet sky across which the shadows of night were imperceptibly creeping, she went over in her mind every step of their wanderings, every mile of the distance they had travelled since they had left home. . . .

First they had boarded the boat at Sandnessjöen. . . . This boat had carried them southward along the coast. . . . In Namsos there had been a large ship with many white sails, that had taken her, with her dear ones, and sailed away—that had carried them off relentlessly, farther and farther from the land they knew. In this ship they had sailed for weeks; the weeks had even grown into months; they had seemed to be crossing an ocean which had no end. . . . There had been something almost laughable in this blind course, steadily fixed on the sunset! When head winds came, they beat up against them; before sweeping fair breezes they scudded along; but always they were westering! . . .

. . . At last they had landed in Quebec. There she had walked about the streets, confused and bewildered by a jargon of unintelligible sounds that did not seem like the speech of people. . . . Was this the Promised Land? Ah no—it was only the beginning of the real journey. . . . Then something within her had risen up in revolt: I will go no farther! . . .

. . . But they had kept on, just the same—had pushed steadily westward, over plains, through deserts, into towns, and out of them again. . . . One fine day they had stood in Detroit, Michigan. This wasn't the place, either, it seemed. . . . Move on! . . . Once more she had felt the spirit of revolt rising to shout aloud: I will go no farther! . . . But it had been as if a resistless flood had torn them loose from their foundations and was carrying them helplessly along on its current—flinging them here and there, hurling them madly onward, with no known destination ahead.

Farther and farther onward . . . always west. . . . For a brief while there had been a chance to relax once more; they had travelled on water again, and she could hear the familiar splash of waves against the ship's side. This language she knew of old, and did not fear; it had lessened the torture of that section of the journey for her, though they had been subjected to much ill-treatment and there had been a great deal of bullying and brawling on board.

At last the day had arrived when they had landed in Milwaukee. But here they were only to make a new start—to take another plunge into the unknown. . . . Farther, and always farther. . . . The relentless current kept whirling them along. . . . Was it bound nowhere, then? . . . Did it have no end? . . .

In the course of time they had come jogging into a place called Prairie du Chien. . . . Had that been in Wisconsin or some other place named after savages? . . . It made no difference—they had gone on. They had floundered along to Lansing, in Iowa. . . . Onward again. Finally they had reached Fillmore County, in Minnesota. . . . But even that wasn't the place, it seemed! . . .

. . . Now she was lying here on a little green hillock, surrounded by the open, endless prairie, far off in a spot from which no road led back! . . . It seemed to her that she had lived many lives already, in each one of which she had done nothing but wander and wander, always straying farther away from the home that was dear to her.

She sat up at last, heaved a deep sigh, and glanced around as if waking from a dream. . . . The unusual blending of the gentle and forceful in her features seemed to be thrown into relief by the scene in which she sat and the twilight hovering about her, as a beautiful picture is enhanced by a well-chosen frame.

The two boys and their little sister were having great fun up here. So many queer things were concealed under the tufts of grass. Store-Hans came running, and brought a handful of little flat, reddish chips of stone that looked as though they had been carved out of the solid rock; they were pointed at one end and broadened out evenly on both sides, like the head of a spear. The edges were quite sharp; in the broad end a deep groove had been filed. Ole brought more of them, and gave a couple to his little sister to play with. . . . The mother sat for a while with the stones in her lap where the children had placed them; at last she took them up, one by one, and examined them closely. . . . These must have been formed by human hands, she thought.

Suddenly Ole made another rare discovery. He brought her a larger stone, that looked like a sledge hammer; in this the groove was deep and broad.

The mother got up hastily.

"Where are you finding these things?"

The boys at once took her to the place; in a moment she, too, was standing beside the little hollow at the brow of the hill, which the men had discovered the night before; the queer stones that the children had been bringing her lay scattered all around.

"Ola says that the Indians made them!" cried Store-Hans, excitedly. "Is it true, mother? . . . Do you suppose they'll ever come back?"

"Yes, maybe—if we stay here long enough. . . ." She remained standing awhile beside the hollow; the same thought possessed her that had seized hold of her husband when he had first found the spot—here a human being lay buried. Strangely enough, it did not frighten her; it only showed her more plainly, in a stronger, harsher light, how unspeakably lonesome this place was.

The evening dusk had now almost deepened into night. It seemed to gather all its strength around her, to close in on every side, to have its centre in the spot where she stood. The wagons had become only a dim speck in the darkness, far, far away; the tent at Hans Olsa's looked like a tuft of grass that had whitened at the top; Tönseten's sod house she was unable to make out at all. . . . She could not bring herself to call aloud to the boys; instead, she walked around the hollow, spoke to them softly, and said that it was time to go home. . . . No, no, they mustn't take the stones with them to-night! But to-morrow they might come up here again to play.

. . . Beret could not go to sleep for a long time that night. At last she grew thoroughly angry with herself; her nerves were taut as bowstrings; her head kept rising up from the pillow to listen—but there was nothing to hear . . . nothing except the night wind, which now had begun to stir.

. . . It stirred with so many unknown things! . . .

Pericles on 31st Street

HARRY MARK PETRAKIS

Louie Debella's bar was located on the corner of 31st Street and Dart Avenue, the last store in a group of five stores owned by Leonard Barsevick, who besides being a landlord operated the Lark Wholesale Clothing Company across the street.

My name is George. My last name is not important. I'm Louie Debella's night bartender and I count myself a good bartender. I might mention a few of the quality places I have tended bar, but that has nothing to do with this story.

If I have learned anything from fifteen years of tending bar it is that a bartender cannot take sides with anything that goes on across the bar. He has got to be strictly nonpartisan. A cousin of mine in South Bend, also in the business, once tried to mediate an argument about Calvin Coolidge. Somebody hit him in the back of the head with a bottle of beer that was not yet empty, and besides needing stitches he got wet. Now when I am on the job I never take sides. That is, I never did until the episode of Pericles.

As I understand it this fellow Pericles was a Greek general and statesman who lived back in those Greek golden years you read about in the school history books. From all reports he was a pretty complete sort of guy who laid down a set of rules and was tough on everybody who did not read them right.

If you are wondering what a Greek who lived a couple of thousand years ago has got to do with this story, I guess it all started because the storekeepers in our row of stores gathered in the bar in the evening after they locked their doors for a glass of beer.

The first man in was usually Dan Ryan, who had the butcher shop. Ryan was a heavy beer man and needed the head start on the others. A little later Olaf Johnson, who ran the Sunlight lunchroom, came in with Sol Reidman the tailor. Olaf had a huge belly that was impossible to keep under a coat.

Sol liked nothing better than to tease Olaf about when the triplets were expected.

The last man in was Bernard Klioris, who had a little grocery next to Sol's tailor shop. Bernard usually got lost in the arguments, and swung back and forth like a kitchen door in a restaurant. He had a sad thin face and was not so bright, but among our patrons you could hardly tell.

Last Tuesday night after I had served Ryan his fourth beer, Olaf and Sol and Bernard came in together, with Olaf and Sol arguing as usual.

"She told me she was a Republican," Olaf said. "They want some lunk for Congress. I told her to come by you and get her petition signed."

Sol waggled his bald head indignantly. "Who gave you leave to advertise my business?" he said. "A man's politics is a sacred trust that belongs to him alone."

"She only had a petition, not a gun," Olaf said. "I knew you was a Republican so I sent her."

"How can anyone," Ryan said from the bar, "be in his right mind and still be a Republican?"

Sol waved a warning finger. "Be careful," he said. "You are stepping on the Constitution when you ridicule a man's politics."

"I read about the Constitution," Bernard said.

They lined up at the bar. I poured them beer. All they ever drank was beer.

The door opened and Nick Simonakis came in. He was the vendor who took his stand at night on the corner of 31st and Dart. He had a glassed-in wagon that he pushed into place under the street lamp, and from the wagon he sold hot dogs and tamales and peanuts. Several times during the evening he locked up the wagon and came into the bar for a glass of wine. He would sit alone at a table to the side of the room, his dark eyes in his hollow-cheeked face glaring at the room from above the white handlebar mustache. Every now and then he would sip his wine and shake his head, making his thick white hair hang more disordered over his forehead.

Other men might have thought he was a little crazy because sometimes he sat there alone talking to himself, but like I said, I do not take sides. At other times he gave up muttering and loudly berated the drinkers of beer. "Only Turks would drink beer," he said, "when they could drink wine. One for the belly and the other for wisdom." He would sip his wine slowly, mocking their guzzling of beer, and the storekeepers would try to ignore him.

"The sun-ripened grapes," Simonakis said, "hanging until they become sweet. Then the trampling by the young maidens to extract the lovely juices. A ceremony of the earth."

"Beer don't just grow in barrels," Olaf said. "Good beer takes a lot of making."

The old man laughed softly as if he was amused. "You are a Turk," he said. "I excuse you because you think and talk like a Turk."

"Say, old man," Sol said. "Someone wants a bag of peanuts. You are losing business."

Simonakis looked at Sol with bright piercing eyes. "I will lose business," he said. "I am drinking my wine."

"He must be rich," Ryan said, "and pushing business away. I wish I had gone into peddling peanuts myself."

"It is not a case of wealth," Simonakis said. "There is a time for labor and a time for leisure. A man must have time to sit and think. This made Greece great."

"Made who what?" Olaf asked with sarcasm.

The old man swept him with contempt. "In ancient Greece," he said coldly, "an elephant like you would have been packed on a mountaintop as bait for buzzards."

"Watch the language," Olaf said. "I don't have to take that stuff from an old goat like you."

"A land of ruined temples," Sol said, and he moved from the bar and carried his beer to a nearby table. "A land of philosophers without shoes."

"A land of men!" Simonakis spit out. "We gave the world learning and courage. We taught men how to live and how to die."

Ryan and Bernard and Olaf had followed Sol to the table, drawing their chairs.

"Would you mind, old man," Ryan said as he sat down, "leaving a little bit of credit to the Irish?"

"I give them credit," Simonakis said, "for inventing the wheelbarrow, and giving the world men to push it."

"Did you hear that!" Ryan said indignantly and looked fiercely at the old man.

The old man went on as if he had not heard. "A model of courage for the world," he said. "Leonidas with three hundred men holding the pass at Thermopylae against the Persian hordes. Themistocles destroying the great fleet of Xerxes at Salamis."

"That's history," Olaf said. "What have they done lately?"

Simonakis ignored him. He motioned to me and I took him the bottle of port. He raised the full glass and held it up and spoke in Greek to the wine as if performing some kind of ceremony. The men watched him and somebody laughed. Simonakis glared at them. "Laugh, barbarians," he said. "Laugh and forget your debt to Greece. Forget the golden age and the men like lions. Hide in your smoking cities and drown in your stinking beer."

"What a goat," Olaf said.

Sol shook his head sadly. "It is a pity to see a man ruined by drink," he said. "That wine he waves has soaked his head."

"Wheelbarrow indeed," Ryan said, and he glared back at the old man.

II

At that moment the front door opened and Leonard Barsevick, the landlord, walked in. He carried an air of elegance into the bar. Maybe because of his Homburg and the black chesterfield coat he wore.

The storekeepers greeted him in a respectful chorus. He waved his hand around like a politician at a beer rally and smiled broadly. "Evening, boys," he said. "Only got a minute but I couldn't pass by without stopping to buy a few of my tenants a beer. George, set up the drinks and mark it on my tab."

"Thank you, Mr. Barsevick," Olaf said. "You sure look like a million bucks tonight."

Barsevick laughed and looked pleased. "Got to keep up a front, Olaf," he said. "If a man in my position gets a spot on his suit he might as well give up."

"That's right, Mr. Barsevick," Ryan said. "A man in your position has got to keep up with the best and you sure do."

"Say, Mr. Barsevick," Bernard said. "You know the leak in the roof at my store I spoke to you about last month. It hasn't been fixed yet and that rain the other night . . ."

"Wait a minute, Bernie," Barsevick laughed. "Not tonight. If I promised to fix it, I'm going to have it fixed. Leonard Barsevick is a man of his word. Ain't that right, boys?"

They all nodded and Olaf said, "Yes, sir," emphatically.

"But not tonight," Barsevick said. "Tonight I'm out for a little relaxation with a baby doll that looks like Jayne Mansfield." He made a suggestive noise with his mouth.

"You're sure a lucky man, Mr. Barsevick," Olaf said admiringly.

"Not luck at all, Olaf," Barsevick said, and his voice took on a tone of serious confidence. "It's perseverance and the ability to get along with people. I always say if I didn't know how to get along with people I wouldn't be where I am today."

"That's sure right, Mr. Barsevick," Ryan said. The others nodded agreement.

"Fine," Barsevick beamed. "All right, boys, drink up, and pass your best wishes to Leonard Barsevick for a successful evening." He winked broadly.

The storekeepers laughed and raised their glasses. Everybody toasted Barsevick but Simonakis. He sat scowling at the landlord from beneath his shaggy brows. Barsevick noticed him.

"You didn't give this gentleman a drink, George," he said. "What are you drinking, sir?"

"He ain't no gentleman," Olaf said. "He is a peanut peddler."

"An authority on wheelbarrows," Ryan said.

Simonakis cocked a thumb at Barsevick. "Hurry, landlord," he said, "your Mansfield is waiting."

Barsevick gave him a cool glance, but the old man just looked bored. Finally the landlord gave up and turned away, pulling on his suede gloves. He strode to the door cutting a fancy figure and waved grandly. "Good night, boys," he said.

The boys wished him good night. Simonakis belched.

III

On the following Thursday the notices came from Barsevick's bookkeeper announcing a fifteen percent rent increase all along the block. All the storekeepers got a notice of the raise becoming effective with the expiration of their leases about a month away. Louie was so disturbed he called me down in the middle of the afternoon and took off early.

That night the storekeepers were a sad bunch. They sat around the table over their beer, looking like their visas had expired.

"I don't understand it," Ryan said. "Mr. Barsevick knows that business has not been good. Fifteen percent at this time makes for an awful load."

"With license fees and the rest," Olaf said, "a lunchroom ain't hardly worthwhile. I was not making nothing before. With this increase it ain't going to get no better."

"Two hands to sew pants will not be enough," Sol said. "I must sew with four hands, all my own."

Bernard looked distressed. "Mr. Barsevick must have a good reason," he said.

"He's got expenses," Olaf said.

"He should have mine," Ryan said. "Beef is up six cents a pound again."

Simonakis came into the bar pulling off his gloves. He ignored the men as he walked by them to his table against the wall and signaled to me for his bottle of wine.

"I am going to buy a wagon," Olaf said loudly, "and sell peanuts and hot dogs on the street."

"You must first," Simonakis said, "have the wisdom to tell them apart."

Olaf flushed and started to get up. Sol shook him down. "No time for games with crazy men tonight," Sol said. "This matter is serious. We must organize a delegation to speak to Mr. Barsevick. It must be explained that this increase imposes a terrible burden on us at this time. Perhaps a little later."

"Shoot him," Simonakis said. He waved the glass I had just filled with dark wine.

"You mind you own business, peddler," Ryan said. "Nobody is talking to you."

"A Greek would shoot him," Simonakis said, "But you are toads."

"I get my rent raised," Olaf said, "and now I got to sit here and be insulted by a peanut peddler."

The front door opened and the room went quiet.

Barsevick closed the door softly behind him and walked over to the storekeepers' table and pulled up a chair and sat down like a sympathetic friend coming to share their grief.

I guess they were all as surprised as I was and for a long moment no one spoke and Barsevick looked solemnly from one to the other. "I hope you do not mind my butting in, boys," he said and he motioned to me. "George, bring the boys a round on me."

"Mr. Barsevick," Ryan said, "the boys and me were just discussing . . ."

Barsevick raised his hand gravely. "I know, Danny," he said. "I know what you are going to say. I want to go on record first as saying there is nobody any sorrier than Leonard Barsevick about this. That is why I am here. My bookkeeper said I did not have to come over tonight and talk to you. I told him I would not stand for that, that you boys were not just tenants, you were friends of mine."

"It is a lot of money, Mr. Barsevick," Olaf said. "I mean if we were making more, things might be different."

"I know that, Olaf," Barsevick said, "Believe me, if there was any other way I would jump at the chance. I said to Jack, my bookkeeper, 'Isn't there any other way?' I swear to you boys he said, 'Mr. Barsevick, if that rent is not increased it will be charity.' " I brought the tray of fresh beer and set the glasses around the table. "Not that I mind a little help to my friends," Barsevick said, "but it is not good for business. I would be shamed before my competitors. 'There's Barsevick,' they would laugh, 'too soft to raise his tenants' rent.' They would put the screws on me and in no time at all I might be out of business."

Everybody was silent for a moment, probably examining the prospect of Leonard Barsevick put out of business because of his soft heart.

"We know you got expenses," Ryan said.

Barsevick shook his head mournfully. "You got no idea," he said. "I mean you boys got no idea. I am afraid sometimes for the whole economy. Costs cannot keep rising and still keep the country sound. Everything is going up. Believe me, boys, being a landlord and a businessman is hell."

"Shoot him," Simonakis said loudly.

Barsevick stopped talking and looked across the tables at the old man.

"He is a crazy man," Sol said. "That wine he drinks makes him talk to himself."

Barsevick turned back to the men but he was disturbed. He looked over at the old man once more like he was trying to understand and then started to get up. "I got to go now, boys," he said. "I'm working late tonight with my bookkeeper. If we see any other way to cut costs I will be glad to reconsider the matter of the increase. That is my promise to you boys as friends."

"We sure appreciate you stopping by, Mr. Barsevick," Ryan said. "We know there is many a landlord would not have bothered."

Barsevick shook his head vigorously. "Not Leonard Barsevick," he said. "Not even his worst enemy will say that Barsevick does not cut a straight corner when it comes to friends."

"We know that, Mr. Barsevick," Olaf said.

"We sure do," Bernard said.

"Shoot him," Simonakis said. "Shoot him before he gets away."

IV

Barsevick whirled around and stared in some kind of shock at the old man. I guess he was trying very fast to figure out if the old man was serious.

"Don't pay him no mind, Mr. Barsevick," Olaf said. "He has been out in the rain too long."

"You are a demagogue." Simonakis spoke loudly to the landlord. "You wave your greedy fingers and tell them you are a friend. Aaaaaaaa!" The old man smiled craftily. "I know your kind. In Athens they would tie you under a bull."

Barsevick stood there like rocks were being bounced off his head, his face turning a bright shade of red.

Sol motioned angrily at the old man. "Somebody wants a hot dog," he said. "You are losing business."

Simonakis looked at Sol for a moment with his mustache bristling, then looked at the others. "I have lost business," he said slowly, "You have lost courage."

A sound of hissing came from Barsevick, his red cheeks shaking off heat like a capped kettle trying to let off steam. "You damn pig," he said huskily. "You unwashed old bum. You damn peddler of peanuts."

The old man would not give an inch. "You are a hypocrite," he said. "A hypocrite and a libertine. You live on the sweat of better men."

Barsevick's jaw was working furiously like he was trying to chew up the right words.

"Let me tell you," Simonakis said, and his voice took on a more moderate tone as if he were pleased to be able to pass information on to the landlord, "let me tell you how the hypocrite goes in the end. One day the people wake up. They know he is a liar and a thief. They pick up stones They aim for his head." He pointed a big long finger at Barsevick and made a rattling sound rise from his throat. "What a mess a big head like yours would make."

Barsevick gasped and whirled to the men at the table. "He's threatening me," he shouted. "Did you hear him? Throw the old bastard out."

No one moved. I kept wiping glasses. A good bartender learns to keep working.

"Did you hear me!" Barsevick yelled. "Somebody throw him out."

"He is a crazy old man," Sol said. "He talks without meaning."

"Shut up!" Barsevick said. "You stick with him because you are no damn good either.

"I do not stick with him," Sol said, and he drew himself up hurt. "I am trying to be fair."

Barsevick turned to me. "George, throw him out!"

I kept wiping the glasses. "I am underpaid, Mr. Barsevick," I said. "My salary barely covers my work. Any extra service would be charity."

The old man took after him again. "Who likes you, landlord?" he said. "Be honest and speak truth before your tenants. Who likes you?"

"You shut up!" Barsevick shouted.

"I mean really likes you," Simonakis said. "I do not mean the poor girls you buy with your tainted money."

"I'll shut the old bastard up!" Barsevick hollered and started for the table against the wall.

Simonakis stood up and Barsevick stopped. The old man looked tall and menacing with his big hands and bright eyes and his white mustache standing out like a joyous challenge to battle. "You cannot shut up truth," Simonakis said. "And the truth is that you are a leech feeding on the labor of better men. You wish to become rich by making them poorer."

Barsevick stood a couple of tables away from the old man with his back bent a little waiting for a word to be raised in his defense. No one spoke and the old man stared at him with eyes like knives.

"You old bastard . . ." Barsevick said weakly.

Ryan made a sound clearing his throat. He wore a stern and studied look on his face. "Fifteen percent is a steep raise," he said. "Right at this time when it is tough to make ends meet."

Barsevick whirled on him. "You keep out of this," he said. "You just mind your own business."

"I would say," Ryan said slowly, "fifteen percent more rent to pay each month is my business."

"I'll make it twenty-five percent," Barsevick shouted. "If you don't like it you can get out!"

"I have a lease," Ryan said quietly. He was looking at the landlord like he was seeing him for the first time.

"I will break it," Barsevick said. He looked angrily around at other storekeepers. "I will break all your leases."

"I did not say nothing!" Bernard protested.

"The way of tyrants and thieves," Simonakis said. "All who oppose them suffer." He raised his head and fixed his eyes upon the ceiling. "O Pericles, lend us a stick so we may drive the tyrant from the market place."

"Stop calling me a tyrant," Barsevick fumed.

Simonakis kept his head raised praying to that guy Pericles.

"I'm going to put every one of you into the street," Barsevick said. "I'm going to teach you all not to be so damn smart."

Sol shook his head with measured contempt for the landlord on his face. "You will not put us out," he said. "First, you are too greedy for the rent. Second, you would not rent those leaking barns again without major repairs, and third . . ." He paused. "Third, I do not admire your personality."

"Amen," Bernard said. "My roof keeps leaking."

"O Pericles!" Simonakis suddenly cried out and everybody looked at him. "They are barbarians and not of Athens but they are honest men and need your help. Give them strength to destroy the common enemy. Lend them your courage to sweep out the tyrant."

"You are all crazy," Barsevick said and he looked driven and disordered. His tie was outside his coat and the Homburg perched lopsided over one ear.

"You are a tiger," Sol said. "Tell me what circus you live in and I will rent a cage to take you home."

"Do not be insulting," Ryan said to Sol. "You will hurt the landlord's feelings. He cannot help he has got a head like a loin of pork."

"You ignorant bastards!" Barsevick shouted.

Ryan got up and came over to the bar. He stepped behind and pulled out the little sawed-off bat Louie kept under the counter. He winked at me. "I am just borrowing it," he said. "I want to put a new crease in the landlord's hat."

Simonakis came back from calling on Pericles. "Do not strike him," he said. "Stone him. Stone him as they stoned tyrants in Athens." He looked at the floor and around the room excitedly searching for stones.

Barsevick in full retreat began to edge toward the door. He opened his mouth to speak some final word of defiance but one look at the bat in Ryan's hand must have choked off his wind.

"Tyrant!" Simonakis shouted.

"Vulture!" Olaf said. "Stop and eat on me, and I'll grind some glass for your salad!"

"Greedy pig!" Ryan said, and he waved the bat. "You try and collect that rent and we all move out!"

"Judas!" Sol said. "Come to me only to sew your shroud!"

"Fix my leaking roof!" Bernard said.

With one last helpless wail, Barsevick stumbled out through the door.

For a long moment after the door closed nobody moved. Then Ryan handed me back the bat. I put it under the counter. Olaf started to the bar with his glass. Bernard came after him. Soon all were lined up at the bar. All except Simonakis, who had gone back to sit down at his table staring moodily into his glass of wine.

Ryan turned his back to the bar and looked across the tables at Simonakis. He looked at him for a long time and no one spoke. The old man kept staring at his wine. Ryan looked helplessly at Olaf and Sol and they watched him struggling. Bernard looked dazed. I held a wet towel in my hands and forgot to wipe the bar. When Ryan finally turned back to Simonakis, you could see he had made up his mind. He spoke slowly and carefully.

"Mr. Simonakis," he said.

The old man raised his head scowling.

"Mr. Simonakis," Ryan said. "Will you be kind enough to join my friends and me in a drink?"

The old man stopped scowling. He nodded gravely and stood up tall and straight, his mustache curved in dignity, and came to the bar. Ryan moved aside to make a place for him.

I began to pour the beer.

"No, George," Ryan said. "We will have wine this trip."

"Yes, sir," I said.

I took down the bottle of port and filled a row of small glasses.

Ryan raised his glass and looked belligerently at the others. "To the glory of Greece," he said.

The rest of them raised their glasses.

"To Athens," Sol said.

"To Mr. Simonakis," Olaf said.

"Ditto," Bernard said.

I took down another wineglass. I poured myself some wine. They all looked at me. I did not care. I was abandoning a professional tradition of neutrality.

"To Pericles," I said.

Simonakis stroked his mustache and sipped his wine. The rest of us sipped right with him.

The Fastest Runner on Sixty-First Street

JAMES T. FARRELL

I

Morty Aiken liked to run and to skate. He liked running games and races. He liked running so much that sometimes he'd go over to Washington Park all by himself and run just for the fun of it. He got a kick out of running, and he had raced every kid he could get to run against him. His love of racing and running had even become a joke among many of the boys he knew. But even when they gave him the horse laugh it was done in a good-natured way, because he was a very popular boy. Older fellows liked him, and when they would see him, they'd say, there's a damn good kid and a damned fast runner.

When he passed his fourteenth birthday, Morty was a trifle smaller than most boys of his own age. But he was well known, and, in a way, almost famous in his own neighborhood. He lived at Sixty-first and Eberhardt, but kids in the whole area had heard of him, and many of them would speak of what a runner and what a skater Morty Aiken was.

He won medals in playground tournaments, and, in fact, he was the only lad from his school who had ever won medals in these tournaments. In these events he became the champion in the fifty- and hundred-yard dash, and with this he gained the reputation of being the best runner, for his age, on the South Side of Chicago.

He was as good a skater as he was a runner. In winter, he was to be seen regularly almost every day on the ice at the Washington Park lagoon or over on the Midway. He had a pair of Johnson racers which his father had given him, and he treasured these more than any other possession. His mother knitted him red socks and a red stocking cap for skating, and he had a red-and-white sweater. When he skated, he was like a streak of red. His form was excellent, and his sense of himself and of his body on the ice was sure and right. Almost every day there would be a game of I-Got-It. The skater who was *it* would skate in a wide circle, chased by the pack until he was caught. Morty loved to play I-Got-It, and on many a day this boy in short pants, wearing the red stocking cap, the red-and-white sweater, and the thick, knitted red woolen socks coming above the black shoes of his Johnson racers, would lead the pack, circling around and around and around, his head forward, his upper torso bent forward, his hands behind his back, his legs working with grace and giving him a speed that sometimes seemed miraculous. And in February, 1919, Morty competed in an ice derby, conducted under the auspices of the Chicago *Clarion*. He won two gold medals. His picture was on the first page of the sports section of the Sunday *Clarion*. All in all, he was a famous and celebrated lad. His father and mother were proud of him. His teacher and Mrs. Bixby, the principal of the school, were proud of him. Merchants on Sixty-first Street were proud of him. There was not a lad in the neighborhood who was greeted on the street by strangers as often as Morty.

Although he was outwardly modest, Morty had his dreams. He was graduated from grammar school in 1919, and was planning to go to Park High in the fall. He was impatient to go to high school and to get into high-school track meets. He'd never been coached, and yet look how good he was! Think of how good he would be when he had some coaching! He'd be a streak of lightning, if there ever was one. He dreamed that he would be called the Human Streak of Lightning. And after high school there would be college, college track meets, and the Big Ten championship, and after that he would join an athletic club and run in track meets, and he would win a place on the Olympic team, and somewhere, in Paris or Rome or some European city, he would beat the best runners in the world, and, like Ty Cobb in baseball and Jess Willard in prize fighting, he'd be the world's greatest runner.

And girls would all like him, and the most beautiful girl in the world would marry him. He liked girls, but girls liked him even more than he liked them. In May, a little while before his graduation, the class had a picnic, and they played post office. The post office was behind a clump of bushes in Jackson Park. He was called to the post office more than any other of the boys. There was giggling and talking and teasing, but it hadn't bothered him, especially because he knew that the other fellows liked and kind of envied him. To Morty, this was only natural. He accepted it. He accepted the fact that he was a streak of lightning on his feet and on the ice, and that this made him feel somehow different from other boys and very important. Even Tony Rabuski looked at him in this way, and if any kid would have picked on him, Tony would have piled into that kid. Tony was the toughest boy in school, and he was also considered to be the dumbest. He was also the poorest. He would often come to school wearing a black shirt, because a black shirt didn't show the dirt the way that other shirts did, and his parents couldn't afford to buy him many shirts. One day Tony was walking away from school with Morty, and Tony said:

"Kid, you run de fastest, I fight de best in de whole school. We make a crack-up team. We're pals. Shake, kid, we're pals."

Morty shook Tony's hand. For a fourteen-year-old boy, Tony had very big and strong hands. The other kids sometimes called them "meat hooks."

Morty looked on this handshake as a pledge. He and Tony became friends, and they were often together. Morty had Tony come over to his house to play, and sometimes Tony stayed for a meal. Tony ate voraciously and wolfishly. When Morty's parents spoke of the way Tony ate and of the quantity of food he ate, Morty would reply by telling them that Tony was his friend.

Because he was poor and somewhat stupid, a dull and fierce resentment smoldered in Tony. Other boys out-talked him, and they were often able to plague and annoy him, and then outrun him because he was heavy footed. The kids used to laugh at Tony because they said he had lead, iron, and bricks in his big feet. After Morty and Tony had shaken hands and become pals, Morty never would join the other boys in razzing Tony. And he and Tony doped out a way that would permit Tony to get even with kids who tried to torment him. If some of the boys made game of Tony until he was confused and enraged and went for them, Morty would chase the boys. He had no difficulty in catching one of them. When he caught any of the boys who'd been teasing and annoying Tony, he'd usually manage to hold the boy until Tony would lumber up and exact his punishment and revenge. Sometimes Tony would be cruel, and on a couple of occasions when Tony, in a dull and stupefied rage, was sitting on a hurt, screaming boy and pounding on him, Morty ordered Tony to lay off. Tony did so instantly. Morty didn't want Tony to be too cruel. He had come to like Tony and to look on him as a big brother. He'd always wanted a brother, and sometimes he would imagine how wonderful it would be if Tony could even come to live at his house.

The system Morty and Tony worked out, with Morty chasing and catching one of the boys who ragged Tony, worked out well. Soon the kids stopped ragging Tony. Because of their fear, and because they liked and respected Morty and wanted him to play with them, they began to accept Tony. And Tony began to change. Once accepted, so that he was no longer the butt of jokes, he looked on all the boys in Morty's gang as his pals. He would protect them as he would protect Morty. Tony then stopped scowling and making fierce and funny faces and acting in many odd little ways. After he became accepted, as a result of being Morty's pal, his behavior changed, and because he was strong and could fight, the boys began to admire him. At times he really hoped for strange boys to come around the neighborhood and act like bullies so he could beat them up. He wanted to fight and punch because he could feel powerful and would be praised and admired.

II

Ever since he had been a little fellow, Tony had often been called a "Polack" or a "dirty Polack." After he became one of the gang or group around Morty, some of the boys would tell him that he was a "white Polack." In his slow way, he thought about these words and what they meant. When you were called certain words, you were laughed at, you were looked at as if something were wrong with you. If you were a Polack, many girls didn't want to have anything to do with you. The boys and girls who weren't Polacks had fun together that Polacks couldn't have. Being a Polack and being called a Polack was like being called a sonofabitch. It was a name. When you were called a name like this, you were looked at as a different kind of kid from one who wasn't called a name. Morty Aiken wasn't called names. Tony didn't want to be called names. And if he fought and beat up those who called him names, they would be afraid of him. He wanted that. But he also wanted to have as much fun as the kids had who weren't called these names. And he worked it out that these kids felt better when they called other kids names. He could fight and he could call names, and if he called a kid a name, and that kid got tough, he could beat him up. He began to call names. And there was a name even worse than Polack—"nigger." If Tony didn't like a kid, he called him a "nigger." And he talked about the "niggers." He felt as good as he guessed these other kids did when he talked about the "niggers." And they could be beat up. They weren't supposed to go to Washington Park because that was a park for the whites. That was what he had often heard.

He heard it said so much that he believed it. He sometimes got a gang of the boys together and they would roam Washington Park, looking for colored boys to beat up. Morty went with them. He didn't particularly like to beat up anyone, but when they saw a colored kid and chased him, he would always be at the head, and he would be the one who caught the colored boy. He could grab or tackle him, and by that time the others would catch up. He worked the same plan that he and Tony had worked against the other boys. And after they caught and beat up a colored boy, they would all talk and shout and brag about what they had done, and talk about how they had each gotten in their licks and punches and kicks, and how fast Morty had run to catch that shine, and what a sock Tony had given him, and, talking all together and strutting and bragging, they felt good and proud of themselves, and they talked about how the Sixty-first Street boys would see to it that Washington Park would stay a white man's park.

And this became more and more important to Tony. There were those names, "Polack," "dirty Polack," "white Polack." If you could be called a "Polack," you weren't considered white. Well, when he beat them up, was he or wasn't he white? They knew. After the way he clouted these black ones, how could the other kids not say that Tony Rabuski wasn't white? That showed them all. That showed he was a hero. He was a hero as much as Morty Aiken was.

III

Morty was a proud boy on the night he graduated from grammar school in June, 1919. When he received his diploma, there was more applause in the auditorium than there was for any other member of the class. He felt good when he heard this clapping, but, then, he expected it. He lived in a world where he was somebody, and he was going into a bigger world where he would still be somebody. He was a fine, clean-looking lad, with dark hair, frank blue eyes, regular and friendly features. He was thin but strong. He wore a blue serge suit with short trousers and a belted jacket, and a white shirt with a white bow tie. His class colors, orange and black ribbons, were pinned on the lapel of his coat. He was scrubbed and washed and combed. And he was in the midst of an atmosphere of gaiety and friendliness. The teachers were happy. There were proud and happy parents and aunts and uncles and older sisters. The local alderman made a speech, praising everybody, and speaking of the graduating boys and girls as fine future Americans. And he declared that in their midst there were many promising lads and lassies who would live to enjoy great esteem and success. He also said that among this group there was also one who not only promised to become a stellar athlete but who had already won gold medals and honors.

And on that night, Morty's father and mother were very happy. They kept beaming with proud smiles. Morty was their only son. Mr. Aiken was a carpenter. He worked steadily, and he had saved his money so that the house he owned was now paid for. He and his wife were quiet-living people who minded their own business. Mr. Aiken was tall and rugged, with swarthy skin, a rough-hewn face, and the look and manner of a workman. He was a gentle but firm man, and was inarticulate with his son. He believed that a boy should have a good time in sports, should fight his own battles, and that boyhood—the best time of one's life—should be filled with happy memories.

The mother was faded and maternal. She usually had little to say; her life was dedicated to caring for her son and her husband and to keeping their home clean and orderly. She was especially happy to know that Morty liked running and skating, because these were not dangerous.

After the graduation ceremonies, the father and mother took Morty home where they had cake and ice cream. The three of them sat together, eating these refreshments, quiet but happy. The two parents were deeply moved. They were filled with gratification because of the applause given their son when he had walked forward on the stage to receive his diploma. They were raising a fine boy, and they could look people in the neighborhood in the eye and know that they had done their duty as parents. The father was putting money by for Morty's college education and hoped that, besides becoming a famous runner, Morty would become a professional man. He talked of this to the son and the mother over their ice cream and cake, and the boy seemed to accept his father's plans. And as the father gazed shyly at Morty he thought of his own boyhood on a Wisconsin farm, and of long summer days there. Morty had the whole summer before him. He would play and grow and enjoy himself. He was not a bad boy, he had never gotten into trouble, he wasn't the kind of boy who caused worry. It was fine. In August there would be his vacation, and they would all go to Wisconsin, and he would go fishing with the boy.

That evening Morty's parents went to bed feeling that this was the happiest day of their lives.

And Morty went to bed, a happy, light-hearted boy, thinking of the summer vacation which had now begun.

IV

The days passed. Some days were better than others. Some days there was little to do, and on other days there was a lot to do. Morty guessed that this was turning out to be as good as any summer he could remember.

Tony Rabuski was working, delivering flowers for a flower merchant, but he sometimes came around after supper, and the kids sat talking or playing on the steps of Morty's house or of another house in the neighborhood. Morty liked to play Run, Sheep, Run, because it gave him a chance to run, and he also liked hiding and searching and hearing the signals called out, and the excitement and tingling and fun when he'd be hiding, perhaps under some porch, and the other side would be near, maybe even passing right by, and he, and the other kids with him, would have to be so still, and he'd even try to hold his breath, and then finally, the signal for which he had been waiting—Run, Sheep, Run—and the race, setting off, tearing away along sidewalks and across streets, running like hell and like a streak of lightning, and feeling your speed in your legs and muscles and getting to the goal first.

The summer was going by, and it was fun. There wasn't anything to worry about, and there were dreams. Edna Purcell, who had been in his class, seemed sweet on him, and she was a wonderful girl. One night she and some other girls came around, and they sat on the steps of Morty's house and played Tin-Tin. Morty had to kiss her. He did, with the kids laughing, and it seemed that something happened to him. He hadn't been shy when he was with girls, but now, when Edna was around, he would be shy. She was wonderful. She was more than wonderful. When he did have the courage to talk to her, he talked about running and ice skating. She told him she knew what a runner and skater he was. A fast skater, such as he was, wouldn't want to think of skating with someone like her. He said that he would, and that next winter he would teach her to skate better. Immediately, he found himself wishing it were next winter already, and he would imagine himself skating with her, and he could see them walking over to the Washington Park lagoon and coming home again. He would carry her skates, and when they breathed they would be able to see their breaths, and the weather would be cold and sharp and would make her red cheeks redder, and they would be alone, walking home, with the snow packed on the park, alone, the two of them walking in the park, with it quiet, so quiet that you would hear nothing, and it would be like they were in another world, and then, there in the quiet park, with white snow all over it, he would kiss Edna Purcell. He had kissed Edna when they'd played Tin-Tin, and Post Office, but he looked forward to the day that he got from her the kiss that would mean that she was his girl, his sweetheart, and the girl who would one day be his wife just like his mother was his father's wife. Everything he dreamed of doing, all the honors he would get, all the medals and cups he dreamed of winning—now all of this would be for Edna. And she was also going to Park High. He would walk to school with her, eat lunch with her, walk her home from school. When he ran in high-school track meets for Park High, Edna would be in the stands. He would give her his medals. He wanted to give her one of his gold skating medals, but he didn't know how to go about asking her to accept it.

No matter what Morty thought about, he thought about Edna at the same time. He thought about her every time he dreamed. When he walked on streets in the neighborhood, he thought of her. When he went to Washington Park or swimming, he thought of Edna. Edna, just to think of her, Edna made everything in the world wonderfully wonderful.

And thus the summer of 1919 was passing for Morty.

V

Morty sat on the curb with a group of boys, and they were bored and restless. They couldn't agree about what game to play, where to go, what to do to amuse themselves. A couple of them started to play Knife but gave it up. Morty suggested a race, but no one would race him. They couldn't agree on playing ball. One boy suggested swimming, but no one would go with him. Several of the boys wrestled, and a fight almost started. Morty sat by himself and thought about Edna. He guessed that he'd rather be with her than with the kids. He didn't know where she was. If he knew that she'd gone swimming, he'd go swimming. He didn't know what to do with himself. If he only could find Edna and if they would do something together, or go somewhere, like Jackson Park Beach, just the two of them, why, then, he knew that today would be the day that he would find a way of giving her one of his *Clarion* gold medals. But he didn't know where she was.

Tony Rabuski came around with four tough-looking kids. Tony had lost his job, and he said the niggers had jumped him when he was delivering flowers down around Forty-seventh Street, and he wanted his pals to stick by him. He told them what had happened, but they didn't get it, because Tony couldn't tell a story straight. Tony asked them didn't they know what was happening? There were race riots, and the beaches and Washington Park and the whole South Side were full of dark clouds, and over on Wentworth Avenue the big guys were fighting, and the dark clouds were out after whites. They didn't believe Tony. But Morty said it was in the newspapers, and that there were race riots. The bored boys became excited. They bragged about what they would do if the jigs came over to their neighborhood. Tony said they had to get some before they got this far. When asked where they were, Tony said all over. Finally, they went over to Washington Park, picking up sticks and clubs and rocks on the way. The park was calm. A few adults were walking and strolling about. A lad of eighteen or nineteen lay under a tree with his head in the lap of a girl who was stroking his hair. Some of the kids smirked and leered as they passed the couple. Morty thought of Edna and wished he could take her to Washington Park and kiss her. There were seven or eight rowboats on the lagoon, but all of the occupants were white. The park sheep were grazing. Tony threw a rock at them, frightening the sheep, and they all ran, but no cop was around to shag them. They passed the boathouse, talking and bragging. They now believed the rumors which they themselves had made up. White girls and women were in danger, and anything might happen. A tall lad sat in the grass with a nursemaid. A baby carriage was near them. The lad called them over and asked them what they were doing with their clubs and rocks. Tony said they were looking for niggers. The lad said that he'd seen two near the goldfish pond and urged the boys to go and get the sonsofbitches. Screaming and shouting, they ran to the goldfish pond. Suddenly, Tony shouted:

"Dark clouds."

VI

They ran. Two Negro boys, near the goldfish pond, heard Tony's cry, and then the others' cry and they ran. The mob of boys chased them. Morty was in the lead. Running at the head of the screaming, angry pack of boys, he forgot everything except how well and how fast he was running, and images of Edna flashed in and out of his mind. If she could see him running! He was running beautifully. He'd catch them. He was gaining. The colored boys ran in a northwest direction. They crossed the drive which flanked the southern end of the Washington Park ball field. Morty was stopped by a funeral procession. The other boys caught up with him. When the funeral procession passed, it was too late to try and catch the colored boys they had been chasing. Angry, bragging, they crossed over to the ball field and marched across it, shouting and yelling. They picked up about eight boys of their own age and three older lads of seventeen or eighteen. The older lads said they knew where they'd find some shines. Now was the time to teach them their place once and for all. Led by the older boys, they emerged from the north end of Washington Park and marched down Grand Boulevard, still picking up men and boys as they went along. One of the men who joined them had a gun. They screamed, looked in doorways for Negroes, believed everything anyone said about Negroes, and kept boasting about what they would do when they found some.

"Dark clouds," Tony boomed.

The mob let out. They crossed to the other side of Grand Boulevard and ran cursing and shouting after a Negro. Morty was in the lead. He was outrunning the men and the older fellows. He heard them shouting behind him. He was running. He was running like the playground hundred-yard champion of the South Side of Chicago. He was running like the future Olympic champion. He was running like he'd run for Edna. He was tearing along, pivoting out of the way of shocked, surprised pedestrians, running, really running. He was running like a streak of lightning.

The Negro turned east on Forty-eighth Street. He had a start of a block. But Morty would catch him. He turned into Forty-eighth Street. He tore along the center of the street. He began to breathe heavily. But he couldn't stop running now. He was outdistancing the gang, and he was racing his own gang and the Negro he was chasing. Down the center of the street and about half a block ahead of him, the Negro was tearing away for dear life. But Morty was gaining on him. Gaining. He was now about a half a block ahead of his own gang. They screamed murderously behind him. And they encouraged him. He heard shouts of encouragement.

"Catch 'em Morty boy!"

"Thata boy, Morty boy!"

He heard Tony's voice. He ran.

The Negro turned into an alley just east of Forestville. Morty ran. He turned into the alley just in time to see the fleeing Negro spurt into a yard in the center of the block. He'd gained more. He was way ahead of the white mob. Somewhere behind him they were coming and yelling. He tore on. He had gained his second wind. He felt himself running, felt the movement of his legs and muscles, felt his arms, felt the sensation of his whole body as he raced down the alley. Never had he run so swiftly. Suddenly Negroes jumped out of yards. He was caught and pinioned. His only thought was one of surprise. Before he even realized what had happened, his throat was slashed. He fell, bleeding. Feebly, he mumbled just once:

"Mother!"

The Negroes disappeared.

He lay bleeding in the center of the dirty alley, and when the gang of whites caught up with him they found him dead in dirt and his own blood in the center of the alley. No Negroes were in sight. The whites surrounded his body. The boys trembled with fear. Some of them cried. One wet his pants. Then they became maddened. And they stood in impotent rage around the bleeding, limp body of Morty Aiken, the fastest runner on Sixty-first Street.

We Wear the Mask

PAUL LAURENCE DUNBAR

We wear the mask that grins and lies,
It hides our cheeks and shades our eyes,—
This debt we pay to human guile;
With torn and bleeding hearts we smile,
And mouth with myriad subtleties.

Why should the world be overwise,
In counting all our tears and sighs?
Nay, let them only see us, while
    We wear the mask.

We smile, but, O great Christ, our cries
To Thee from tortured souls arise.
We sing, but oh, the clay is vile
Beneath our feet, and long the mile;
But let the world dream otherwise,
    We wear the mask.

I, Too, Sing America

LANGSTON HUGHES

I, too, sing America.

I am the darker brother.
They send me to eat in the kitchen
When company comes,
But I laugh,
And eat well,
And grow strong.

Tomorrow,
I'll sit at the table
When company comes.
Nobody'll dare
Say to me,
"Eat in the kitchen,"
Then.

Besides,
They'll see how beautiful I am
And be ashamed,—

I, too, am America.

Jazz, Jive, and Jam

LANGSTON HUGHES

"It being Negro History Week," said Simple, "Joyce took me to a pay lecture to hear some Negro hysterian—"

"Historian," I corrected.

"—hysterian speak," continued Simple, "and he laid our Negro race low. He said we was misbred, misread, and misled, also losing our time good-timing. Instead of time-taking and money-making, we are jazz-shaking. Oh, he enjoyed his self at the expense of the colored race—and him black as me. He really delivered a lecture—in which, no doubt, there is some truth."

"Constructive criticism, I gather—a sort of tearing down in order to build up."

"He tore us down good," said Simple. "Joyce come out saying to me, her husband, that he had really got my number. I said 'Baby, he did not miss you, neither.' But Joyce did not consider herself included in the bad things he said.

"She come telling me on the way home by subway, 'Jess Semple, I have been pursuing culture since my childhood. But you, when I first met you, all you did was drape yourself over some beer bar and argue with the barflies. The higher things of life do not come out of a licker trough.'

"I replied, 'But, Joyce, how come culture has got to be so dry?'

"She answers me back, 'How come your gullet has got to be so wet? You are sitting in this subway right now looking like you would like to have a beer.'

" 'Solid!' I said. 'I would. How did you guess it?'

" 'Married to you for three years. I can read your mind,' said Joyce. 'We'll buy a couple of cans to take home. I might even drink one myself.'

" 'Joyce, baby,' I said, 'in that case, let's buy three cans.'

"Joyce says, 'Remember the budget, Jess.'

"I says, 'Honey, you done busted the budget going to that lecture program which cost One Dollar a head, also we put some small change in the collection to help Negroes get ahead.'

" 'Small change?' says Joyce. 'I put a dollar.'

" 'Then our budget is busted real good,' I said, 'so we might as well dent it some more. Let's get six cans of beer.'

" 'All right,' says Joyce, 'go ahead, drink yourself to the dogs—instead of saving for that house we want to buy!'

" 'Six cans of beer would not pay for even the bottom front step,' I said. 'But they would lift my spirits this evening. That Negro high-speaking doctor done tore my spirits down. I did not know before that the colored race was so misled, misread, and misbred. According to him there is hardly a pure black man left. But I was setting in the back, so I guess he did not see me.'

" 'Had you not had to go to sleep in the big chair after dinner,' says Joyce, 'we would have been there on time and had seats up front.'

" 'I were near enough to that joker,' I said. 'Loud as he could holler, we did not need to set no closer. And he certainly were nothing to look at!'

" 'Very few educated men look like Harry Belafonte,' said Joyce.

" 'I am glad I am handsome instead of wise,' I said. But Joyce did not crack a smile. She had that lecture on her mind.

" 'Dr. Conboy is smart,' says Joyce. 'Did you hear him quoting Aristotle?'

" 'Who were Harry Stottle?' I asked.

" 'Some people are not even misread,' said Joyce. 'Aristotle was a Greek philosopher like Socrates, a great man of ancient times.'

" 'He must of been before Booker T. Washington then,' I said, 'because, to tell the truth, I has not heard of him at all. But tonight being *Negro* History Week, how come Dr. Conboy has to quote some Greek?'

" 'There were black Greeks,' said Joyce. 'Did you not hear him say that Negroes have played a part in all history, throughout all time, from Eden to now?'

" 'Do you reckon Eve was brownskin?' I requested.

" 'I do not know about Eve,' said Joyce, 'but Cleopatra was of the colored race, and the Bible says Sheba, beloved of Solomon, was black but comely.'

" 'I wonder would she come to me?' I says.

" 'Solomon also found Cleopatra comely. He was a king,' says Joyce.

" 'And I am Jesse B. Semple,' I said.

"But by that time the subway had got to our stop. At the store Joyce broke the budget again, opened up her pocket purse, and bought us six cans of beer. So it were a good evening. It ended well—except that I ain't for going to any more meetings—especially interracial meetings."

"Come now! Don't you want to improve race relations?"

"Sure," said Simple, "but in my opinion, jazz, jive, and jam would be better for race relations than all this high-flown gab, gaff, and gas the orators put out. All this talking that white folks do at meetings, and big Negroes, too, about how to get along together—just a little jam session would have everybody getting along fine without having to listen to so many speeches. Why, last month Joyce took me to a Race Relations Seminar which her club and twenty other clubs gave, and man, it lasted three days! It started on a Friday night and it were not over until Sunday afternoon. They had sessions' mammy! Joyce is a fiend for culture."

"And you sat through all that?"

"I did not set," said Simple. "I stood. I walked in and walked out. I smoked on the corner and snuck two drinks at the bar. But I had to wait for Joyce, and I thought them speeches would never get over! My wife were a delegate from her club, so she had to stay, although I think Joyce got tired her own self. But she would not admit it. Joyce said, 'Dr. Hillary Thingabod was certainly brilliant, were he not?'

"I said, 'He were not.'

"Joyce said, 'What did you want the man to say?'

"I said, 'I wish he had sung, instead of *said*. That program needed some music to keep folks awake.'

"Joyce said, 'Our forum was not intended for a musical. It was intended to see how we can work out integration.'

"I said, 'With a jazz band, they could work out integration in ten minutes. Everybody would have been dancing together like they all did at the Savoy—colored and white—or down on the East Side at them Casinos on a Friday night where jam holds forth—and we would have been integrated.'

"Joyce said, 'This was a serious seminar, aiming at facts, not fun.'

" 'Baby,' I said, 'what is more facts than acts? Jazz makes people get into action, move! Didn't nobody move in that hall where you were—except to jerk their head up when they went to sleep, to keep anybody from seeing that they was nodding. Why, that chairman, Mrs. Maxwell-Reeves, almost lost her glasses off her nose, she jerked her head up so quick one time when that man you say was so brilliant were speaking!'

" 'Jess Semple, that is not so!' yelled Joyce. 'Mrs. Maxwell-Reeves were just lost in thought. And if you think you saw *me* sleeping——'

" 'You was too busy trying to look around and see where I was,' I said. 'Thank God, I did not have to set up there like you with the delegation. I would not be a delegate to no such gabfest for nothing on earth.'

" 'I thought you was so interested in saving the race!' said Joyce. 'Next time I will not ask you to accompany me to no cultural events, Jesse B., because I can see you do not appreciate them. That were a discussion of ways and means. And you were talking about jazz bands!'

" 'There's more ways than one to skin a cat,' I said. 'A jazz band like Duke's or Hamp's or Basie's sure would of helped that meeting. At least on Saturday afternoon, they could have used a little music to put some pep into the proceedings. Now, just say for instant, baby, they was to open with jazz and close with jam—and do the talking in between. Start out, for example, with "The St. Louis Blues," which is a kind of colored national anthem. That would put every human in a good humor. Then play "Why Don't You Do Right?" which could be addressed to white folks. They could pat their feet to that. Then for a third number before introducing the speaker, let some guest star like Pearl Bailey sing "There'll Be Some Changes Made"—which, as I understand it, were the theme of the meeting, anyhow—and all the Negroes could say *Amen!*

" 'Joyce, I wish you would let me plan them interracial seminaries next time. After the music, let the speechmaking roll for a while—with maybe a calypso between speeches. Then, along about five o'clock, bring on the jam session, extra-special. Start serving tea to "Tea For Two," played real cool. Whilst drinking tea and dancing, the race relationers could relate, the integraters could integrate, and desegregators desegregate. Joyce, you would not have to beg for a crowd to come out and support your efforts then. Jam—and the hall would be jammed! Even I would stick around, and not be outside sneaking a smoke, or trying to figure how I can get to the bar before the resolutions are voted on. *Resolved: that we solve* the race problem! Strike up the band! Hit it, men! Aw, play that thing! "How High the Moon!" How high! Wheee-ee-e!' "

"What did Joyce say to that?" I demanded.

"Joyce just thought I was high," said Simple.

Frederick Douglass

ROBERT HAYDEN

When it is finally ours, this freedom, this liberty, this
beautiful and terrible thing, needful to man as air,
usable as earth; when it belongs at last to our children,
when it is truly instinct, brain matter, diastole, systole,
reflex action; when it is finally won; when it is more
than the gaudy mumbo jumbo of politicians:
this man, this Douglass, this former slave, this Negro
beaten to his knees, exiled, visioning a world
where none is lonely, none hunted, alien,
this man, superb in love and logic, this man
shall be remembered. Oh, not with statues' rhetoric,
not with legends and poems and wreaths of bronze alone,
but with the lives grown out of his life, the lives
fleshing his dream of the beautiful, needful thing.

Runagate Runagate

ROBERT HAYDEN

I

Runs falls rises stumbles on from darkness into darkness
and the darkness thicketed with shapes of terror
and the hunters pursuing and the hounds pursuing
and the night cold and the night long and the river
to cross and the jack-muh-lanterns beckoning beckoning
and blackness ahead and when shall I reach that somewhere
morning and keep on going and never turn back and keep on
going

Runagate
Runagate
Runagate

Many thousands rise and go
many thousand crossing over

O mythic North
O star-shaped yonder Bible city

Some go weeping and some rejoicing
some in coffins and some in carriages
some in silks and some in shackles

Rise and go or fare you well

No more auction block for me
no more driver's lash for me

If you see my Pompey, 30 yrs of age,
new breeches, plain stockings, negro shoes;
if you see my Anna, likely young mulatto
branded E on thr right cheek, R on the left,
catch them if you can and notify subscriber.
Catch them if you can, but it won't be easy.
They'll dart underground when you try to catch them.
plunge into quicksand, whirlpools, mazes,
turn into scorpions when you try to catch them.

And before I'll be a slave
I'll be buried in my grave

North star and bonanza gold
I'm bound for the freedom, freedom-bound
and oh Susyanna don't you cry for me
Runagate
Runagate

II

Rises from their anguish and their power,

Harriet Tubman,

woman of earth, whip-
scarred,
a summoning, a shining

Mean to be free

And this was the way of it, brethren brethren,
way we journeyed from Can't to Can.
Moon so bright and no place to hide,
the cry up and the patterollers riding,
hound dogs belling in bladed air.

And fear starts a-murbling. Never make it,
we'll never make it. *Hush that now,*
and she's turned upon us, levelled pistol
glinting in the moonlight:
Dead folks can't jaybird-talk, she says:
you keep on going now or die, she says.

Wanted   Harriet Tubman   alias The General
alias Moses   Stealer of Slaves

In league with Garrison   Alcott   Emerson
Garrett   Douglass   Thoreau   John Brown

Armed and known to be Dangerous

Wanted   Reward   Dead or Alive

Tell me, Ezekiel, oh tell me do you see
mailed Jehovah coming to deliver me?

Hoot-owl calling in the ghosted air,
five times calling to the hants in the air.
Shadow of a face in the scary leaves,
shadow of a voice in the talking leaves:

Come ride-a my train

Oh that train, ghost-story train
through swamp and savanna movering movering,
over trestles of dew, through caves of the wish,
Midnight Special on a sabre track movering movering,
first stop Mercy and the last Hallelujah.

Come ride-a my train

Mean mean mean to be free.

Traditional and Material Realities

American literature produced by midwesterners expressed a desire for the good life in its defense of traditional values and in its criticism of materialism, the ethical attitude focusing on physical well-being and hence on the material possessions to bring it about.

The midwestern frontier—seated amid a wealth of material advantages—represented opportunity, competition for achievement and, above all, the idea of success to both native migrants and European immigrants. According to historian Frederick Jackson Turner in his study *The Frontier in American History*, they saw "in the free and competitive movement the chance to break the bondage of social rank, and to rise to a higher plane of existence." Being idealists, they measured success by struggle and reward, with individuals deserving only what they had worked hard to obtain. The significance or worth was not in the end of labor—profit—but in the act of labor itself, which was a confirmation of the individual experience. For these pioneering settlers, monetary gain was important only insofar as it provided the means for a life of human dignity. Put simply, theirs was a tradition of toil, of energetic competition, of individualism.

Although the frontier consciousness with its sense of struggle and its principle of reward remained alive after the wilderness was tamed and made to yield life, a subtle corruptive change took place. As Willa Cather indicated in her own writings of the experiences on the Nebraska plains, she saw the idealism often overrun by a pragmatic or practical materialism. Cather granted the validity of the American success formula based on hard work plus the resources of the fertile farmlands in the Midwest. Yet she questioned whether human factors like warmth and familial closeness needed to be sacri-

American Gothic, Grant Wood

ficed in return for a prosperous life. As Cather illustrated in the short story "The Sentimentality of William Tavener," *ambition* implied a narrowness of pursuit as well as positive virtues like hard work, self-improvement and self-discipline.

Since the 1920s literary figures like Sinclair Lewis and F. Scott Fitzgerald have analyzed the American character and manners with regard to the inner emotional life of the victims of success. Enormously familiar with urban middle-class life, Lewis condemned the preoccupation with financial success as a means of securing economic power and a network of social alliances: lodges, parties, clubs, and the like. Setting his novel *Babbit* in an intermediate-sized city more characteristic of the Midwest, Lewis typified the conformist businessman whose thinking and lifestyle were shaped by the mechanized process of standardization upon which an industrial and business society depended. His novel also exposed the elasticity of business ethics, the sacrifice of personal joy and freedom to transient gain, and the yearning for self-realization and fulfillment.

Raised in "a house below the average on a street above the average" in St. Paul, Minnesota, Fitzgerald grew up dazzled by the lives of the wealthy and by the efforts of the near rich to move into the coveted circle. The insights he gained about youth, money and success became dominant subjects for social commentary in his fiction. As an illustration, his short story "Winter Dreams" opened with two lovers separated by money—Dexter Green was the grocer's son and Judy Jones's father was as wealthy as his Pierce-Arrow automobile signified. The rest of the narrative delineated Dexter's rise into sufficient wealth and power to claim the rich girl of his dreams. Furthermore, it made clear that without the capacity for love a life of materialistic acquisition ultimately yielded to disillusionment.

Upholding traditional values of goodness, simplicity and natural beauty, other contemporary authors revealed humaneness in the midst of commonplace surroundings. Such poets as James Wright, William Stafford and Robert Hayden portrayed families that seemed to find whatever psychological support and reassurance they needed within the limits of their own lives and communities. Others like Gwendolyn Brooks characterized ordinary people who substituted the struggles against economic uncertainty for the subtleties of social position, and a little anticipation for a big dream. The tradition-directed reality for these writers represented a sense of past, of place, of social and spiritual well-being.

The Sentimentality of William Tavener

WILLA CATHER

It takes a strong woman to make any sort of success of living in the West, and Hester undoubtedly was that. When people spoke of William Tavener as the most prosperous farmer in McPherson County, they usually added that his wife was a "good manager." She was an executive woman, quick of tongue and something of an imperatrix. The only reason her husband did not consult her about his business was that she did not wait to be consulted.

It would have been quite impossible for one man, within the limited sphere of human action, to follow all Hester's advice, but in the end William usually acted upon some of her suggestions. When she incessantly denounced the "shiftlessness" of letting a new threshing machine stand unprotected in the open, he eventually built a shed for it. When she sniffed contemptuously at his notion of fencing a hog corral with sod walls, he made a spiritless beginning on the structure—merely to "show his temper," as she put it—but in the end he went off quietly to town and bought enough barbed wire to complete the fence. When the first heavy rains came on, and the pigs rooted down the sod wall and made little paths all over it to facilitate their ascent, he heard his wife relate with relish the story of the little pig that built a mud house, to the minister at the dinner table, and William's gravity never relaxed for an instant. Silence, indeed, was William's refuge and his strength.

William set his boys a wholesome example to respect their mother. People who knew him very well suspected that he even admired her. He was a hard man towards his neighbors, and even towards his sons: grasping, determined and ambitious.

There was an occasional blue day about the house when William went over the store bills, but he never objected to items relating to his wife's gowns or bonnets. So it came about that many of the foolish, unnecessary little things that Hester bought for boys, she had charged to her personal account.

One spring night Hester sat in a rocking chair by the sitting room window, darning socks. She rocked violently and sent her long needle vigorously back and forth over her gourd, and it took only a very casual glance to see that she was wrought up over something. William sat on the other side of the table reading his farm paper. If he had noticed his wife's agitation, his calm, clean-shaven face betrayed no sign of concern. He must have noticed the sarcastic turn of her remarks at the supper table, and he must have noticed the moody silence of the older boys as they ate. When supper was but half over little Billy, the youngest, had suddenly pushed back his plate and slipped away from the table, manfully trying to swallow a sob. But William Tavener never heeded ominous forecasts in the domestic horizon, and he never looked for a storm until it broke.

After supper the boys had gone to the pond under the willows in the big cattle corral, to get rid of the dust of plowing. Hester could hear an occasional spash and a laugh ringing clear through the stillness of the night, as she sat by the open window. She sat silent for almost an hour reviewing in her mind many plans of attack. But she was too vigorous a woman to be much of a strategist, and she usually came to her point with directness. At last she cut her thread and suddenly put her darning down, saying emphatically:

"William, I don't think it would hurt you to let the boys go to that circus in town tomorrow."

William continued to read his farm paper, but it was not Hester's custom to wait for an answer. She usually divined his arguments and assailed them one by one before he uttered them.

"You've been short of hands all summer, and you've worked the boys hard, and a man ought use his own flesh and blood as well as he does his hired hands. We're plenty able to afford it, and it's little enough our boys ever spend. I don't see how you can expect 'em to be steady and hard workin', unless you encourage 'em a little. I never could see much harm in circuses, and our boys have never been to one. Oh, I know Jim Howley's boys get drunk an' carry on when they go, but our boys ain't that sort, an' you know it, William. The animals are real instructive, an' our boys don't get to see much out here on the prairie. It was different where we were raised, but the boys have got no advantages here, an' if you don't take care, they'll grow up to be greenhorns."

Hester paused a moment, and William folded up his paper, but vouchsafed no remark. His sisters in Virginia had often said that only a quiet man like William could ever have lived with Hester Perkins. Secretly, William was rather proud of his wife's "gift of speech," and of the fact that she could talk in prayer meeting as fluently as a man. He confined his own efforts in that line to a brief prayer at Covenant meetings.

Hester shook out another sock and went on.

"Nobody was ever hurt by goin' to a circus. Why, law me! I remember I went to one myself once, when I was little. I had most forgot about it. It was over at Pewtown, an' I remember how I had set my heart on going. I don't think I'd ever forgiven my father if he hadn't taken me, though that red clay road was in a frightful way after the rain. I mind they had an elephant and six poll parrots, an' a Rocky Mountain lion, an' a cage of monkeys, an' two camels. My! but they were a sight to me then!"

Hester dropped the black sock and shook her head and smiled at the recollection. She was not expecting anything from William yet, and she was fairly startled when he said gravely, in much the same tone in which he announced the hymns in prayer meeting:

"No, there was only one camel. The other was a dromedary."

She peered around the lamp and looked at him keenly.

"Why, William, how come you to know?"

William folded his paper and answered with some hesitation, "I was there, too."

Hester's interest flashed up. "Well, I never, William! To think of my finding it out after all these years! Why, you couldn't have been much bigger'n our Billy then. It seems queer I never saw you when you was little, to remember about you. But then you Back Creek folks never have anything to do with us Gap people. But how come you to go? Your father was stricter with you than you are with your boys."

"I reckon I shouldn't 'a gone," he said slowly, "but boys will do foolish things. I had done a good deal of fox hunting the winter before, and father let me keep the bounty money. I hired Tom Smith's Tap to weed the corn for me, an' I slipped off unbeknownst to father an' went to the show."

Hester spoke up warmly: "Nonsense, William! It didn't do you no harm,

I guess. You was always worked hard enough. It must have been a big sight for a little fellow. That clown must have just tickled you to death."

William crossed his knees and leaned back in his chair.

"I reckon I could tell all that fool's jokes now. Sometimes I can't help thinkin' about 'em in meetin' when the sermon's long. I mind I had on a pair of new boots that hurt me like the mischief, but I forgot all about 'em when that fellow rode the donkey. I recall I had to take them boots off as soon as I got out of sight o' town, and walked home in the mud barefoot."

"O poor little fellow!" Hester ejaculated, drawing her chair nearer and leaning her elbows on the table. "What cruel shoes they did use to make for children. I remember I went up to Back Creek to see the circus wagons go by. They came down from Romney, you know. The circus men stopped at the creek to water the animals, an' the elephant got stubborn an' broke a big limb off the yellow willow tree that grew there by the toll house porch, an' the Scribners were 'fraid as death he'd pull the house down. But this much I saw him do; he waded in the creek an' filled his trunk with water and squirted it in at the window and nearly ruined Ellen Scribner's pink lawn dress that she had just ironed an' laid out on the bed ready to wear to the circus."

"I reckon that must have been a trial to Ellen," chuckled William, "for she was mighty prim in them days."

Hester drew her chair still nearer William's. Since the children had begun growing up, her conversation with her husband had been almost wholly confined to questions of economy and expense. Their relationship had become purely a business one, like that between landlord and tenant. In her desire to indulge her boys she had unconsciously assumed a defensive and almost hostile attitude towards her husband. No debtor ever haggled with his usurer more doggedly than did Hester with her husband in behalf of her sons. The strategic contest had gone on so long that it had almost crowded out the memory of a closer relationship. This exchange of confidences tonight, when common recollections took them unawares and opened their hearts, had all the miracle of romance. They talked on and on; of old neighbors, of old familiar faces in the valley where they had grown up, of long forgotten incidents of their youth—weddings, picnics, sleighing parties and baptizings. For years they had talked of nothing else but butter and eggs and the prices of things, and now they had as much to say to each other as people who meet after a long separation.

Cradling wheat to check maturity of kernels

When the clock struck ten, William rose and went over to his walnut secretary and unlocked it. From his red leather wallet he took out a ten dollar bill and laid it on the table beside Hester.

"Tell the boys not to stay late, an' not to drive the horses hard," he said quietly, and went off to bed.

Hester blew out the lamp and sat still in the dark a long time. She left the bill lying on the table where William had placed it. She had a painful sense of having missed something, or lost something; she felt that somehow the years had cheated her.

The little locust trees that grew by the fence were white with blossoms. Their heavy odor floated in to her on the night wind and recalled a night long ago, when the first whippoorwill of the Spring was heard, and the rough, buxom girls of Hawkins Gap had held her laughing and struggling under the locust trees, and searched in her bosom for a lock of her sweetheart's hair, which is supposed to be on every girl's breast when the first whippoorwill sings. Two of those same girls had been her bridesmaids. Hester had been a very happy bride. She rose and went softly into the room where William lay. He was sleeping heavily, but occasionally moved his hand before his face to ward off the flies. Hester went into the parlor and took the piece of mosquito net from the basket of wax apples and pears that her sister had made before she died. One of the boys had brought it all the way from Virginia, packed in a tin pail, since Hester would not risk shipping so precious an ornament by freight. She went back to the bedroom and spread the net over William's head. Then she sat down by the bed and listened to his deep, regular breathing until she heard the boys returning. She went out to meet them and warn them not to waken their father.

"I'll be up early to get your breakfast, boys. Your father says you can go to the show." As she handed the money to the eldest, she felt a sudden throb of allegiance to her husband and said sharply, "And you be careful of that, an' don't waste it. Your father works hard for his money."

The boys looked at each other in astonishment and felt that they had lost a powerful ally.

Kitchenette Building

GWENDOLYN BROOKS

We are things of dry hours and the involuntary plan
Grayed in, and gray. "Dream" makes a giddy sound, not strong
Like "rent," "feeding a wife," "satisfying a man."

But could a dream send up through onion fumes
Its white and violet, fight with fried potatoes
And yesterday's garbage ripening in the hall,
Flutter, or sing an aria down these rooms

Even if we were willing to let it in,
Had time to warm it, keep it very clean,
Anticipate a message, let it begin?

We wonder. But not well! not for a minute!
Since Number Five is out of the bathroom now,
We think of lukewarm water, hope to get in it.

What Shall I Give My Children? Who Are Poor

GWENDOLYN BROOKS

What shall I give my children? who are poor,
Who are adjudged the leastwise of the land,
Who are my sweetest lepers, who demand
No velvet and no velvety velour;
But who have begged me for a brisk contour,
Crying that they are quasi, contraband
Because unfinished, graven by a hand
Less than angelic, admirable or sure.
My hand is stuffed with mode, design, device.
But I lack access to my proper stone.
And plentitude or plan shall not suffice
Nor grief nor love shall be enough alone
To ratify my little halves who bear
Across an autumn freezing everywhere.

Life for My Child Is Simple, and Is Good

GWENDOLYN BROOKS

Life for my child is simple, and is good.
He knows his wish. Yes, but that is not all,
Because I know mine too.
And we both want joy of undeep and unabiding things,
Like kicking over a chair or throwing blocks out of a window
Or tipping over an icebox pan
Or snatching down curtains or fingering an electric outlet
Or a journey or a friend or an illegal kiss.
No. There is more to it than that.
It is that he has never been afraid.
Rather, he reaches out and lo the chair falls with a beautiful
crash,
And the blocks fall, down on the people's heads,
And the water comes slooshing sloppily out across the floor.
And so forth.
Not that success, for him, is sure, infallible.
But never has he been afraid to reach.
His lesions are legion.
But reaching is his rule.

The Bean Eaters

GWENDOLYN BROOKS

They eat beans mostly, this old yellow pair.
Dinner is a casual affair.
Plain chipware on a plain and creaking wood,
Tin flatware.

Two who are Mostly Good.
Two who have lived their day,
But keep on putting on their clothes
And putting things away.

And remembering . . .
Remembering, with twinklings and twinges,
As they lean over the beans in their rented back room that is
        full of beads and receipts and dolls and cloths, tobacco
        crumbs, vases and fringes.

Winter Dreams

F. SCOTT FITZGERALD

Some of the caddies were poor as sin and lived in one-room houses with a neurasthenic cow in the front yard, but Dexter Green's father owned the second best grocery-store in Black Bear—the best one was "The Hub," patronized by the wealthy people from Sherry Island—and Dexter caddied only for pocket-money.

In the fall when the days became crisp and gray, and the long Minnesota winter shut down like the white lid of a box, Dexter's skis moved over the snow that hid the fairways of the golf course. At these times the country gave him a feeling of profound melancholy—it offended him that the links should lie in enforced fallowness, haunted by ragged sparrows for the long season. It was dreary, too, that on the tees where the gay colors fluttered in summer there were now only the desolate sand-boxes knee-deep in crusted ice. When he crossed the hills the wind blew cold as misery, and if the sun was out he tramped with his eyes squinted up against the hard dimensionless glare.

In April the winter ceased abruptly. The snow ran down into Black Bear Lake scarcely tarrying for the early golfers to brave the season with red and black balls. Without elation, without an interval of moist glory, the cold was gone.

Dexter knew that there was something dismal about this Northern spring, just as he knew there was something gorgeous about the fall. Fall made him clinch his hands and tremble and repeat idiotic sentences to himself, and make brisk abrupt gestures of command to imaginary audiences and armies. October filled him with hope which November raised to a sort of ecstatic triumph, and in this mood the fleeting brilliant impressions of the summer at Sherry Island were ready grist to his mill. He became a golf champion and defeated Mr. T. A. Hedrick in a marvellous match played a hundred times over the fairways of his imagination, a match each detail of which he changed about untiringly—sometimes he won with almost laughable ease, sometimes he came up magnificently from behind. Again, stepping from a Pierce-Arrow automobile, like Mr. Mortimer Jones, he strolled frigidly into the lounge of the Sherry Island Golf Club—or perhaps, surrounded by an admiring crowd, he gave an exhibition of fancy diving from the spring-board of the club raft. . . . Among those who watched him in open-mouthed wonder was Mr. Mortimer Jones.

And one day it came to pass that Mr. Jones—himself and not his ghost—came up to Dexter with tears in his eyes and said that Dexter was the —— —— best caddy in the club, and wouldn't he decide not to quit if Mr. Jones made it worth his while, because every other —— —— caddy in the club lost one ball a hole for him—regularly—

"No, sir," said Dexter decisively, "I don't want to caddy any more." Then, after a pause: "I'm too old."

"You're not more than fourteen. Why the devil did you decide just this morning that you wanted to quit? You promised that next week you'd go over to the State tournament with me."

"I decided I was too old."

Dexter handed in his "A Class" badge, collected what money was due him from the caddy master, and walked home to Black Bear Village.

"The best —— —— caddy I ever saw," shouted Mr. Mortimer Jones over a drink that afternoon. "Never lost a ball! Willing! Intelligent! Quiet! Honest! Grateful!"

The little girl who had done this was eleven—beautifully ugly as little girls are apt to be who are destined after a few years to be inexpressibly lovely and bring no end of misery to a great number of men. The spark, however, was perceptible. There was a general ungodliness in the way her lips twisted down at the corners when she smiled, and in the—Heaven help us!—in the almost passionate quality of her eyes. Vitality is born early in such women. It was utterly in evidence now, shining through her thin frame in a sort of glow.

She had come eagerly out on to the course at nine o'clock with a white linen nurse and five small new golf-clubs in a white canvas bag which the nurse was carrying. When Dexter first saw her she was standing by the caddy house, rather ill at ease and trying to conceal the fact by engaging her nurse in an obviously unnatural conversation graced by startling and irrelevant grimaces from herself.

"Well, it's certainly a nice day, Hilda," Dexter heard her say. She drew down the corners of her mouth, smiled, and glanced furtively around, her eyes in transit falling for an instant on Dexter.

Then to the nurse:

"Well, I guess there aren't very many people out here this morning, are there?"

The smile again—radiant, blatantly artificial—convincing.

"I don't know what we're supposed to do now," said the nurse looking nowhere in particular.

"Oh, that's all right. I'll fix it up."

Dexter stood perfectly still, his mouth slightly ajar. He knew that if he moved forward a step his stare would be in her line of vision—if he moved backward he would lose his full view of her face. For a moment he had not realized how young she was. Now he remembered having seen her several times the year before—in bloomers.

Suddenly, involuntarily, he laughed, a short abrupt laugh—then, startled by himself, he turned and began to walk quickly away.

"Boy!"

Dexter stopped.

"Boy——"

Beyond question he was addressed. Not only that, but he was treated to that absurd smile, that preposterous smile—the memory of which at least a dozen men were to carry into middle age.

"Boy, do you know where the golf teacher is?"

"He's giving a lesson."

"Well, do you know where the caddy-master is?"

"He isn't here yet this morning."

"Oh." For a moment this baffled her. She stood alternately on her right and left foot.

"We'd like to get a caddy," said the nurse. "Mrs. Mortimer Jones sent us out to play golf, and we don't know how without we get a caddy."

Here she was stopped by an ominous glance from Miss Jones, followed by the smile.

"There aren't any caddies here except me," said Dexter to the nurse, "and I got to stay here in charge until the caddy-master gets here."

"Oh."

Miss Jones and her retinue now withdrew, and at a proper distance from Dexter became involved in a heated conversation, which was concluded by

Miss Jones taking one of the clubs and hitting it on the ground with violence. For further emphasis she raised it again and was about to bring it down smartly upon the nurse's bosom, when the nurse seized the club and twisted it from her hands.

"You damn little mean old *thing!*" cried Miss Jones wildly.

Another argument ensued. Realizing that the elements of the comedy were implied in the scene, Dexter several times began to laugh, but each time restrained the laugh before it reached audibility. He could not resist the monstrous conviction that the little girl was justified in beating the nurse.

The situation was resolved by the fortuitous appearance of the caddy-master, who was appealed to immediately by the nurse.

"Miss Jones is to have a little caddy, and this one says he can't go."

"Mr. McKenna said I was to wait here till you came," said Dexter quickly.

"Well, he's here now." Miss Jones smiled cheerfully at the caddy-master. Then she dropped her bag and set off at a haughty mince toward the first tee.

"Well?" The caddy-master turned to Dexter. "What you standing there like a dummy for? Go pick up the young lady's clubs."

"I don't think I'll go out today," said Dexter.

"You don't—"

"I think I'll quit."

The enormity of his decision frightened him. He was a favorite caddy, and the thirty dollars a month he earned through the summer were not to be made elsewhere around the lake. But he had received a strong emotional shock, and his perturbation required a violent and immediate outlet.

It is not so simple as that, either. As so frequently would be the case in the future, Dexter was unconsciously dictated to by his winter dreams.

II

Now, of course, the quality and the seasonability of these winter dreams varied, but the stuff of them remained. They persuaded Dexter several years later to pass up a business course at the State university—his father, prospering now, would have paid his way—for the precarious advantage of attending an older and more famous university in the East, where he was bothered by his scanty funds. But do not get the impression, because his winter dreams happened to be concerned at first with musings on the rich, that there was anything merely snobbish in the boy. He wanted not association with glittering things and glittering people—he wanted the glittering things themselves. Often he reached out for the best without knowing why he wanted it—and sometimes he ran up against the mysterious denials and prohibitions in which life indulges. It is with one of those denials and not with his career as a whole that this story deals.

He made money. It was rather amazing. After college he went to the city from which Black Bear Lake draws its wealthy patrons. When he was only twenty-three and had been there not quite two years, there were already people who liked to say: "Now *there's* a boy—" All about him rich men's sons were peddling bonds precariously, or investing patrimonies precariously, or plodding through the two dozen volumes of the "George Washington Commercial Course," but Dexter borrowed a thousand dollars on his college degree and his confident mouth, and bought a partnership in a laundry.

It was a small laundry when he went into it, but Dexter made a specialty of learning how the English washed fine woolen golfstockings without shrinking them, and within a year he was catering to the trade that wore knickerbockers. Men were insisting that their Shetland hose and sweaters go to his laundry, just as they had insisted on a caddy who could find golfballs. A little later he was doing their wives' lingerie as well—and running five branches in different parts of the city. Before he was twenty-seven he owned the largest string of laundries in his section of the country. It was then that he sold out and went to New York. But the part of his story that concerns us goes back to the days when he was making his first big success.

When he was twenty-three Mr. Hart—one of the gray-haired men who liked to say "Now there's a boy"—gave him a guest card to the Sherry Island Golf Club for a week-end. So he signed his name one day on the register, and that afternoon played golf in a foursome with Mr. Hart and Mr. Sandwood and Mr. T. A. Hedrick. He did not consider it necessary to remark that he had once carried Mr. Hart's bag over this same links, and that he knew every trap and gully with his eyes shut—but he found himself glancing at the four caddies who trailed them, trying to catch a gleam or gesture that would remind him of himself, that would lessen the gap which lay between his present and his past.

It was a curious day, slashed abruptly with fleeting, familiar impressions. One minute he had the sense of being a trespasser—in the next he was impressed by the tremendous superiority he felt toward Mr. T. A. Hedrick, who was a bore and not even a good golfer any more.

Then, because of a ball Mr. Hart lost near the fifteenth green, an enormous thing happened. While they were searching the stiff grasses of the rough there was a clear call of "Fore!" from behind a hill in their rear. And as they all turned abruptly from their search a bright new ball sliced abruptly over the hill and caught Mr. T. A. Hedrick in the abdomen.

"By Gad!" cried Mr. T. A. Hedrick, "they ought to put some of these crazy women off the course. It's getting to be outrageous."

A head and a voice came up together over the hill:

"Do you mind if we go through?"

"You hit me in the stomach!" declared Mr. Hedrick wildly.

"Did I?" The girl approached the group of men. "I'm sorry. I yelled 'Fore!' "

Her glance fell casually on each of the men—then scanned the fairway for her ball.

"Did I bounce into the rough?"

It was impossible to determine whether this question was ingenuous or malicious. In a moment, however, she left no doubt, for as her partner came up over the hill she called cheerfully:

"Here I am! I'd have gone on the green except that I hit something."

As she took her stance for a short mashie shot, Dexter looked at her closely. She wore a blue gingham dress, rimmed at throat and shoulders with a white edging that accentuated her tan. The quality of exaggeration, of thinness, which had made her passionate eyes and down-turning mouth absurd at eleven, was gone now. She was arrestingly beautiful. The color in her cheeks was centred like the color in a picture—it was not a "high" color, but a sort of fluctuating and feverish warmth, so shaded that it seemed at any moment it would recede and disappear. This color and the mobility of her mouth gave a continual impression of flux, of intense life, of passionate vitality—balanced only partially by the sad luxury of her eyes.

She swung her mashie impatiently and without interest, pitching the ball into a sand-pit on the other side of the green. With a quick, insincere smile and a careless "Thank you!" she went on after it.

"That Judy Jones!" remarked Mr. Hedrick on the next tee, as they waited—some moments—for her to play on ahead. "All she needs is to be turned up and spanked for six months and then to be married off to an old-fashioned cavalry captain."

"My God, she's good-looking!" said Mr. Sandwood, who was just over thirty.

"Good-looking!" cried Mr. Hedrick contemptuously, "she always looks as if she wanted to be kissed! Turning those big cow-eyes on every calf in town!"

It was doubtful if Mr. Hedrick intended a reference to the maternal instinct.

"She'd play pretty good golf if she'd try," said Mr. Sandwood.

"She has no form," said Mr. Hedrick solemnly.

"She has a nice figure," said Mr. Sandwood.

"Better thank the Lord she doesn't drive a swifter ball," said Mr. Hart, winking at Dexter.

Later in the afternoon the sun went down with a riotous swirl of gold and varying blues and scarlets, and left the dry, rustling night of Western summer. Dexter watched from the veranda of the Golf Club, watched the even overlap of the waters in the little wind, silver molasses under the harvest moon. Then the moon held a finger to her lips and the lake became a clear pool, pale and quiet. Dexter put on his bathing suit and swam out to the farthest raft, where he stretched dripping on the wet canvas of the springboard.

There was a fish jumping and a star shining and the lights around the lake were gleaming. Over on a dark peninsula a piano was playing the songs of last summer and of summers before that—songs from *Chin-Chin* and *The Count of Luxemburg* and *The Chocolate Soldier*—and because the sound of a piano over a stretch of water had always seemed beautiful to Dexter he lay perfectly quiet and listened.

The tune the piano was playing at that moment had been gay and new five years before when Dexter was a sophomore at college. They had played it at a prom once when he could not afford the luxury of proms, and he had stood outside the gymnasium and listened. The sound of the tune precipitated in him a sort of ecstasy and it was with that ecstasy he viewed what happened to him now. It was a mood of intense appreciation, a sense that, for once, he was magnificently attune to life and that everything about him was radiating a brightness and a glamour he might never know again.

A low pale oblong detached itself suddenly from the darkness of the

Island, spitting forth the reverberate sound of a racing motor-boat. Two white streamers of cleft water rolled themselves out behind it and almost immediately the boat was beside him, drowning out the hot tinkle of the piano in the drone of its spray. Dexter raising himself on his arms was aware of a figure standing at the wheel, of two dark eyes regarding him over the lengthening space of water—then the boat had gone by and was sweeping in an immense and purposeless circle of spray round and round in the middle of the lake. With equal eccentricity one of the circles flattened out and headed back toward the raft.

"Who's that?" she called, shutting off her motor. She was so near now that Dexter could see her bathing suit, which consisted apparently of pink rompers.

The nose of the boat bumped the raft, and as the latter tilted rakishly he was precipitated toward her. With different degrees of interest they recognized each other.

"Aren't you one of those men we played through this afternoon?" she demanded.

He was.

"Well, do you know how to drive a motor-boat? Because if you do I wish you'd drive this one so I can ride on the surfboard behind. My name is Judy Jones"—she favored him with an absurd smirk—rather, what tried to be a smirk, for, twist her mouth as she might, it was not grotesque, it was merely beautiful—"and I live in a house over there on the Island, and in that house there is a man waiting for me. When he drove up at the door I drove out of the dock because he says I'm his ideal."

There was a fish jumping and a star shining and the lights around the lake were gleaming. Dexter sat beside Judy Jones and she explained how her boat was driven. Then she was in the water, swimming to the floating surfboard with a sinuous crawl. Watching her was without effort to the eye, like watching a branch waving or a sea gull flying. Her arms, burned to butternut, moved sinuously among the dull platinum ripples, elbow appearing first, casting the forearm back with a cadence of falling water, then reaching out and down, stabbing a path ahead.

They moved out into the lake; turning, Dexter saw that she was kneeling on the low rear of the now uptilted surfboard.

"Go faster," she called, "fast as it'll go."

Obediently he jammed the lever forward and the white spray mounted at the bow. When he looked around again the girl was standing up on the rushing board, her arms spread wide, her eyes lifted toward the moon.

"It's awful cold," she shouted. "What's your name?"

He told her.

"Well, why don't you come to dinner tomorrow night?"

His heart turned over like the fly-wheel of the boat, and, for the second time, her casual whim gave a new direction to his life.

III

Next evening while he waited for her to come downstairs, Dexter peopled the soft deep summer room and the sun porch that opened from it with the men who had already loved Judy Jones. He knew the sort of men they were—the men who when he first went to college had entered from the great prep schools with graceful clothes and the deep tan of healthy summers. He had seen that, in one sense, he was better than these men. He was newer and stronger. Yet in acknowledging to himself that he wished his children to be like them he was admitting that he was but the rough, strong stuff from which they eternally sprang.

When the time had come for him to wear good clothes, he had known who were the best tailors in America, and the best tailors in America had made him the suit he wore this evening. He had acquired that particular reserve peculiar to his university, that set it off from other universities. He recognized the value to him of such a mannerism and he had adopted it; he knew that to be careless in dress and manner required more confidence than to be careful. But carelessness was for his children. His mother's name had been Krimslich. She was a Bohemian of the peasant class and she had talked broken English to the end of her days. Her son must keep to the set patterns.

At a little after seven Judy Jones came downstairs. She wore a blue silk afternoon dress, and he was disappointed at first that she had not put on something more elaborate. This feeling was accentuated when, after a brief greeting, she went to the door of a butler's pantry and pushing it open called: "You can serve dinner, Martha." He had rather expected that a butler would announce dinner, that there would be a cocktail. Then he put these thoughts behind him as they sat down side by side on a lounge and looked at each other.

"Father and Mother won't be here," she said thoughtfully.

He remembered the last time he had seen her father, and he was glad the parents were not to be here tonight—they might wonder who he was. He had been born in Keeble, a Minnesota village fifty miles farther north, and he always gave Keeble as his home instead of Black Bear Village. Country towns were well enough to come from if they weren't inconveniently in sight and used as footstools by fashionable lakes.

They talked of his university, which she had visited frequently during the past two years, and of the nearby city which supplied Sherry Island with its patrons, and whither Dexter would return next day to his prospering laundries.

During dinner she slipped into a moody depression which gave Dexter a feeling of uneasiness. Whatever petulance she uttered in her throaty voice worried him. Whatever she smiled at—at him, at a chicken liver, at nothing—it disturbed him that her smile could have no root in mirth, or even in amusement. When the scarlet corners of her lips curved down, it was less a smile than an invitation to a kiss.

Then, after dinner, she led him out on the dark sun porch and deliberately changed the atmosphere.

"Do you mind if I weep a little?" she said.

"I'm afraid I'm boring you," he responded quickly.

"You're not. I like you. But I've just had a terrible afternoon. There was a man I cared about, and this afternoon he told me out of a clear sky that he was poor as a church mouse. He'd never even hinted it before. Does this sound horribly mundane?"

"Perhaps he was afraid to tell you."

"Suppose he was," she answered. "He didn't start right. You see, if I'd thought of him as poor—well, I've been mad about loads of poor men, and fully intended to marry them all. But in this case, I hadn't thought of him that way, and my interest in him wasn't strong enough to survive the shock. As if a girl calmly informed her fiancé that she was a widow. He might not object to widows, but—"

"Let's start right," she interrupted herself suddenly. "Who are you, anyhow?"

For a moment Dexter hesitated. Then:

"I'm nobody," he announced. "My career is largely a matter of futures."

"Are you poor?"

"No," he said frankly, "I'm probably making more money than any man my age in the Northwest. I know that's an obnoxious remark, but you advised me to start right."

There was a pause. Then she smiled and the corners of her mouth drooped and an almost imperceptible sway brought her closer to him, looking up into his eyes. A lump rose in Dexter's throat, and he waited breathless for the experiment, facing the unpredictable compound that would form mysteriously from the elements of their lips. Then he saw—she communicated her excitement to him, lavishly, deeply, with kisses that were not a promise but a fulfillment. They aroused in him not hunger demanding renewal but surfeit that would demand more surfeit . . . kisses that were like charity, creating want by holding back nothing at all.

It did not take him many hours to decide that he had wanted Judy Jones ever since he was a proud, desirous little boy.

IV

It began like that—and continued, with varying shades of intensity, on such a note right up to the dénouement. Dexter surrendered a part of himself to the most direct and unprincipled personality with which he had ever come in contact. Whatever Judy wanted, she went after with the full pressure of her charm. There was no divergence of method, no jockeying for position or premeditation of effects—there was a very little mental side to any of her affairs. She simply made men conscious to the highest degree of her physical loveliness. Dexter had no desire to change her. Her deficiencies were knit up with a passionate energy that transcended and justified them.

When, as Judy's head lay against his shoulder that first night, she whispered, "I don't know what's the matter with me. Last night I thought I was in love with a man and tonight I think I'm in love with you—" —it seemed to him a beautiful and romantic thing to say. It was the exquisite excitability that for the moment he controlled and owned. But a week later he was compelled to view this same quality in a different light. She took him in her roadster to a picnic supper, and after supper she disappeared, likewise in her roadster, with another man. Dexter became enormously upset and was scarcely able to be decently civil to the other people present. When she assured him that she had not kissed the other man, he knew she was lying—yet he was glad that she had taken the trouble to lie to him.

He was, as he found before the summer ended, one of a varying dozen who circulated about her. Each of them had at one time been favored above all others—about half of them still basked in the solace of occasional sentimental revivals. Whenever one showed signs of dropping out through long neglect, she granted him a brief hour, which encouraged him to tag along for a year or so longer. Judy made these forays upon the helpless and defeated without malice, indeed half unconscious that there was anything mischievous in what she did.

When a new man came into town everyone dropped out—dates were automatically cancelled.

The helpless part of trying to do anything about it was that she did it all herself. She was not a girl who could be "won" in the kinetic sense—she was proof against cleverness, she was proof against charm; if any of these assailed her too strongly she would immediately resolve the affair to a physical basis, and under the magic of her physical splendor the strong as well as the brilliant played her game and not their own. She was entertained only by the gratification of her desires and by the direct exercise of her own charm. Perhaps from so much youthful love, so many youthful lovers, she had come, in self-defense, to nourish herself wholly from within.

Succeeding Dexter's first exhilaration came restlessness and dissatisfaction. The helpless ecstasy of losing himself in her was opiate rather than tonic. It was fortunate for his work during the winter that those moments of ecstasy came infrequently. Early in their acquaintance it had seemed for a while that there was a deep and spontaneous mutual attraction—that first August, for example—three days of long evenings on her dusky veranda, of strange wan kisses through the late afternoon, in shadowy alcoves or behind the protecting trellises of the garden arbors, of mornings when she was fresh as a dream and almost shy at meeting him in the clarity of the rising day. There was all the ecstasy of an engagement about it, sharpened by his realization that there was no engagement. It was during those three days that, for the first time, he had asked her to marry him. She said "maybe some day," she said "kiss me," she said "I'd like to marry you," she said "I love you"—she said—nothing.

The three days were interrupted by the arrival of a New York man who visited at her house for half September. To Dexter's agony, rumor engaged them. The man was the son of the president of a great trust company. But at the end of a month it was reported that Judy was yawning. At a dance one night she sat all evening in a motor-boat with a local beau, while the New

Yorker searched the club for her frantically. She told the local beau that she was bored with her visitor, and two days later he left. She was seen with him at the station, and it was reported that he looked very mournful indeed.

On this note the summer ended. Dexter was twenty-four, and he found himself increasingly in a position to do as he wished. He joined two clubs in the city and lived at one of them. Though he was by no means an integral part of the stag lines at these clubs, he managed to be on hand at dances where Judy Jones was likely to appear. He could have gone out socially as much as he liked—he was an eligible young man, now, and popular with downtown fathers. His confessed devotion to Judy Jones had rather solidified his position. But he had no social aspirations and rather despised the dancing men who were always on tap for the Thursday or Saturday parties and who filled in at dinners with the younger married set. Already he was playing with the idea of going East to New York. He wanted to take Judy Jones with him. No disillusion as to the world in which she had grown up could cure his illusion as to her desirability.

Remember that—for only in the light of it can what he did for her be understood.

Eighteen months after he first met Judy Jones he became engaged to another girl. Her name was Irene Scheerer, and her father was one of the men who had always believed in Dexter. Irene was light-haired and sweet and honorable, and a little stout, and she had two suitors whom she pleasantly relinquished when Dexter formally asked her to marry him.

Summer, fall, winter, spring, another summer, another fall—so much he had given of his active life to the incorrigible lips of Judy Jones. She had treated him with interest, with encouragement, with malice, with indifference, with contempt. She had inflicted on him the innumerable little slights and indignities possible in such a case—as if in revenge for having ever cared for him at all. She had beckoned him and yawned at him and beckoned him again and he had responded often with bitterness and narrowed eyes. She had brought him ecstatic happiness and intolerable agony of spirit. She had caused him untold inconvenience and not a little trouble. She had insulted him, and she had ridden over him, and she had played his interest in her against his interest in his work—for fun. She had done everything to him except to criticize him—this she had not done—it seemed to him only because it might have sullied the utter indifference she manifested and sincerely felt toward him.

When autumn had come and gone again it occurred to him that he could not have Judy Jones. He had to beat this into his mind but he convinced himself at last. He lay awake at night for a while and argued it over. He told himself the trouble and the pain she had caused him, he enumerated her glaring deficiencies as a wife. Then he said to himself that he loved her, and after a while he fell asleep. For a week, lest he imagined her husky voice over the telephone or her eyes opposite him at lunch, he worked hard and late, and at night he went to his office and plotted out his years.

At the end of a week he went to a dance and cut in on her once. For almost the first time since they had met he did not ask her to sit out with him or tell her that she was lovely. It hurt him that she did not miss these things—that was all. He was not jealous when he saw that there was a new man tonight. He had been hardened against jealousy long before.

He stayed late at the dance. He sat for an hour with Irene Scheerer and talked about books and about music. He knew very little about either. But he was beginning to be master of his own time now, and he had a rather priggish notion that he—the young and already fabulously successful Dexter Green—should know more about such things.

That was in October, when he was twenty-five. In January, Dexter and Irene became engaged. It was to be announced in June, and they were to be married three months later.

The Minnesota winter prolonged itself interminably, and it was almost May when the winds came soft and the snow ran down into Black Bear Lake at last. For the first time in over a year Dexter was enjoying a certain tranquility of spirit. Judy Jones had been in Florida, and afterward in Hot Springs, and somewhere she had been engaged, and somewhere she had broken it off. At first, when Dexter had definitely given her up, it had made him sad that people still linked them together and asked for news of her, but when he began to be placed at dinner next to Irene Scheerer people didn't ask him about her any more—they told him about her. He ceased to be an authority on her.

May at last. Dexter walked the streets at night when the darkness was damp as rain, wondering that so soon, with so little done, so much of ecstasy had gone from him. May one year back had been marked by Judy's poignant, unforgivable, yet forgiven turbulence—it had been one of those rare times when he fancied she had grown to care for him. That old penny's worth of happiness he had spent for this bushel of content. He knew that Irene would be no more than a curtain spread behind him, a hand moving among gleaming tea cups, a voice calling to children . . . fire and loveliness were gone, the magic of nights and the wonder of the varying hours and seasons . . . slender lips, down-turning, dropping to his lips and bearing him up into a heaven of eyes . . . The thing was deep in him. He was too strong and alive for it to die lightly.

In the middle of May when the weather balanced for a few days on the thin bridge that led to deep summer he turned in one night at Irene's house. Their engagement was to be announced in a week now—no one would be surprised at it. And tonight they would sit together on the lounge at the University Club and look on for an hour at the dancers. It gave him a sense of solidity to go with her—she was so sturdily popular, so intensely "great."

He mounted the steps of the brownstone house and stepped inside.

"Irene," he called.

Mrs. Scheerer came out of the living room to meet him.

"Dexter," she said, "Irene's gone upstairs with a splitting headache. She wanted to go with you but I made her go to bed."

"Nothing serious, I—"

"Oh, no. She's going to play golf with you in the morning. You can spare her for just one night, can't you, Dexter?"

Her smile was kind. She and Dexter liked each other. In the living room he talked for a moment before he said goodnight.

Returning to the University Club, where he had rooms, he stood in the doorway for a moment and watched the dancers. He leaned against the doorpost, nodded at a man or two—yawned.

"Hello, darling."

The familiar voice at his elbow startled him. Judy Jones had left a man and crossed the room to him—Judy Jones, a slender enameled doll in cloth of gold: gold in a band at her head, gold in two slipper points at her dress's hem. The fragile glow of her face seemed to blossom as she smiled at him. A breeze of warmth and light blew through the room. His hands in the pockets of his dinner jacket tightened spasmodically. He was filled with a sudden excitement.

"When did you get back?" he asked casually.

"Come here and I'll tell you about it."

She turned and he followed her. She had been away—he could have wept at the wonder of her return. She had passed through enchanted streets, doing things that were like provocative music. All mysterious happenings, all fresh and quickening hopes, had gone away with her, come back with her now.

She turned in the doorway.

"Have you a car here? If you haven't, I have."

"I have a coupé."

In then, with a rustle of golden cloth. He slammed the door. Into so many cars she had stepped—like this—like that—her back against the leather, so—her elbow resting on the door—waiting. She would have been soiled long since had there been anything to soil her—except herself—but this was her own self outpouring.

With an effort he forced himself to start the car and back into the street. This was nothing, he must remember. She had done this before, and he had put her behind him, as he would have crossed a bad account from his books.

He drove slowly downtown and, affecting abstraction, traversed the deserted streets of the business section, peopled here and there where a movie was giving out its crowd or where consumptive or pugilistic youth lounged in front of pool halls. The clink of glasses and the slap of hands on the bars issued from saloons, cloisters of glazed glass and dirty yellow light.

She was watching him closely and the silence was embarrassing, yet in this crisis he could find no casual word with which to profane the hour. At a convenient turning he began to zigzag back toward the University Club.

"Have you missed me?" she asked suddenly.

"Everybody missed you."

He wondered if she knew of Irene Scheerer. She had been back only a day—her absence had been almost contemporaneous with his engagement.

"What a remark!" Judy laughed sadly—without sadness. She looked at him searchingly. He became absorbed in the dashboard.

"You're handsomer than you used to be," she said thoughtfully. "Dexter, you have the most rememberable eyes."

He could have laughed at this, but he did not laugh. It was the sort of thing that was said to sophomores. Yet it stabbed at him.

"I'm awfully tired of everything, darling." She called everyone darling, endowing the endearment with careless, individual camaraderie. "I wish you'd marry me."

The directness of this confused him. He should have told her now that he was going to marry another girl, but he could not tell her. He could as easily have sworn that he had never loved her.

"I think we'd get along," she continued, on the same note, "unless probably you've forgotten me and fallen in love with another girl."

Her confidence was obviously enormous. She had said, in effect, that she found such a thing impossible to believe, that if it were true he had merely committed a childish indiscretion—and probably to show off. She would forgive him, because it was not a matter of any moment but rather something to be brushed aside lightly.

"Of course you could never love anybody but me," she continued, "I like the way you love me. Oh, Dexter, have you forgotten last year?"

"No, I haven't forgotten."

"Neither have I!"

Was she sincerely moved—or was she carried along by the wave of her own acting?

"I wish we could be like that again," she said, and he forced himself to answer:

"I don't think we can."

"I suppose not. . . . I hear you're giving Irene Scheerer a violent rush."

There was not the faintest emphasis on the name, yet Dexter was suddenly ashamed.

"Oh, take me home," cried Judy suddenly; "I don't want to go back to that idiotic dance—with those children."

Then, as he turned up the street that led to the residence district, Judy began to cry quietly to herself. He had never seen her cry before.

The dark street lightened, the dwellings of the rich loomed up around them, he stopped his coupé in front of the great white bulk of the Mortimer Joneses' house, somnolent, gorgeous, drenched with the splendor of the damp moonlight. Its solidity startled him. The strong walls, the steel of the girders, the breadth and beam and pomp of it were there only to bring out the contrast with the young beauty beside him. It was sturdy to accentuate her slightness—as if to show what a breeze could be generated by a butterfly's wings.

He sat perfectly quiet, his nerves in wild clamor, afraid that if he moved he would find her irresistibly in his arms. Two tears had rolled down her wet face and trembled on her upper lip.

"I'm more beautiful than anybody else," she said brokenly, "Why can't I be happy?" Her moist eyes tore at his stability—her mouth turned slowly downward with an exquisite sadness: "I'd like to marry you if you'll have me, Dexter. I suppose you think I'm not worth having, but I'll be so beautiful for you, Dexter."

A million phrases of anger, pride, passion, hatred, tenderness fought on his lips. Then a perfect wave of emotion washed over him, carrying off with it a sediment of wisdom, of convention, of doubt, of honor. This was his girl who was speaking, his own, his beautiful, his pride.

"Won't you come in?" He heard her draw in her breath sharply.

Waiting.

"All right," his voice was trembling, "I'll come in."

V

It was strange that neither when it was over nor a long time afterward did he regret that night. Looking at it from the perspective of ten years, the fact that Judy's flare for him endured just one month seemed of little importance. Nor did it matter that by his yielding he subjected himself to a deeper agony in the end and gave serious hurt to Irene Scheerer and to Irene's parents, who had befriended him. There was nothing sufficiently pictorial about Irene's grief to stamp itself on his mind.

Dexter was at bottom hard-minded. The attitude of the city on his action was of no importance to him, not because he was going to leave the city, but because any outside attitude on the situation seemed superficial. He was completely indifferent to popular opinion. Nor, when he had seen that it was no use, that he did not possess in himself the power to move fundamentally or to hold Judy Jones, did he bear any malice toward her. He loved her, and he would love her until the day he was too old for loving—but he could not have her. So he tasted the deep pain that is reserved only for the strong, just as he had tasted for a little while the deep happiness.

Even the ultimate falsity of the grounds upon which Judy terminated the engagement that she did not want to "take him away" from Irene—Judy, who had wanted nothing else—did not revolt him. He was beyond any revulsion or any amusement.

He went East in February with the intention of selling out his laundries and settling in New York—but the war came to America in March and changed his plans. He returned to the West, handed over the management of the business to his partner, and went into the first officers' training camp in late April. He was one of those young thousands who greeted the war with a certain amount of relief, welcoming the liberation from webs of tangled emotion.

VI

This story is not his biography, remember, although things creep into it which have nothing to do with those dreams he had when he was young. We are almost done with them and with him now. There is only one more incident to be related here, and it happens seven years farther on.

It took place in New York, where he had done well—so well that there were no barriers too high for him. He was thirty-two years old, and, except for one flying trip immediately after the war, he had not been West in seven years. A man named Devlin from Detroit came into his office to see him in a business way, and then and there this incident occurred, and closed out, so to speak, this particular side of his life.

"So you're from the Middle West," said the man Devlin with careless curiosity. "That's funny—I thought men like you were probably born and raised on Wall Street. You know—wife of one of my best friends in Detroit came from your city. I was an usher at the wedding."

Dexter waited with no apprehension of what was coming.

"Judy Simms," said Devlin with no particular interest; "Judy Jones she was once."

"Yes, I knew her." A dull impatience spread over him. He had heard, of course, that she was married—perhaps deliberately he had heard no more.

"Awfully nice girl," brooded Devlin meaninglessly, "I'm sort of sorry for her."

"Why?" Something in Dexter was alert, receptive, at once.

"Oh, Lud Simms has gone to pieces in a way. I don't mean he ill-uses her, but he drinks and runs around—"

"Doesn't she run around?"

"No. Stays at home with her kids."

"Oh."

"She's a little too old for him," said Devlin.

"Too old!" cried Dexter. "Why, man, she's only twenty-seven."

He was possessed with a wild notion of rushing out into the streets and taking a train to Detroit. He rose to his feet spasmodically.

"I guess you're busy," Devlin apoligized quickly. "I didn't realize—"

"No, I'm not busy," said Dexter, steadying his voice. "I'm not busy at all. Not busy at all. Did you say she was—twenty-seven? No, I said she was twenty-seven."

"Yes, you did," agreed Devlin dryly.

"Go on, then. Go on."

"What do you mean?"

"About Judy Jones."

Devlin looked at him helplessly.

"Well, that's—I told you all there is to it. He treats her like the devil. Oh, they're not going to get divorced or anything. When he's particularly outrageous she forgives him. In fact, I'm inclined to think she loves him. She was a pretty girl when she first came to Detroit."

A pretty girl! The phrase struck Dexter as ludicrous.

"Isn't she—a pretty girl, any more?"

"Oh, she's all right."

"Look here," said Dexter, sitting down suddenly, "I don't understand. You say she was a 'pretty girl' and now you say she's 'all right.' I don't understand what you mean—Judy Jones wasn't a pretty girl, at all. She was a great beauty. Why, I knew her, I knew her. She was—"

Devlin laughed pleasantly.

"I'm not trying to start a row," he said. "I think Judy's a nice girl and I like her. I can't understand how a man like Lud Simms could fall madly in love with her, but he did." Then he added: "Most of the women like her."

Dexter looked closely at Devlin, thinking wildly that there must be a reason for this, some insensitivity in the man or some private malice.

"Lots of women fade just like *that,*" Devlin snapped his fingers. "You must have seen it happen. Perhaps I've forgotten how pretty she was at her wedding. I've seen her so much since then, you see. She has nice eyes."

A sort of dullness settled down upon Dexter. For the first time in his life he felt like getting very drunk. He knew that he was laughing loudly at something Devlin had said, but he did not know what it was or why it was funny. When, in a few minutes, Devlin went he lay down on his lounge and looked out the window at the New York sky line into which the sun was sinking in dull lovely shades of pink and gold.

He had thought that having nothing else to lose he was invulnerable at last—but he knew that he had just lost something more, as surely as if he had married Judy Jones and seen her fade away before his eyes.

The dream was gone. Something had been taken from him. In a sort of panic he pushed the palms of his hands into his eyes and tried to bring up a picture of the waters lapping on Sherry Island and the moonlit veranda, and gingham on the golf links and the dry sun and the gold color of her neck's soft down. And her mouth damp to his kisses and her eyes plaintive with melancholy and her freshness like new fine linen in the morning. Why, these things were no longer in the world! They had existed and they existed no longer.

For the first time in years the tears were streaming down his face. But they were for himself now. He did not care about mouth and eyes and moving hands. He wanted to care, and he could not care. For he had gone away and he could never go back any more. The gates were closed, the sun was gone down, and there was no beauty but the gray beauty of steel that withstands all time. Even the grief he could have borne was left behind in the country of illusion, of youth, of the richness of life, where his winter dreams had flourished.

"Long ago," he said, "long ago, there was something in me, but now that thing is gone. Now that thing is gone, that thing is gone. I cannot cry. I cannot care. That thing will come back no more."

Complaint

JAMES WRIGHT

She's gone. She was my love, my moon or more.
She chased the chickens out and swept the floor,
Emptied the bones and nut-shells after feasts,
And smacked the kids for leaping up like beasts.
Now morbid boys have grown past awkwardness;
The girls let stitches out, dress after dress,
To free some swinging body's riding space
And form the new child's unimagined face.
Yet, while vague nephews, spitting on their curls,
Amble to pester winds and blowsy girls,
What arm will sweep the room, what hand will hold
New snow against the milk to keep it cold?
And who will dump the garbage, feed the hogs,
And pitch the chickens' heads to hungry dogs?
Now my lost hag who dumbly bore such pain:
Childbirth and midnight sassafras and rain.
New snow against her face and hands she bore,
And now lies down, who was my moon or more.

One Home

WILLIAM STAFFORD

Mine was a Midwest home—you can keep your world.
Plain black hats rode the thoughts that made our code.
We sang hymns in the house; the roof was near God.

The light bulb that hung in the pantry made a wan light,
but we could read by it the names of preserves—
outside, the buffalo grass, and the wind in the night.

A wildcat sprang at Grandpa on the Fourth of July
when he was cutting plum bushes for fuel,
before Indians pulled the West over the edge of the sky.

To anyone who looked at us we said, "My friend";
liking the cut of a thought, we could say, "Hello."
(But plain black hats rode the thoughts that made our code.)

The sun was over our town; it was like a blade.
Kicking cottonwood leaves we ran toward storms.
Wherever we looked the land would hold us up.

Father's Voice

WILLIAM STAFFORD

"No need to get home early;
the car can see in the dark."
He wanted me to be rich
the only way we could,
easy with what we had.

And always that was his gift,
given for me ever since,
easy gift, a wind
that keeps on blowing for flowers
or birds wherever I look.

World, I am your slow guest,
one of the common things
that move in the sun and have
close, reliable friends
in the earth, in the air, in the rock.

Those Winter Sundays

ROBERT HAYDEN

Sundays too my father got up early
and put his clothes on in the blueblack cold,
then with cracked hands that ached
from labor in the weekday weather made
banked fires blaze. No one ever thanked him.

I'd wake and hear the cold splintering, breaking.
When the rooms were warm, he'd call,
and slowly I would rise and dress,
fearing the chronic angers of that house,

Speaking indifferently to him,
who had driven out the cold
and polished my good shoes as well.
What did I know, what did I know
of love's austere and lonely offices?

CHAPTER ONE FROM *Babbitt*

SINCLAIR LEWIS

I

The towers of Zenith aspired above the morning mist; austere towers of steel and cement and limestone, sturdy as cliffs and delicate as silver rods. They were neither citadels nor churches, but frankly and beautifully office-buildings.

The mist took pity on the fretted structures of earlier generations: the Post Office with its shingle-tortured mansard, the red brick minarets of hulking old houses, factories with stingy and sooted windows, wooden tenements colored like mud. The city was full of such grotesqueries, but the clean towers were thrusting them from the business center, and on the farther hills were shining new houses, homes—they seemed—for laughter and tranquillity.

Over a concrete bridge fled a limousine of long sleek hood and noiseless engine. These people in evening clothes were returning from an all-night rehearsal of a Little Theater play, an artistic adventure considerably illuminated by champagne. Below the bridge curved a railroad, a maze of green and crimson lights. The New York Flyer boomed past, and twenty lines of polished steel leaped into the glare.

In one of the skyscrapers the wires of the Associated Press were closing down. The telegraph operators wearily raised their celluloid eye-shades after a night of talking with Paris and Peking. Through the building crawled the scrubwomen, yawning, their old shoes slapping. The dawn mist spun away. Cues of men with lunch-boxes clumped toward the immensity of new factories, sheets of glass and hollow tile, glittering shops where five thousand men worked beneath one roof, pouring out the honest wares that would be sold up the Euphrates and across the veldt. The whistles rolled out in greeting a chorus cheerful as the April dawn; the song of labor in a city built—it seemed—for giants.

II

There was nothing of the giant in the aspect of the man who was beginning to awaken on the sleeping-porch of a Dutch Colonial house in that residential district of Zenith known as Floral Heights.

His name was George F. Babbitt. He was forty-six years old now, in April, 1920, and he made nothing in particular, neither butter nor shoes nor poetry, but he was nimble in the calling of selling houses for more than people could afford to pay.

His large head was pink, his brown hair thin and dry. His face was babyish in slumber, despite his wrinkles and the red spectacle-dents on the slopes of his nose. He was not fat but he was exceedingly well fed; his cheeks were pads, and the unroughened hand which lay helpless upon the khaki-colored blanket was slightly puffy. He seemed prosperous, extremely married and unromantic; and altogether unromantic appeared this sleeping-porch, which looked on one sizable elm, two respectable grass-plots, a cement driveway, and a corrugated iron garage. Yet Babbitt was again dreaming of the fairy child, a dream more romantic than scarlet pagodas by a silver sea.

For years the fairy child had come to him. Where others saw but Georgie Babbitt, she discerned gallant youth. She waited for him, in the darkness beyond mysterious groves. When at last he could slip away from the crowded house he darted to her. His wife, his clamoring friends, sought to follow, but he escaped, the girl fleet beside him, and they crouched together on a shadowy hillside. She was so slim, so white, so eager! She cried that he was gay and valiant, that she would wait for him, that they would sail—

Rumble and bang of the milk-truck.

Babbitt moaned, turned over, struggled back toward his dream. He could see only her face now, beyond misty waters. The furnace-man slammed the basement door. A dog barked in the next yard. As Babbitt sank blissfully into a dim warm tide, the paper-carrier went by whistling, and the rolled-up *Advocate* thumped the front door. Babbitt roused, his stomach constricted with alarm. As he relaxed, he was pierced by the familiar and irritating rattle of some one cranking a Ford: snap-ah-ah, snap-ah-ah, snap-ah-ah. Himself a pious motorist, Babbitt cranked with the unseen driver, with him waited through taut hours for the roar of the starting engine, with him agonized as the roar ceased and again began the infernal patient snap-ah-ah—a round, flat sound, a shivering cold-morning sound, a sound infuriating and inescapable. Not till the rising voice of the motor told him that the Ford was moving was he released from the panting tension. He glanced once at his favorite tree, elm twigs against the gold patina of sky, and fumbled for sleep as for a drug. He who had been a boy very credulous of life was no longer greatly interested in the possible and improbable adventures of each new day.

He escaped from reality till the alarm-clock rang, at seven-twenty.

III

It was the best of nationally advertised and quantitatively produced alarm-clocks, with all modern attachments, including cathedral chime, intermittent alarm, and a phosphorescent dial. Babbitt was proud of being awakened by such a rich device. Socially it was almost as creditable as buying expensive cord tires.

He sulkily admitted now that there was no more escape, but he lay and detested the grind of the real-estate business, and disliked his family, and disliked himself for disliking them. The evening before, he had played poker at Vergil Gunch's till midnight, and after such holidays he was irritable before breakfast. It may have been the tremendous home-brewed beer of the prohibition-era and the cigars to which that beer enticed him; it may have been resentment of return from this fine, bold man-world to a restricted region of wives and stenographers, and of suggestions not to smoke so much.

From the bedroom beside the sleeping-porch, his wife's detestably cheerful "Time to get up, Georgie boy," and the itchy sound, the brisk and scratchy sound, of combing hairs out of a stiff brush.

He grunted; he dragged his thick legs, in faded baby-blue pajamas, from under the khaki blanket; he sat on the edge of the cot, running his fingers through his wild hair, while his plump feet mechanically felt for his slippers. He looked regretfully at the blanket—forever a suggestion to him of freedom and heroism. He had bought it for a camping trip which had never come off. It symbolized gorgeous loafing, gorgeous cursing, virile flannel shirts.

He creaked to his feet, groaning at the waves of pain which passed behind his eyeballs. Though he waited for their scorching recurrence, he looked blurrily out at the yard. It delighted him, as always; it was the neat yard of a successful business man of Zenith, that is, it was perfection, and made him also perfect. He regarded the corrugated iron garage. For the three-hundred-and-sixty-fifth time in a year he reflected, "No class to that tin shack. Have to build me a frame garage. But by golly it's the only thing on the place that isn't up-to-date!" While he stared he thought of a community garage for his acreage development, Glen Oriole. He stopped puffing and jiggling. His arms were akimbo. His petulant, sleep-swollen face was set in harder lines. He suddenly seemed capable, an official, a man to contrive, to direct, to get things done.

On the vigor of his idea he was carried down the hard, clean, unused-looking hall into the bathroom.

Though the house was not large it had, like all houses on Floral Heights, an altogether royal bathroom of porcelain and glazed tile and metal sleek as silver. The towel-rack was a rod of clear glass set in nickel. The tub was long enough for a Prussian Guard, and above the set bowl was a sensational exhibit of tooth-brush holder, shaving-brush holder, soap-dish, sponge-dish, and medicine-cabinet, so glittering and so ingenious that they resembled an electrical instrument-board. But the Babbitt whose god was Modern Appliances was not pleased. The air of the bathroom was thick with the smell of a heathen toothpaste. "Verona been at it again! 'Stead of sticking to Lilidol, like I've re-peat-ed-ly asked her, she's gone and gotten some confounded stinkum stuff that makes you sick!"

The bath-mat was wrinkled and the floor was wet. (His daughter Verona eccentrically took baths in the morning, now and then.) He slipped on the mat, and slid against the tub. He said "Damn!" Furiously he snatched up his tube of shaving-cream, furiously he lathered, with a belligerent slapping of the unctuous brush, furiously he raked his plump cheeks with a safety-razor. It pulled. The blade was dull. He said, "Damn—oh—oh—damn it!"

He hunted through the medicine-cabinet for a packet of new razor-blades (reflecting, as invariably, "Be cheaper to buy one of these dinguses and strop your own blades,") and when he discovered the packet, behind the round box of bicarbonate of soda, he thought ill of his wife for putting it there and very well of himself for not saying "Damn." But he did say it, immediately afterward, when with wet and soap-slippery fingers he tried to remove the horrible little envelope and crisp clinging oiled paper from the new blade.

Then there was the problem, oft-pondered, never solved, of what to do with the old blade, which might imperil the fingers of his young. As usual, he tossed it on top of the medicine-cabinet, with a mental note that some day he must remove the fifty or sixty other blades that were also temporarily, piled up there. He finished his shaving in a growing testiness increased by his spinning headache and by the emptiness in his stomach. When he was done, his round face smooth and streamy and his eyes stinging from soapy water, he reached for a towel. The family towels were wet, wet and clammy and vile, all of them wet, he found, as he blindly snatched them—his own face-towel, his wife's, Verona's, Ted's, Tinka's, and the lone bath-towel with the huge welt of initial. Then George F. Babbitt did a dismaying thing. He wiped his face on the guest-towel! It was a pansy-emboidered trifle which always hung there to indicate that the Babbitts were in the best Floral Heights society. No one had ever used it. No guest had ever dared to. Guests secretively took a corner of the nearest regular towel.

He was raging, "By golly, here they go and use up all of the towels, every doggone one of 'em, and they use 'em and get 'em all wet and sopping, and never put out a dry one for me—of course, I'm the goat!—and then I want one and— I'm the only person in the doggone house that's got the slightest doggone bit of consideration for other people and thoughtfulness and consider there may be others that may want to use the doggone bathroom after me and consider—"

He was pitching the chill abominations into the bath-tub, pleased by the vindictiveness of that desolate flapping sound; and in the midst his wife serenely trotted in, observed serenely, "Why Georgie dear, what are you doing? Are you going to wash out the towels? Why, you needn't wash out the towels. Oh, Georgie, you didn't go and use the guest-towel, did you?"

It is not recorded that he was able to answer.

For the first time in weeks he was sufficiently roused by his wife to look at her.

IV

Myra Babbitt—Mrs. George F. Babbitt—was definitely mature. She had creases from the corners of her mouth to the bottom of her chin, and her plump neck bagged. But the thing that marked her as having passed the line was that she no longer had reticences before her husband, and no longer worried about not having reticences. She was in a petticoat now, and corsets which bulged, and unaware of being seen in bulgy corsets. She had become so dully habituated to married life that in her full matronliness she was as sexless as an anemic nun. She was a good woman, a kind woman, a diligent woman, but no one, save perhaps Tinka her ten-year-old, was at all interested in her or entirely aware that she was alive.

After a rather thorough discussion of all the domestic and social aspects of towels she apologized to Babbitt for his having an alcoholic headache; and he recovered enough to endure the search for a B.V.D. undershirt which had, he pointed out, malevolently been concealed among his clean pajamas.

He was fairly amiable in the conference on the brown suit.

"What do you think, Myra?" He pawed at the clothes hunched on a chair in their bedroom, while she moved about mysteriously adjusting and patting her petticoat and, to his jaundiced eye, never seeming to get on with her dressing. "How about it? Shall I wear the brown suit another day?"

"Well, it looks awfully nice on you."

"I know, but gosh, it needs pressing."

"That's so. Perhaps it does."

"It certainly could stand being pressed, all right."

"Yes, perhaps it wouldn't hurt it to be pressed."

"But gee, the coat doesn't need pressing. No sense in having the whole darn suit pressed, when the coat doesn't need it."

"That's so."

"But the pants certainly need it, all right. Look at them—look at those wrinkles—the pants certainly do need pressing."

"That's so. Oh, Georgie, why couldn't you wear the brown coat with the blue trousers we were wondering what we'd do with them?"

"Good Lord! Did you ever in all my life know me to wear the coat of one suit and the pants of another? What do you think I am? A busted book-keeper?"

"Well, why don't you put on the dark gray suit to-day, and stop in at the tailor and leave the brown trousers?"

"Well, they certainly need— Now where the devil is that gray suit? Oh, yes, here we are."

He was able to get through the other crises of dressing with comparative resoluteness and calm.

His first adornment was the sleeveless dimity B.V.D. undershirt, in which he resembled a small boy humorlessly wearing a cheesecloth tabard at a civic pageant. He never put on B.V.D.'s without thanking the God of Progress that he didn't wear tight, long, old-fashioned undergarments, like his father-in-law and partner, Henry Thompson. His second embellishment was combing and slicking back his hair. It gave him a tremendous forehead, arching up two inches beyond the former hair-line. But most wonder-working of all was the donning of his spectacles.

There is character in spectacles—the pretentious tortoise-shell, the meek pince-nez of the school teacher, the twisted silver-framed glasses of the old villager. Babbitt's spectacles had huge, circular, frameless lenses of the very best glass; the ear-pieces were thin bars of gold. In them he was the modern business man; one who gave orders to clerks and drove a car and played occasional golf and was scholarly in regard to Salesmanship. His head suddenly appeared not babyish but weighty, and you noted his heavy, blunt nose, his straight mouth and thick, long upper lip, his chin overfleshy but strong; with respect you beheld him put on the rest of his uniform as a Solid Citizen.

The gray suit was well cut, well made, and completely undistinguished. It was a standard suit. White piping on the V of the vest added a flavor of law and learning. His shoes were black laced boots, good boots, honest boots, standard boots, extraordinarily uninteresting boots. The only frivolity was in his purple knitted scarf. With considerable comment on the matter to Mrs. Babbitt (who, acrobatically fastening the back of her blouse to her skirt with a safety-pin, did not hear a word he said), he chose between the purple scarf and a tapestry effect with stringless brown harps among blown palms, and into it he thrust a snake-head pin with opal eyes.

A sensational event was changing from the brown suit to the gray the contents of his pockets. He was earnest about these objects. They were of eternal importance, like baseball or the Republican Party. They included a fountain pen and a silver pencil (always lacking a supply of new leads) which belonged in the righthand upper vest pocket. Without them he would have felt naked. On his watch-chain were a gold penknife, silver cigar-cutter, seven keys (the use of two of which he had forgotten), and incidentally a good watch. Depending from the chain was a large, yellowish elk's-tooth—proclamation of his membership in the Brotherly and Protective Order of Elks. Most significant of all was his loose-leaf pocket note-book, that modern and efficient note-book which contained the addresses of people whom he had forgotten, prudent memoranda of postal money-orders which had reached their destinations months ago, stamps which had lost their mucilage, clippings of verses by T. Cholmondeley Frink and of the newspaper editorials from which Babbitt got his opinions and his polysyllables, notes to be sure and do things which he did not intend to do, and one curious inscription—D.S.S.D.M.Y.P.D.F.

But he had no cigarette-case. No one had ever happened to give him one, so he hadn't the habit, and people who carried cigarette-cases he regarded as effeminate.

Last, he stuck in his lapel the Boosters' Club button. With the conciseness of great art the button displayed two words: "Boosters—Pep!" It made Babbitt feel loyal and important. It associated him with Good Fellows, with men who were nice and human, and important in business circles. It was his V.C., his Legion of Honor ribbon, his Phi Beta Kappa key.

With the subtleties of dressing ran other complex worries. "I feel kind of punk this morning," he said. "I think I had too much dinner last evening. You oughtn't to serve those heavy banana fritters."

"But you asked me to have some."

"I know, but— I tell you, when a fellow gets past forty he has to look after his digestion. There's a lot of fellows that don't take proper care of themselves. I tell you at forty a man's a fool or his doctor—I mean, his own doctor. Folks don't give enough attention to this matter of dieting. Now I think— Course a man ought to have a good meal after the day's work, but it would be a good thing for both of us if we took lighter lunches."

"But Georgie, here at home I always do have a light lunch."

"Mean to imply I make a hog of myself, eating down-town? Yes, sure! You'd have a swell time if you had to eat the truck that new steward hands out to us at the Athletic Club! But I certainly do feel out of sorts, this morning. Funny, got a pain down here on the left side—but no, that wouldn't be appendicitis, would it? Last night, when I was driving over to Verg Gunch's, I felt a pain in my stomach, too. Right here it was—kind of a sharp shooting pain. I— Where'd that dime go to? Why don't you serve more prunes at breakfast? Of course I eat an apple every evening—an apple a day keeps the doctor away—but still, you ought to have more prunes, and not all these fancy doodads."

"The last time I had prunes you didn't eat them."

"Well, I didn't feel like eating 'em, I suppose. Matter of fact, I think I did eat some of 'em. Anyway— I tell you it's mighty important to— I was saying to Verg Gunch, just last evening, most people don't take sufficient care of their diges—"

"Shall we have the Gunches for our dinner, next week?"

"Why sure; you bet."

"Now see here, George: I want you to put on your nice dinner-jacket that evening."

"Rats! The rest of 'em won't want to dress."

"Of course they will. You remember when you didn't dress for the Littlefields' supper-party, and all the rest did, and how embarrassed you were."

"Embarrassed, hell! I wasn't embarrassed. Everybody knows I can put on as expensive a Tux. as anybody else, and I should worry if I don't happen to have it on sometimes. All a darn nuisance, anyway. All right for a woman, that stays around the house all the time, but when a fellow's worked like the dickens all day, he doesn't want to go and hustle his head off getting into the soup-and-fish for a lot of folks that he's seen in just reg'lar ordinary clothes that same day."

"You know you enjoy being seen in one. The other evening you admitted you were glad I'd insisted on your dressing. You said you felt a lot better for it. And oh, Georgie, I do wish you wouldn't say 'Tux.' It's 'dinner-jacket.' "

"Rats, what's the odds?"

"Well, it's what all the nice folks say. Suppose Lucile McKelvey heard you calling it a 'Tux.' "

"Well, that's all right now! Lucile McKelvey can't pull anything on me! Her folks are common as mud, even if her husband and her dad are millionaires! I suppose you're trying to rub in *your* exalted social position! Well, let me tell you that your revered paternal ancestor, Henry T., doesn't even call it a 'Tux.'! He calls it a 'bobtail jacket for a ringtail monkey,' and you couldn't get him into one unless you chloroformed him!"

"Now don't be horrid, George."

"Well, I don't want to be horrid, but Lord! you're getting as fussy as Verona. Ever since she got out of college she's been too rambunctious to live with—doesn't know what she wants—well, I know what she wants!—all she wants is to marry a millionaire, and live in Europe, and hold some preacher's hand, and simultaneously at the same time stay right here in Zenith and be some blooming kind of a socialist agitator or boss charity-worker or some damn thing! Lord, and Ted is just as bad! He wants to go to college, and he doesn't want to go to college. Only one of the three that knows her own mind is Tinka. Simply can't understand how I ever came to have a pair of shillyshallying children like Rone and Ted. I may not be any Rockefeller or James J. Shakespeare, but I certainly do know my own mind, and I do keep right on plugging along in the office and— Do you know the latest? Far as I can figure out, Ted's new bee is he'd like to be a movie actor and— And here I've told him a hundred times, if he'll go to college and law-school and make good, I'll set him up in business and— Verona just exactly as bad. Doesn't know what she wants. Well, well, come on! Aren't you ready yet? The girl rang the bell three minutes ago."

V

Before he followed his wife, Babbitt stood at the westernmost window of their room. This residential settlement, Floral Heights, was on a rise; and though the center of the city was three miles away—Zenith had between three and four hundred thousand inhabitants now—he could see the top of the Second National Tower, an Indiana limestone building of thirty-five stories.

Its shining walls rose against April sky to a simple cornice like a streak of white fire. Integrity was in the tower, and decision. It bore its strength lightly as a tall soldier. As Babbitt stared, the nervousness was soothed from his face, his slack chin lifted in reverence. All he articulated was "That's one lovely sight!" but he was inspired by the rhythm of the city; his love of it renewed. He beheld the tower as a temple-spire of the religion of business, a faith passionate, exalted, surpassing common men; and as he clumped down to breakfast he whistled the ballad "Oh, by gee, by gosh, by jingo" as though it were a hymn melancholy and noble.

*Washington McNeely**

EDGAR LEE MASTERS

Rich, honored by my fellow citizens,
The father of many children, born of a noble mother,
All raised there
In the great mansion-house, at the edge of town.
Note the cedar tree on the lawn!
I sent all the boys to Ann Arbor, all the girls to Rockford.
The while my life went on, getting more riches and honors—
Resting under my cedar tree at evening.
The years went on.
I sent the girls to Europe;
I dowered them when married.
I gave the boys money to start in business.
They were strong children, promising as apples
Before the bitten places show.
But John fled the country in disgrace.
Jenny died in child-birth—
I sat under my cedar tree.
Harry killed himself after a debauch,
Susan was divorced—
I sat under my cedar tree.
Paul was invalided from over study,
Mary became a recluse at home for love of a man—
I sat under my cedar tree.
All were gone, or broken-winged or devoured by life—
I sat under my cedar tree.

* From *Spoon River Anthology*.

My mate, the mother of them, was taken—
I sat under my cedar tree,
Till ninety years were tolled.
O maternal Earth, which rocks the fallen leaf to sleep!

Protests and Affirmations

That authors with a midwestern background often adhered to an egalitarian tradition was evident both in their protests against social inequities and in their affirmations of patriotic fervor, faith in democracy, and personal fulfillment.

The promise of free land which had drawn settlers westward throughout the first half of the nineteenth century changed after the Civil War as repeated natural disasters and growing problems with land speculators, mortgagors, and railroad monopolists turned a vision of earthly paradise into a discontented reality. As a result of this discontentment, the Populist—or People's—movement was organized. The literary Populism of Hamlin Garland and Vachel Lindsay represented part of this collective protest by midwestern agrarians between the 1890s and the early 1900s. Garland's *Main-Travelled Roads,* the earliest rural fiction of social criticism, reflected his strong objection to the social injustice of which the prairie farmers were victims. Despite the note of protest, he avoided using the obvious tone of a tract in his best stories such as "The Return of a Private," a narrative with distinctive regional flavor and both social and artistic significance. Though also reactionary, Lindsay's Populist poetry scorned industrialization, urbanization and the railroads. More importantly, it showed that Populism signified a shift in agrarian attitudes from a hope for an agricultural utopia in the future to a memory of an imagined golden age in the preindustrial past.

Published in 1940 as an expression of racial protest, Richard Wright's propaganda novel *Native Son* delivered to the consciousness and conscience of urban America a portrait of one unfortunate byproduct of American culture—the alienated black—as symbolized by Bigger Thomas. Set in Chicago, his novel depicted a negro youth banished to the Black Belt district to search for his humanity amid the rubble of old buildings and shattered personalities. Rather than defending his protagonist's actions, Wright attempted to explain that Bigger's consistent response to his emotional pattern of fear, shame, and hatred was conditioned by a white-dominant, capitalistic, urban society. This novel eventually became a turning point in black literature, liberating other negro authors to write about what they knew to be true in America.

Other authors revealed a wishful optimism, writing of the human spirit's eventual triumph over adversity. Abraham Lincoln, one of the Midwest's great folk heroes, applied social idealism to politics, affirming a way of life and a system of government of, by and for the people. In the "Gettysburg Address", for instance, he voiced a sincere and deep belief concerning the responsibilities of a democracy to eliminate war and inspire patriotism. His biographer, Carl Sandburg, thought the nation's hope lay in the decency and endurance of its people. A lyric rather than narrative poet, he expressed his faith in democracy with subjectivity and emotion. In *The People, Yes* Sandburg fused aspects of folk wisdom and commentary to assure the masses that they would eventually receive their due.

The subject of an overwhelming portion of Langston Hughes's poetry was the black struggle for freedom and equal opportunity. The poet coded this struggle into his theme of the dream deferred. However, broadening this concept in "Let America Be America Again" to include all whose sense of fulfillment had been thwarted, Hughes indicated disappointment and anger that the American dream had not yet been realized, but he also affirmed hope and determination that it eventually would be. Similarly, Eric Sevareid, an essayist from the Midwest, illuminated the nation's problems and progress in "The American Dream," a testimony of patriotic love and reassurance. In spite of a tone of weariness and subdued indignation, the fiction of Kurt Vonnegut, Jr., too, revealed an abiding optimism and asserted the good and the joyful in life. However troubled by a lack of communication and a rigid conformity in American society, Vonnegut argued that life could be lent authenticity, especially through compassion and understanding. That genuine love proved the most satisfying source of personal fulfillment was illustrated in his short story "Adam."

For the most part, the midwestern egalitarian literary tradition demonstrated a faith in the land, and a faith in the people, their strength and their will to survive.

The Return of a Private

HAMLIN GARLAND

The nearer the train drew toward La Crosse, the soberer the little group of "vets" became. On the long way from New Orleans they had beguiled tedium with jokes and friendly chaff; or with planning with elaborate detail what they were going to do now, after the war. A long journey, slowly, irregularly, yet persistently pushing northward. When they entered on Wisconsin territory they gave a cheer, and another when they reached Madison, but after that they sank into a dumb expectancy. Comrades dropped off at one or two points beyond, until there were only four or five left who were bound for La Crosse County.

Three of them were gaunt and brown, the fourth was gaunt and pale, with signs of fever and ague upon him. One had a great scar down his temple, one limped, and they all had unnaturally large, bright eyes, showing emaciation. There were no hands greeting them at the station, no banks of gayly dressed ladies waving handkerchiefs and shouting "Bravo!" as they came in on the caboose of a freight train into the towns that had cheered and blared at them on their way to war. As they looked out or stepped upon the platform for a moment, while the train stood at the station, the loafers looked at them indifferently. Their blue coats, dusty and grimy, were too familiar now to excite notice, much less a friendly word. They were the last of the army to return, and the loafers were surfeited with such sights.

The train jogged forward so slowly that it seemed likely to be midnight before they should reach La Crosse. The little squad grumbled and swore, but it was no use; the train would not hurry, and, as a matter of fact, it was nearly two o'clock when the engine whistled "down brakes."

All of the group were farmers, living in districts several miles out of the town, and all were poor.

"Now boys," said Private Smith, he of the fever and ague, "we are landed in La Crosse in the night. We've got to stay somewhere till mornin'. Now I ain't got no two dollars to waste on a hotel. I've got a wife and children, so I'm goin' to roost on a bench and take the cost of a bed out of my hide."

"Same here," put in one of the other men. "Hide'll grow on again, dollar'll come hard. It's going to be mighty hot skirmishin' to find a dollar these days."

"Don't think they'll be a deputuation of citizens waitin' to 'scort us to a hotel, eh?" said another. His sarcasm was too obvious to require an answer.

Smith went on, "Then at daybreak we'll start for home—at least, I will."

"Well, I'll be dummed if I'll take two dollars out o' *my* hide," one of the younger men said. "I'm goin' to a hotel, ef I don't never lay up a cent."

"That'll do f'r you," said Smith; "but if you had a wife an' three young uns dependin' on yeh—"

"Which I ain't, thank the Lord! and don't intend havin' while the court knows itself."

The station was deserted, chill, and dark, as they came into it at exactly a quarter to two in the morning. Lit by the oil lamps that flared a dull red light over the dingy benches, the waiting room was not an inviting place. The younger man went off to look up a hotel, while the rest remained and prepared to camp down on the floor and benches. Smith was attended to tenderly by the other men, who spread their blankets on the bench for him, and, by robbing themselves, made quite a comfortable bed, though the narrowness of the bench made his sleeping precarious.

It was chill, though August, and the two men, sitting with bowed heads, grew stiff with cold and weariness, and were forced to rise now and again and walk about to warm their stiffened limbs. It did not occur to them, probably, to contrast their coming home with their going forth, or with the coming home of the generals, colonels, or even captains——but to Private Smith, at any rate, there came a sickness at heart almost deadly as he lay there on his hard bed and went over his situation.

In the deep of the night, lying on a board in the town where he had enlisted three years ago, all elation and enthusiasm gone out of him, he faced the fact that with the joy of home-coming was already mingled the bitter juice of care. He saw himself sick, worn out, taking up the work on his half-cleared farm, the inevitable mortgage standing ready with open jaw to swallow half his earnings. He had given three years of his life for a mere pittance of pay, and now!—

Morning dawned at last, slowly, with a pale yellow dome of light rising silently above the bluffs, which stand like some huge storm-devastated castle, just east of the city. Out to the left the great river swept on its massive yet silent way to the south. Bluejays called across the water from hillside to hillside through the clear, beautiful air, and hawks began to skim the tops of the hills. The older men were astir early, but Private Smith had fallen at last into a sleep, and they went out without waking him. He lay on his knapsack, his gaunt face turned toward the ceiling, his hands clasped on his breast, with a curious pathetic effect of weakness and appeal.

An engine switching near woke him at last, and he slowly sat up and stared about. He looked out of the window and saw that the sun was lightening the hills across the river. He rose and brushed his hair as well as he could, folded his blankets up, and went out to find his companions. They stood gazing silently at the river and at the hills.

"Looks natcher'l, don't it?" they said, as he came out.

"That's what it does," he replied. "An' it looks good. D' yeh see that peak?" He pointed at a beautiful symmetrical peak, rising like a slightly truncated cone, so high that it seemed the very highest of them all. It was touched by the morning sun and it glowed like a beacon, and a light scarf of gray morning fog was rolling up its shadowed side.

"My farm's just beyond that. Now, if I can only ketch a ride, we'll be home by dinner-time."

"I'm talkin' about breakfast," said one of the others.

"I guess it's one more meal o' hardtack f'r me," said Smith.

They foraged around, and finally found a restaurant with a sleepy old German behind the counter, and procured some coffee, which they drank to wash down their hardtack.

"Time'll come," said Smith, holding up a piece by the corner, "when this'll be a curiosity."

"I hope to God it will! I bet I've chawed hardtack enough to shingle every house in the coolly. I've chawed it when my lampers was down, and when they wasn't. I've took it dry, soaked, and mashed. I've had it wormy, musty, sour, and blue-mouldy. I've had it in little bits and big bits; 'fore coffee an' after coffee. I'm ready f'r a change. I'd like t' git holt jest about now o' some of the hot biscuits my wife c'n make when she lays herself out f'r company."

"Well, if you set there gabblin', you'll never *see* yer wife."

"Come on," said Private Smith. "Wait a moment, boys; less take suthin.'

It's on me." He led them to the rusty tin dipper which hung on a nail beside the wooden water-pail, and they grinned and drank. Then shouldering their blankets and muskets, which they were "takin' home to the boys," they struck out on their last march.

"They called that coffee Jayvy," grumbled one of them, "but it never went by the road where government Jayvy resides. I reckon I know coffee from peas."

They kept together on the road along the turnpike, and up the winding road by the river, which they followed for some miles. The river was very lovely, curving down along its sandy beds, pausing now and then under broad basswood trees, or running in dark, swift, silent currents under tangles of wild grapevines, and drooping alders, and haw trees. At one of these lovely spots the three vets sat down on the thick green sward to rest, "on Smith's account." The leaves of the trees were as fresh and green as in June, the jays called cheery greetings to them, and kingfishers darted to and fro with swooping, noiseless flight.

"I tell yeh, boys, this knocks the swamps of Loueesiana into kingdom come."

"You bet. All they c'n raise down there is snakes, niggers, and p'rticler hell."

"An' fighting men," put in the older man.

"An' fightin' men. If I had a good hook an' line I'd sneak a pick'rel out o' that pond. Say, remember that time I shot that alligator——"

"I guess we'd better be crawlin' along," interrupted Smith, rising and shouldering his knapsack, with considerable effort, which he tried to hide.

"Say, Smith, lemme give you a lift on that."

"I guess I c'n manage," said Smith, grimly.

"Course. But, yo' see, I may not have a chance right off to pay yeh back for the times you've carried my gun and hull caboodle. Say, now, gimme that gun, anyway."

"All right, if yeh feel like it, Jim," Smith replied, and they trudged along doggedly in the sun, which was getting higher and hotter each half-mile.

"Ain't it queer there ain't no teams comin' along," said Smith, after a long silence.

"Well, no, seein's it's Sunday."

"By jinks, that's a fact. It *is* Sunday. I'll git home in time f'r dinner, sure!" he exulted. "She don't hev dinner usially till about *one* on Sundays." And he fell into a muse, in which he smiled.

"Well, I'll git home jest about six o'clock, jest about when the boys are milkin' the cows," said old Jim Cranby. "I'll step into the barn, an' then I'll say: '*Heah!* why ain't this milkin' done before this time o' day?' An' then won't they yell!" he added, slapping his thigh in great glee.

Smith went on. "I'll jest go up the path. Old Rover'll come down the road to meet me. He won't bark; he'll know me, an' he'll come down waggin' his tail an' showin' his teeth. That's his way of laughin'. An' so I'll walk up to the kitchen door, an' I'll say, '*Dinner* f'r a hungry man!' An' then she'll jump up, an'——"

He couldn't go on. His voice choked at the thought of it. Saunders, the third man, hardly uttered a word, but walked silently behind the others. He had lost his wife the first year he was in the army. She died of pneumonia, caught in the autumn rains while working in the fields in his place.

They plodded along till at last they came to a parting of the ways. To the right the road continued up the main valley; to the left it went over the big ridge.

"Well, boys," began Smith, as they grounded their muskets and looked away up the valley, "here's where we shake hands. We've marched together a good many miles, an' now I s'pose we're done."

"Yes, I don't think we'll do any more of it f'r a while. I don't want to, I know."

"I hope I'll see yeh once in a while, boys, to talk over old times."

"Of course," said Saunders, whose voice trembled a little, too. "It ain't *exactly* like dyin'." They all found it hard to look at each other.

"But we'd ought'r go home with you,' said Cranby. "You'll never climb that ridge with all them things on yer back."

"Oh, I'm all right! Don't worry about me. Every step takes me nearer home, yeh see. Well, good-by, boys."

They shook hands. "Good-by. Good luck!"

"Same to you. Lemme know how you find things at home."

"Good-by."

"Good-by."

He turned once before they passed out of sight, and waved his cap, and they did the same, and all yelled. Then all marched away with their long, steady, loping, veteran step. The solitary climber in blue walked on for a time, with his mind filled with the kindness of his comrades, and musing upon the many wonderful days they had had together in camp and field.

He thought of his chum, Billy Tripp. Poor Billy! A "minie" ball fell into his breast one day, fell wailing like a cat, and tore a great ragged hole in his heart. He looked forward to a sad scene with Billy's mother and sweetheart. They would want to know all about it. He tried to recall all that Billy had said, and the particulars of it, but there was little to remember, just that wild wailing sound high in the air, a dull slap, a short, quick expulsive groan, and the boy lay with his face in the dirt in the ploughed field they were marching across.

That was all. But all the scenes he had since been through had not dimmed the horror, the terror of that moment, when his boy comrade fell, with only a breath between a laugh and a death-groan. Poor handsome Billy! Worth millions of dollars was his young life.

These sombre recollections gave way at length to more cheerful feelings as he began to approach his home coolly. The fields and houses grew familiar, and in one or two he was greeted by people seated in the doorways. But he was in no mood to talk, and pushed on steadily, though he stopped and accepted a drink of milk once at the well-side of a neighbor.

The sun was burning hot on that slope, and his step grew slower, in spite of his iron resolution. He sat down several times to rest. Slowly he crawled up the rough, reddish-brown road, which wound along the hillside, under great trees, through dense groves of jack oaks, with tree-tops far below him on his left hand, and the hills far above him on his right. He crawled along like some minute, wingless variety of fly.

He ate some hardtack, sauced with wild berries, when he reached the summit of the ridge, and sat there for some time, looking down into his home coolly.

Sombre, pathetic figure! His wide, round, gray eyes gazing down into the beautiful valley, seeing and not seeing, the splendid cloud-shadows sweeping over the western hills and across the green and yellow wheat far below. His head drooped forward on his palm, his shoulders took on a tired stoop, his cheek-bones showed painfully. An observer might have said, "He is looking down upon his own grave."

II

Sunday comes in a Western wheat harvest with such sweet and sudden relaxation to man and beast that it would be holy for that reason, if for

no other, and Sundays are usually fair in harvest-time. As one goes out into the field in the hot morning sunshine, with no sound abroad save the crickets and the indescribably pleasant silken rustling of the ripened grain, the reaper and the very sheaves in the stubble seem to be resting, dreaming.

Around the house, in the shade of the trees, the men sit, smoking, dozing, or reading the papers, while the women, never resting, move about at the housework. The men eat on Sundays about the same as the other days, and breakfast is no sooner over and out of the way than dinner begins.

But at the Smith farm there were no men dozing or reading. Mrs. Smith was alone with her three children, Mary, nine, Tommy, six, and little Ted, just past four. Her farm, rented to a neighbor, lay at the head of a coolly or narrow gully, made at some far-off post-glacial period by the vast and angry floods of water which gullied these tremendous furrows in the level prairie—furrows so deep that undisturbed portions of the original level rose like hills on either side, rose to quite considerable mountains.

The chickens wakened her as usual that Sabbath morning from dreams of her absent husband, from whom she had not heard for weeks. The shadows drifted over the hills, down the slopes, across the wheat, and up the opposite wall in leisurely way, as if, being Sunday, they could take it easy also. The fowls clustered about the housewife as she went out into the yard. Fuzzy little chickens swarmed out from the coops, where their clucking and perpetually disgruntled mothers tramped about, petulantly thrusting their heads through the spaces between the slats.

A cow called in a deep, musical bass, and a calf answered from a little pen near by, and a pig scurried guiltily out of the cabbages. Seeing all this, seeing the pig in the cabbages, the tangle of grass in the garden, the broken fence which she had mended again and again—the little woman, hardly more than a girl, sat down and cried. The bright Sabbath morning was only a mockery without him!

A few years ago they had bought this farm, paying part, mortgaging the rest in the usual way. Edward Smith was a man of terrible energy. He worked "nights and Sundays," as the saying goes, to clear the farm of its brush and of its insatiate mortgage! In the midst of his Herculean struggle came the call for volunteers, and with the grim and unselfish devotion to his country which made the Eagle Brigade able to "whip its weight in wildcats," he threw down his scythe and grub-axe, turned his cattle loose, and became a blue-coated cog in a vast machine for killing men, and not thistles. While the millionaire sent his money to England for safe-keeping, this man, with his girl-wife and three babies, left them on a mortgaged farm, and went away to fight for an idea. It was foolish, but it was sublime for all that.

That was three years before, and the young wife, sitting on the well-curb on this bright Sabbath harvest morning, was righteously rebellious. It seemed to her that she had borne her share of the country's sorrow. Two brothers had been killed, the renter in whose hands her husband had left the farm had proved a villain; one year the farm had been without crops, and now the overripe grain was waiting the tardy hand of the neighbor who had rented it, and who was cutting his own grain first.

About six weeks before, she had received a letter saying, "We'll be discharged in a little while." But no other word had come from him. She had seen by the papers that his army was being discharged, and from day to day other soldiers slowly percolated in blue streams back into the State and county, but still *her* hero did not return.

Each week she had told the children that he was coming, and she had watched the road so long that it had become unconscious; and as she stood at the well, or by the kitchen door, her eyes were fixed unthinkingly on the road that wound down the coolly.

Nothing wears on the human soul like waiting. If the stranded mariner, searching the sun-bright seas, could once give up hope of a ship, that horrible grinding on his brain would cease. It was this waiting, hoping, on the edge of despair, that gave Emma Smith no rest.

Neighbors said, with kind intentions: "He's sick, maybe, an' can't start north just yet. He'll come along one o' these days."

"Why don't he write?" was her question, which silenced them all. This Sunday morning it seemed to her as if she could not stand it longer. The house seemed intolerably lonely. So she dressed the little ones in their best calico dresses and home-made jackets, and, closing up the house, set off down the coolly to old Mother Gray's.

"Old Widder Gray" lived at the "mouth of the coolly." She was a widow woman with a large family of stalwart boys and laughing girls. She was the visible incarnation of hospitality and optimistic poverty. With Western open-heartedness she fed every mouth that asked food of her, and worked herself to death as cheerfully as her girls danced in the neighborhood harvest dances.

She waddled down the path to meet Mrs. Smith with a broad smile on her face.

"Oh, you little dears! Come right to your granny. Gimme me a kiss! Come right in, Mis' Smith. How are yeh, anyway? Nice mornin', ain't it? Come in an' set down. Everything's in a clutter, but that won't scare you any."

She led the way into the best room, a sunny, square room, carpeted with a faded and patched rag carpet, and papered with white-and-green wall-paper, where a few faded effigies of dead members of the family hung in variously sized oval walnut frames. The house resounded with singing, laughter, whistling, tramping of heavy boots, and riotous scufflings. Half-grown boys came to the door and crooked their fingers at the children, who ran out, and were soon heard in the midst of the fun.

"Don't s'pose you've heard from Ed?" Mrs. Smith shook her head. "He'll turn up some day, when you ain't lookin' for 'im." The good old soul had said that so many times that poor Mrs. Smith derived no comfort from it any longer.

"Liz heard from Al the other day. He's comin' some day this week. Anyhow, they expect him."

"Did he say anything of——"

"No, he didn't," Mrs. Gray admitted. "But then it was only a short letter, anyhow. Al ain't much for writin', anyhow.—But come out and see my new cheese. I tell yeh, I don't believe I ever had better luck in my life. If Ed should come, I want you should take him up a piece of this cheese."

It was beyond human nature to resist the influence of that noisy, hearty, loving household, and in the midst of the singing and laughing the wife forgot her anxiety, for the time at least, and laughed and sang with the rest.

About eleven o'clock a wagon-load more drove up to the door, and Bill Gray, the widow's oldest son, and his whole family, from Sand Lake Coolly, piled out amid a good-natured uproar. Every one talked at once, except Bill, who sat in the wagon with his wrists on his knees, a straw in his mouth, and an amused twinkle in his blue eyes.

"Ain't heard nothin' o' Ed, I s'pose?" He asked in a kind of bellow. Mrs. Smith shook her head. Bill, with a delicacy very striking in such a great giant, rolled his quid in his mouth, and said: "Didn't know but you had. I hear two or three of the Sand Lake boys are comin'. Left New Orleenes some time this week. Didn't write nothin' about Ed, but no news is good news in such cases, mother always says."

"Well, go put out yer team," said Mrs. Gray, "an' go'n bring me in some taters, an', Sim, you go see if you c'n find some corn. Sadie, you put on the water to bile. Come now, hustle yer boots, all o' yeh. If I feed this yer crowd, we've got to have some raw materials. If y' think I'm goin' to feed yeh on pie—you're just mightily mistaken."

The children went off into the field, the girls put dinner on to boil, and then went to change their dresses and fix their hair. "Somebody might come," they said.

"Land sakes, *I hope* not! I don't know where in time I'd set 'em 'less they'd eat at the second table," Mrs. Gray laughed, in pretended dismay.

The two older boys, who had served their time in the army, lay out on the grass before the house, and whittled and talked desultorily about the war and the crops, and planned buying a threshing-machine. The older girls and Mrs. Smith helped enlarge the table and put on the dishes, talking all the time in that cheery, incoherent, and meaningful way a group of such women have,—a conversation to be taken for its spirit rather than for its letter, though Mrs. Gray at last got the ear of them all and dissertated at length on girls.

"Girls in love ain' no use in the whole blessed week," she said. "Sundays they're a-lookin' down the road, expectin' he'll *come*. Sunday afternoons they can't think o' nothin' else, 'cause he's *here*. Monday mornin's they're sleepy and kind o' dreamy and slimpsy, and good f'r nothin' on Tuesday and Wednesday. Thursday they git absent-minded, an' begin to look off toward Sunday agin, an' mope aroun' and let the dishwater git cold, right under their noses. Friday they break dishes, an' go off in the best room an' snivel, an' look out o' the winder. Saturdays they have queer spurts o' workin' like all p'ssessed, an' spurts o' frizzin' their hair. An' Sunday they begin it all over agin."

The girls giggled and blushed, all through this tirade from their mother, their broad faces and powerful frames anything but suggestive of lackadaisical sentiment. But Mrs. Smith said:

"Now, Mrs. Gray, I hadn't ought to stay to dinner. You've got——"

"Now you set right down! If any of them girls' beaus comes, they'll have to take what's left, that's all. They ain't s'posed to have much appetite, nohow. No, you're goin' to stay if they starve, an' they ain't no danger o' that."

At one o'clock the long table was piled with boiled potatoes, cords of boiled corn on the cob, squash and pumpkin pies, hot biscuit, sweet pickles, bread and butter, and honey. Then one of the girls took down a conch-shell from a nail, and going to the door, blew a long, fine, free blast, that showed there was no weakness of lungs in her ample chest.

Then the children came out of the forest of corn, out of the creek, out of the loft of the barn, and out of the garden.

"They come to their feed f'r all the world jest like the pigs when y' holler 'poo-ee!' See 'em scoot!" laughed Mrs. Gray, every wrinkle on her face shining with delight.

The men shut up their jack-knives, and surrounded the horsetrough to souse their faces in the cold, hard water, and in a few moments the table was filled with a merry crowd, and a row of wistful-eyed youngsters circled the kitchen wall, where they stood first on one leg and then on the other, in impatient hunger.

"Now pitch in, Mrs. Smith," said Mrs. Gray, presiding over the table. "You know these men critters. They'll eat every grain of it, if yeh give 'em a chance. I swan, they're made o' India-rubber, their stomachs is, I know it."

"Haf to eat to work," said Bill, gnawing a cob with a swift, circular motion that rivalled a corn-sheller in results.

"More like workin' to eat," put in one of the girls, with a giggle. "More eat 'n work with you."

"*You* needn't say anything, Net. Any one that'll eat seven ears——"

"I didn't, no such thing. You piled your cobs on my plate."

"That'll do to tell Ed Varney. It won't go down here where we know yeh."

"Good land! Eat all yeh want! They's plenty more in the fiel's, but I can't afford to give you young uns tea. The tea is for us women-folks, and 'specially f'r Mis' Smith an' Bill's wife. We're a-goin' to tell fortunes by it."

One by one the men filled up and shoved back, and one by one the children slipped into their places, and by two o'clock the women alone remained around the débris-covered table, sipping their tea and telling fortunes.

As they got well down to the grounds in the cup, they shook them with a circular motion in the hand, and then turned them bottom-side-up quickly in the saucer, then twirled them three or four times one way, and three or four times the other, during a breathless pause. Then Mrs. Gray lifted the cup, and, gazing into it with profound gravity, pronounced the impending fate.

It must be admitted that, to a critical observer, she had abundant preparation for hitting close to the mark, as when she told the girls that "somebody was comin'." "It's a man," she went on gravely. "He is cross-eyed——"

"Oh, you hush!" cried Nettie.

"He has red hair, and is death on b'iled corn and hot biscuit."

The other shrieked with delight.

"But he's goin' to get the mitten, that red-headed feller is, for I see another feller comin' up behind him."

"Oh, lemme see, lemme see!" cried Nettie.

"Keep off," said the priestess, with a lofty gesture. "His hair is black. He don't eat so much, and he works more."

The girls exploded in a shriek of laughter, and pounded their sister on the back.

At last came Mrs. Smith's turn, and she was trembling with excitement as Mrs. Gray again composed her jolly face to what she considered a proper solemnity of expression.

"Somebody is comin' to *you*," she said, after a long pause. "He's got a musket on his back. He's a soldier. He's almost here. See?"

She pointed at two little tea-stems, which really formed a faint suggestion of a man with a musket on his back. He had climbed nearly to the edge of the cup. Mrs. Smith grew pale with excitement. She trembled so she could hardly hold the cup in her hand as she gazed into it.

"It's Ed," cried the old woman. "He's on the way home. Heavens an' earth! There he is now!" She turned and waved her hand out toward the road. They rushed to the door to look where she pointed.

A man in a blue coat, with a musket on his back, was toiling slowly up the hill on the sun-bright, dusty road, toiling slowly, with bent head half hidden by a heavy knapsack. So tired it seemed that walking was indeed a process of falling. So eager to get home he would not stop, would not look aside, but plodded on, amid the cries of the locusts, the welcome of the crickets, and the rustle of the yellow wheat. Getting back to God's country, and his wife and babies!

Laughing, crying, trying to call him and the children at the same time, the little wife, almost hysterical, snatched her hat and ran out into the yard. But the soldier had disappeared over the hill into the hollow beyond, and, by the time she had found the children, he was too far away for her voice to reach him. And, besides, she was not sure it was her husband, for he had not turned his head at their shouts. This seemed so strange. Why didn't he stop to rest at his old neighbor's house? Tortured by hope and doubt, she hurried up the coolly as fast as she could push the baby wagon, the blue-coated figure just ahead pushing steadily, silently forward up the coolly.

When the excited, panting little group came in sight of the gate they saw the blue-coated figure standing, leaning upon the rough rail fence, his chin on his palms, gazing at the empty house. His knapsack, canteen, blankets, and musket lay upon the dusty grass at his feet.

He was like a man lost in a dream. His wide, hungry eyes devoured the scene. The rough lawn, the little unpainted house, the field of clear yellow wheat behind it, down across which streamed the sun, now almost ready to touch the high hill to the west, the crickets crying merrily, a cat on the fence near by, dreaming, unmindful of the stranger in blue——

How peaceful it all was. O God! How far removed from all camps, hospitals, battle lines. A little cabin in a Wisconsin coolly, but it was majestic in its peace. How did he ever leave it for those years of tramping, thirsting, killing?

Trembling, weak with emotion, her eyes on the silent figure, Mrs. Smith hurried up to the fence. Her feet made no noise in the dust and grass, and they were close upon him before he knew of them. The oldest boy ran a little ahead. He will never forget that figure, that face. It will always remain as something epic, that return of the private. He fixed his eyes on the pale face covered with a ragged beard.

"Who *are* you, sir?" asked the wife, or, rather, started to ask, for he turned, stood a moment, and then cried:

"Emma!"

"Edward!"

The children stood in a curious row to see their mother kiss this bearded, strange man, the elder girl sobbing sympathetically with her mother. Illness had left the soldier partly deaf, and this added to the strangeness of his manner.

But the youngest child stood away, even after the girl had recognized her father and kissed him. The man turned then to the baby, and said in a curiously unpaternal tone:

"Come here, my little man; don't you know me?" But the baby backed away under the fence and stood peering at him critically.

"My little man!" What meaning in those words! This baby seemed like some other woman's child, and not the infant he had left in his wife's arms. The war had come between him and his baby—he was only a strange man to him, with big eyes; a soldier, with mother hanging to his arm, and talking in a loud voice.

"And this is Tom," the private said, drawing the oldest boy to him. "*He'll* come and see me. *He* knows his poor old pap when he comes home from the war."

The mother heard the pain and reproach in his voice and hastened to apologize.

"You've changed so, Ed. He can't know yeh. This is papa, Teddy; come and kiss him—Tom and Mary do. Come, won't you?" But Teddy still peered through the fence with solemn eyes, well out of reach. He resembled a half-wild kitten that hesitates, studying the tones of one's voice.

"I'll fix him," said the soldier, and sat down to undo his knapsack, out of which he drew three enormous and very red apples. After giving one to each of the older children, he said:

"*Now* I guess he'll come. Eh, my little man? Now come see your pap."

Teddy crept slowly under the fence, assisted by the overzealous Tommy, and a moment later was kicking and squalling in his father's arms. Then they entered the house, into the sitting room, poor, bare, art-forsaken little room, too, with its rag carpet, its square clock, and its two or three chromos and pictures from *Harper's Weekly* pinned about.

"Emma, I'm all tired out," said Private Smith, as he flung himself down on the carpet as he used to do, while his wife brought a pillow to put under his head, and the children stood about munching their apples.

"Tommy, you run and get me a pan of chips, and Mary, you get the teakettle on, and I'll go and make some biscuit."

And the soldier talked. Question after question he poured forth about the crops, the cattle, the renter, the neighbors. He slipped his heavy government brogan shoes off his poor, tired, blistered feet, and lay out with utter, sweet relaxation. He was a free man again, no longer a soldier under a command. At supper he stopped once, listened and smiled. "That's old Spot. I know her voice. I s'pose that's her calf out there in the pen. I can't milk her to-night, though. I'm too tired. But I tell you, I'd like a drink of her milk. What's become of old Rove?"

"He died last winter. Poisoned, I guess." There was a moment of sadness for them all. It was some time before the husband spoke again, in a voice that trembled a little.

"Poor old feller! He'd 'a' known me half a mile away. I expected him to come down the hill to meet me. It 'ud 'a' been more like comin' home if I could 'a' seen him comin' down the road an' waggin' his tail, an' laughin' that way he has. I tell yeh, it kind o' took hold o' me to see the blinds down an' the house shut up."

"But, yeh see, we—we expected you'd write again 'fore you started. And then we thought we'd see you if you *did* come," she hastened to explain.

"Well, I ain't worth a cent on writin'. Besides, it's just as well yeh didn't know when I was comin'. I tell you, it sounds good to hear them chickens out there, an' turkeys, an' the crickets. Do you know they don't have just the same kind o' crickets down South? Who's Sam hired t' help cut yer grain?"

"The Ramsey boys."

"Looks like a good crop; but I'm afraid I won't do much gettin' it cut. This cussed fever an' ague has got me down pretty low. I don't know when I'll get rid of it. I'll bet I've took twenty-five pounds of quinine if I've taken a bit. Gimme another biscuit. I tell yeh, they taste good, Emma. I ain't had anything like it——Say, if you'd 'a' hear'd me braggin' to th' boys about your butter 'n' biscuits I'll bet your ears 'ud 'a' burnt.'

The private's wife colored with pleasure. "Oh, you're always a-braggin' about your things. Everybody makes good butter."

"Yes; old lady Snyder, for instance."

"Oh, well, she ain't to be mentioned. She's Dutch."

"Or old Mis' Snively. One more cup o' tea, Mary. That's my girl! I'm feeling better already. I just b'lieve the matter with me is, I'm *starved.*"

This was a delicious hour, one long to be remembered. They were like lovers again. But their tenderness, like that of a typical American family, found utterance in tones, rather than in words. He was praising her when praising her biscuit, and she knew it. They grew soberer when he showed where he had been struck, one ball burning the back of his hand, one cutting away a lock of hair from his temple, and one passing through the calf of his leg. The wife shuddered to think how near she had come to being a soldier's widow. Her waiting no longer seemed hard. This sweet, glorious hour effaced it all.

Then they rose, and all went out into the garden and down to the barn. He stood beside her while she milked old Spot. They began to plan fields and crops for next year.

His farm was weedy and encumbered, a rascally renter had run away with his machinery (departing between two days), his children needed clothing, the years were coming upon him, he was sick and emaciated, but his heroic soul did not quail. With the same courage with which he had faced his Southern march he entered upon a still more hazardous future.

Oh, that mystic hour! The pale man with big eyes standing there by the well, with his young wife by his side. The vast moon swinging above the eastern peaks, the cattle winding down the pasture slopes with jangling bells, the crickets singing, the stars blooming out sweet and far and serene; the katydids rhythmically calling, the little turkeys crying querulously, as they settled to roost in the poplar tree near the open gate. The voices at the well drop lower, the little ones nestle in their father's arms at last, and Teddy falls asleep there.

The common soldier of the American volunteer army had returned. His war with the South was over, and his fight, his daily running fight with nature and against the injustice of his fellow-men, was begun again.

Flower-Fed Buffaloes

VACHEL LINDSAY

The flower-fed buffaloes of the spring
In the days of long ago,
Ranged where the locomotives sing
And the prairie flowers lie low;—
The tossing, blooming, perfumed grass
Is swept away by wheat,
Wheels and wheels and wheels spin by
In the spring that still is sweet,
But the flower-fed buffaloes of the spring
Left us long ago.
They gore no more, they bellow no more,
They trundle around the hills no more:—
With the Blackfeet, lying low,
With the Pawnees, lying low.
Lying low.

Factory Windows Are Always Broken

VACHEL LINDSAY

Factory windows are always broken.
Somebody's always throwing bricks,
Somebody's always heaving cinders,
Playing ugly Yahoo tricks.

Factory windows are always broken.
Other windows are let alone.
No one throws through the chapel window
The bitter, snarling derisive stone.

Factory windows are always broken.
Something or other is going wrong.
Something is rotten—I think, in Denmark.
End of the factory-window song.

FROM *Native Son*

RICHARD WRIGHT

"You know, Bigger," his mother said, "if you don't take that job the relief'll cut us off. We won't have any food."

"I told you I'd take it!" he shouted and slammed the door.

He went down the steps into the vestibule and stood looking out into the street through the plate glass of the front door. Now and then a street car rattled past over steel tracks. He was sick of his life at home. Day in and day out there was nothing but shouts and bickering. But what could he do? Each time he asked himself that question his mind hit a blank wall and he stopped thinking. Across the street directly in front of him, he saw a truck pull to a stop at the curb and two white men in overalls got out with pails and brushes. Yes, he could take the job at Dalton's and be miserable, or he could refuse it and starve. It maddened him to think that he did not have a wider choice of action. Well, he could not stand here all day like this. What was he to do with himself? He tried to decide if he wanted to buy a ten-cent magazine, or go to a movie, or go to the poolroom and talk with the gang, or just loaf around. With his hands deep in his pockets, another cigarette slanting across his chin, he brooded and watched the men at work across the street. They were pasting a huge colored poster to a signboard. The poster showed a white face.

"That's Buckley!" He spoke softly to himself. "He's running for State's Attorney again." The men were slapping the poster with wet brushes. He looked at the round florid face and wagged his head. "I bet that sonofabitch rakes off a million bucks in graft a year. Boy, if I was in his shoes for just one day I'd *never* have to worry again."

When the men were through they gathered up their pails and brushes and got into the truck and drove off. He looked at the poster: the white face was fleshy but stern; one hand was uplifted and its index finger pointed straight out into the street at each passer-by. The poster showed one of those faces that looked straight at you when you looked at it and all the while you were walking and turning your head to look at it it kept looking unblinkingly back at you until you got so far from it you had to take your eyes away, and then it stopped, like a movie blackout. Above the top of the poster were tall red letters: IF YOU BREAK THE LAW, YOU CAN'T WIN!

He snuffed his cigarette and laughed silently. "You crook," he mumbled, shaking his head. "You let whoever pays *you* off win!" He opened the door and met the morning air. He went along the sidewalk with his head down, fingering the quarter in his pocket. He stopped and searched all of his pockets; in his vest pocket he found a lone copper cent. That made a total of twenty-six cents, fourteen cents of which would have to be saved for carfare to Mr. Dalton's; that is, if he decided to take the job. In order to buy a magazine and go to the movies he would have to have at least twenty cents more. "Goddammit, I'm always broke!" he mumbled.

He stood on the corner in the sunshine, watching cars and people pass. He needed more money; if he did not get more than he had now he would not know what to do with himself for the rest of the day. He wanted to see a movie; his senses hungered for it. In a movie he could dream without effort; all he had to do was lean back in a seat and keep his eyes open.

He thought of Gus and G.H. and Jack. Should he go to the poolroom and talk with them? But there was no use in his going unless they were ready to do what they had been long planning to do. If they could, it would mean some sure and quick money. From three o'clock to four o'clock in the afternoon there was no policeman on duty in the block where Blum's Delicatessen was and it would be safe. One of them could hold a gun on Blum and keep him from yelling; one could watch the front door; one could watch the back; and one could get the money from the box under the counter. Then all four of them could lock Blum in the store and run out through the back and duck down the alley and meet an hour later, either at Doc's poolroom or at the South Side Boys' Club, and split the money.

Holding up Blum ought not take more than two minutes, at the most. And it would be their last job. But it would be the toughest one that they had ever pulled. All the other times they had raided newsstands, fruit stands, and apartments. And, too, they had never held up a white man before. They had always robbed Negroes. They felt that it was much easier and safer to rob their own people, for they knew that white policemen never really searched diligently for Negroes who committed crimes against other Negroes. For months they had talked of robbing Blum's, but had not been able to bring themselves to do it. They had the feeling that the robbing of Blum's would be a violation of ultimate taboo; it would be a trespassing into territory where the full wrath of an alien white world would be turned loose upon them; in short, it would be a symbolic challenge of the white world's rule over them; a challenge which they yearned to make, but were afraid to. Yes; if they could rob Blum's, it would be a real hold-up, in more senses than one. In comparison, all of their other jobs had been play.

"Good-bye, Bigger."

He looked up and saw Vera passing with a sewing kit dangling from her arm. She paused at the corner and came back to him.

"Now, what you want?"

"Bigger, please. . . . You're getting a good job now. Why don't you stay away from Jack and Gus and G.H. and keep out of trouble?"

"You keep your big mouth out of my business!"

"But, Bigger!"

"Go on to school, will you!"

She turned abruptly and walked on. He knew that his mother had been talking to Vera and Buddy about him, telling them that if he got into any more trouble he would be sent to prison and not just to the reform school, where they sent him last time. He did not mind what his mother said to Buddy about him. Buddy was all right. Tough, plenty. But Vera was a sappy girl; she did not have any more sense than to believe everything she was told.

He walked toward the poolroom. When he got to the door he saw Gus half a block away, coming toward him. He stopped and waited. It was Gus who had first thought of robbing Blum's.

"Hi, Bigger!"

"What you saying, Gus?"

"Nothing. Seen G.H. or Jack yet?"

"Naw. You?"

"Naw. Say, got a cigarette?"

"Yeah."

Bigger took out his pack and gave Gus a cigarette; he lit his and held the match for Gus. They leaned their backs against the red-brick wall of a building, smoking, their cigarettes slanting white across their black chins. To the east Bigger saw the sun burning a dazzling yellow. In the sky above him a few big white clouds drifted. He puffed silently, relaxed, his mind pleasantly vacant of purpose. Every slight movement in the street evoked a casual curiosity in him. Automatically, his eyes followed each car as it whirred over the smooth black asphalt. A woman came by and he watched the gentle sway of her body until she disappeared into a doorway. He sighed, scratched his chin and mumbled.

"Kinda warm today."

"Yeah," Gus said.

"You get more heat from this sun than from them old radiators at home."

"Yeah; them old white landlords sure don't give much heat."

"And they always knocking at your door for money."

"I'll be glad when summer comes."

"Me too," Bigger said.

He stretched his arms above his head and yawned; his eyes moistened. The sharp precision of the world of steel and stone dissolved into blurred waves. He blinked and the world grew hard again, mechanical, distinct. A weaving motion in the sky made him turn his eyes upward; he saw a slender streak of billowing white blooming against the deep blue. A plane was writing high up in the air.

"Look!" Bigger said.

"What?"

"That plane writing up there," Bigger said, pointing.

"Oh!"

They squinted at a tiny ribbon of unfolding vapor that spelled out the word: USE. . . . The plane was so far away that at times the strong glare of the sun blanked it from sight.

"You can hardly see it," Gus said.

"Looks like a little bird," Bigger breathed with childlike wonder.

"Them white boys sure can fly," Gus said.

"Yeah," Bigger said, wistfully. "They get a chance to do everything."

Noiselessly, the tiny plane looped and veered, vanishing and appearing, leaving behind it a long trail of white plumage, like coils of fluffy paste being squeezed from a tube; a plume-coil that grew and swelled and slowly began to fade into the air at the edges. The plane wrote another word: SPEED. . . .

"How high you reckon he is?" Bigger asked.

"I don't know. Maybe a hundred miles; maybe a thousand."

"I could fly one of them things if I had a chance," Bigger mumbled reflectively, as though talking to himself.

Gus pulled down the corners of his lips, stepped out from the wall, squared his shoulders, doffed his cap, bowed low and spoke with mock deference:

"Yessuh."

"You go to hell," Bigger said, smiling.

"Yessuh," Gus said again.

"I *could* fly a plane if I had a chance," Bigger said.

"If you wasn't black and if you had some money and if they'd let you go to that aviation school, you *could* fly a plane," Gus said.

For a moment Bigger contemplated all the "ifs" that Gus had mentioned. Then both boys broke into hard laughter, looking at each other through squinted eyes. When their laughter subsided, Bigger said in a voice that was half-question and half-statement:

"It's funny how the white folks treat us, ain't it?"

"It better be funny," Gus said.

"Maybe they right in not wanting us to fly," Bigger said. " 'Cause if I took a plane up I'd take a couple of bombs along and drop 'em as sure as hell. . . ."

They laughed again, still looking upward. The plane sailed and dipped and spread another word against the sky: GASOLINE. . . .

"Use Speed Gasoline," Bigger mused, rolling the words slowly from his lips. "God, I'd like to fly up there in that sky."

"God'll let you fly when He gives you your wings up in heaven," Gus said.

They laughed again, reclining against the wall, smoking, the lids of their eyes drooped softly against the sun. Cars whizzed past on rubber tires. Bigger's face was metallically black in the strong sunlight. There was in his eyes a pensive, brooding amusement, as of a man who had been long confronted and tantalized by a riddle whose answer seemed always just on the verge of escaping him, but prodding him irresistibly on to seek solution. The silence irked Bigger; he was anxious to do something to evade looking so squarely at this problem.

"Let's play 'white,' " Bigger said, referring to a game of play-acting in which he and his friends imitated the ways and manners of white folks.

"I don't feel like it," Gus said.

"General!" Bigger pronounced in a sonorous tone, looking at Gus expectantly.

"Aw, hell! I don't want to play," Gus whined.

"You'll be court-martialed," Bigger said, snapping out his words with military precision.

"Nigger, you nuts!" Gus laughed.

"General!" Bigger tried again, determinedly.

Gus looked wearily at Bigger, then straightened, saluted and answered:

"Yessuh."

"Send your men over the river at dawn and attack the enemy's left flank," Bigger ordered.

"Yessuh."

"Send the Fifth, Sixth, and Seventh Regiments," Bigger said, frowning. "And attack with tanks, gas, planes, and infantry."

"Yessuh!" Gus said again, saluting and clicking his heels.

For a moment they were silent, facing each other, their shoulders thrown back, their lips compressed to hold down the mounting impulse to laugh. Then they guffawed, partly at themselves and partly at the vast white world that sprawled and towered in the sun before them.

"Say, what's a 'left flank'?" Gus asked.

"I don't know," Bigger said. "I heard it in the movies."

They laughed again. After a bit they relaxed and leaned against the wall, smoking. Bigger saw Gus cup his left hand to his ear, as though holding a telephone receiver; and cup his right hand to his mouth, as though talking into a transmitter.

"Hello," Gus said.

"Hello," Bigger said. "Who's this?"

"This is Mr. J. P. Morgan speaking," Gus said.

"Yessuh, Mr. Morgan," Bigger said; his eyes filled with mock adulation and respect.

"I want you to sell twenty thousand shares of U.S. Steel in the market this morning," Gus said.

"At what price, suh?" Bigger asked.

"Aw, just dump 'em at any price," Gus said with casual irritation. "We're holding too much."

"Yessuh," Bigger said.

"And call me at my club at two this afternoon and tell me if the President telephoned," Gus said.

"Yessuh, Mr. Morgan," Bigger said.

Both of them made gestures signifying that they were hanging up telephone receivers; then they bent double, laughing.

"I bet that's *just* the way they talk," Gus said.

"I wouldn't be surprised," Bigger said.

They were silent again. Presently, Bigger cupped his hand to his mouth and spoke through an imaginary telephone transmitter.

"Hello."

"Hello," Gus answered. "Who's this?"

"This is the President of the United States speaking," Bigger said.

"Oh, yessuh, Mr. President," Gus said.

"I'm calling a cabinet meeting this afternoon at four o'clock and you, as Secretary of State, *must* be there."

"Well, now, Mr. President," Gus said, "I'm pretty busy. They raising sand over there in Germany and I got to send 'em a note. . . .

"But this is important," Bigger said.

"What you going to take up at this cabinet meeting?" Gus asked.

"Well, you see, the niggers is raising sand all over the country," Bigger said, struggling to keep back his laughter. "We've got to do something with these black folks. . . ."

"Oh, if it's about the niggers, I'll be right there, Mr. President," Gus said.

They hung up imaginary receivers and leaned against the wall and laughed. A street car rattled by. Bigger sighed and swore.

"Goddammit!"

"What's the matter?"

"They don't let us do *nothing*."

"Who?"

"The *white* folks."

"You talk like you just now finding that out," Gus said.

"Naw. But I just can't get used to it," Bigger said. "I swear to God I can't. I know I oughtn't think about it, but I can't help it. Every time I think about it I feel like somebody's poking a red-hot iron down my throat. Goddammit, look! We live here and they live there. We black and they white. They got things and we ain't. They do things and we can't. It's just like living in jail. Half the time I feel like I'm on the outside of the world peeping in through a knot-hole in the fence. . . ."

"Aw, ain't no use feeling that way about it. It don't help none," Gus said.

"You know one thing?" Bigger said.

"What?"

"Sometimes I feel like something awful's going to happpen to me," Bigger spoke with a tinge of bitter pride in his voice.

"What you mean?" Gus asked, looking at him quickly. There was fear in Gus's eyes.

"I don't know. I just feel that way. Every time I get to thinking about me being black and they being white, me being here and they being there, I feel like something awful's going to happen to me. . . ."

"Aw, for Chrissakes! There ain't nothing you can do about it. How come you want to worry yourself? You black and they make the laws. . . ."

"Why they make us live in one corner of the city? Why don't they let us fly planes and run ships. . . ."

Gus hunched Bigger with his elbow and mumbled good-naturedly, "Aw, nigger, quit thinking about it. You'll go nuts."

The plane was gone from the sky and the white plumes of floating smoke were thinly spread, vanishing. Because he was restless and had time on his hands, Bigger yawned again and hoisted his arms high above his head.

"Nothing ever happens," he complained.

"What you want to happen?"

"Anything," Bigger said with a wide sweep of his dingy palm, a sweep that included all the possible activities of the world.

Then their eyes were riveted; a slate-colored pigeon swooped down to the middle of the steel car tracks and began strutting to and fro with ruffled feathers, its fat neck bobbing with regal pride. A street car rumbled forward and the pigeon rose swiftly through the air on wings stretched so taut and sheer that Bigger could see the gold of the sun through their translucent tips. He tilted his head and watched the slate-colored bird flap and wheel out of sight over the edge of a high roof.

"Now, if I could only do that," Bigger said.

Gus laughed.

"Nigger, you nuts."

"I reckon we the only things in this city that can't go where we want to go and do what we want to do."

"Don't think about it," Gus said.

"I can't help it."

"That's why you feeling like something awful's going to happen to you," Gus said. "You think too much."

"What in hell can a man do?" Bigger asked, turning to Gus.

"Get drunk and sleep it off."

"I can't. I'm broke."

Bigger crushed his cigarette and took out another one and offered the package to Gus. They continued smoking. A huge truck swept past, lifting scraps of white paper into the sunshine; the bits settled down slowly.

"Gus?"

"Hunh?"

"You know where the white folks live?"

"Yeah," Gus said, pointing eastward. "Over across the 'line'; over there on Cottage Grove Avenue."

"Naw; they don't," Bigger said.

"What you mean?" Gus asked, puzzled. "Then, where do they live?"

Bigger doubled his fist and struck his solar plexus.

"Right down here in my stomach," he said.

Gus looked at Bigger searchingly, then away, as though ashamed.

"Yeah; I know what you mean," he whispered.

"Every time I think of 'em, I *feel* 'em," Bigger said.

"Yeah; and in your chest and throat, too," Gus said.

"It's like fire."

"And sometimes you can't hardly breathe. . . ."

Bigger's eyes were wide and placid, gazing into space.

"That's when I feel like something awful's going to happen to me. . . ." Bigger paused, narrowed his eyes. "Naw; it ain't like something going to happen to me. It's. . . . It's like I was going to do something I can't help. . . ."

"Yeah!" Gus said with uneasy eagerness. His eyes were full of a look compounded of fear and admiration for Bigger. "Yeah; I know what you mean. It's like you going to fall and don't know where you going to land. . . ."

Gus's voice trailed off. The sun slid behind a big white cloud and the street was plunged in cool shadow; quickly the sun edged forth again and it was bright and warm once more. A long sleek black car, its fenders glinting like glass in the sun, shot past them at high speed and turned a corner a few blocks away. Bigger pursed his lips and sang:

"Zoooooooooom!"

"They got everything," Gus said.

"They own the world," Bigger said.

"Aw, what the hell," Gus said. "Let's go in the poolroom."

"OK."

They walked toward the door of the poolroom.

"Say, you taking that job you told us about?" Gus asked.

"I don't know."

"You talk like you don't want it."

"Oh, hell, yes! I want the job," Bigger said.

They looked at each other and laughed. They went inside. The poolroom was empty, save for a fat, black man who held a half-smoked, unlit cigar in his mouth and leaned on the front counter. To the rear burned a single green-shaded bulb.

"Hi, Doc," Bigger said.

"You boys kinda early this morning," Doc said.

"Jack or G.H. around yet?" Bigger asked.

"Naw," Doc said.

"Let's shoot a game," Gus said.

"I'm broke," Bigger said.

"I got some money."

"Switch on the light. The balls are racked," Doc said.

Bigger turned on the light. They lagged for first shot. Bigger won. They started playing. Bigger's shots were poor; he was thinking of Blum's, fascinated with the idea of the robbery, and a little afraid of it.

Gettysburg Address

ABRAHAM LINCOLN

Four score and seven years ago our fathers brought forth on this continent, a new nation, conceived in Liberty, and dedicated to the proposition that all men are created equal.

Now we are engaged in a great civil war, testing whether that nation, or any nation so conceived and so dedicated, can long endure. We are met on a great battlefield of that war. We have come to dedicate a portion of that field, as a final resting place for those who here gave their lives that that nation might live. It is altogether fitting and proper that we should do this.

But, in a larger sense, we can not dedicate—we can not consecrate—we can not hallow—this ground. The brave men, living and dead, who struggled here, have consecrated it, far above our poor power to add or detract. The world will little note, nor long remember what we say here, but it can never forget what they did here. It is for us the living, rather, to be dedicated here to the unfinished work which they who fought here have thus far so nobly advanced. It is rather for us to be here dedicated to the great task remaining before us—that from these honored dead we take increased devotion to that cause for which they gave the last full measure of devotion—that we here highly resolve that these dead shall not have died in vain—that this nation, under God, shall have a new birth of freedom—and that government of the people, by the people, for the people, shall not perish from the earth.

*The People Will Live On**

CARL SANDBURG

The people will live on.
The learning and blundering people will live on.
They will be tricked and sold and again sold
And go back to the nourishing earth for rootholds,
The people so peculiar in renewal and comeback,
You can't laugh off their capacity to take it.
The mammoth rests between his cyclonic dramas.

The people so often sleepy, weary, enigmatic,
is a vast huddle with many units saying:
"I earn my living.
I make enough to get by
and it takes all my time.
If I had more time
I could do more for myself
and maybe for others.
I could read and study
and talk things over
and find out about things.
It takes time.
I wish I had the time."

The people is a tragic and comic two-face:
hero and hoodlum: phantom and gorilla twist-
ing to moan with a gargoyle mouth: "They

* From *The People, Yes.*

buy me and sell me . . . it's a game . . .
sometime I'll break loose . . ."

Once having marched
Over the margins of animal necessity,
Over the grim line of sheer subsistence
Then man came
To the deeper rituals of his bones,
To the lights lighter than any bones,
To the time for thinking things over,
To the dance, the song, the story,
Or the hours given over to dreaming,
Once having so marched.

Between the finite limitations of the five senses
and the endless yearnings of man for the beyond
the people hold to the humdrum bidding of work and food
while reaching out when it comes their way
for lights beyond the prison of the five senses,
for keepsakes lasting beyond any hunger or death.
This reaching is alive.
The panderers and liars have violated and smutted it.
Yet this reaching is alive yet
for lights and keepsakes.

The people know the salt of the sea
and the strength of the winds
lashing the corners of the earth.
The people take the earth
as a tomb of rest and a cradle of hope.
Who else speaks for the Family of Man?
They are in tune and step
with constellations of universal law.

The people is a polychrome,
a spectrum and a prison
held in a moving monolith,
a console organ of changing themes,
a clavilux of color poems
wherein the sea offers fog
and the fog moves off in rain
and the labrador sunset shortens
to a nocturne of clear stars
serene over the shot spray
of northern lights.

The steel mill sky is alive.
The fire breaks white and zigzag
shot on a gun-metal gloaming.
Man is a long time coming.
Man will yet win.
Brother may yet line up with brother:

This old anvil laughs at many broken hammers.
There are men who can't be bought.
The fireborn are at home in fire.
The stars make no noise.
You can't hinder the wind from blowing.
Time is a great teacher.
Who can live without hope?
In the darkness with a great bundle of grief
the people march.
In the night, and overhead a shovel of stars for
keeps, the people march:
"Where to? What next?"

Let America Be America Again

LANGSTON HUGHES

Let America be America again.
Let it be the dream it used to be.
Let it be the pioneer on the plain
Seeking a home where he himself is free.

(America never was America to me.)

Let America be the dream the dreamers dreamed—
Let it be that great strong land of love
Where never kings connive nor tyrants scheme
That any man be crushed by one above.

(It never was America to me.)

O, let my land be a land where Liberty
Is crowned with no false patriotic wreath,
But opportunity is real, and life is free,
Equality is in the air we breathe.

(There's never been equality for me,
Nor freedom in this "homeland of the free.")

*Say who are you that mumbles in the dark?
And who are you that draws your veil across the stars?*

I am the poor white, fooled and pushed apart,
I am the Negro bearing slavery's scars.

I am the red man driven from the land,
I am the immigrant clutching the hope I seek—
And finding only the same old stupid plan.
Of dog eat dog, of mighty crush the weak.

I am the young man, full of strength and hope,
Tangled in that ancient endless chain
Of profit, power, gain, of grab the land!
Of grab the gold! Of grab the ways of satisfying need!
Of work the men! Of take the pay!
Of owning everything for one's own greed!

I am the farmer, bondsman to the soil.
I am the worker sold to the machine.
I am the Negro, servant to you all.
I am the people, humble, hungry, mean—
Hungry yet today despite the dream.
Beaten yet today—O, Pioneers!
I am the man who never got ahead,
The poorest worker bartered through the years.

Yet I'm the one who dreamt our basic dream
In that Old World while still a serf of kings,
Who dreamt a dream so strong, so brave, so true,
That even yet its mighty daring sings
In every brick and stone, in every furrow turned
That's made America the land it has become.
O, I'm the man who sailed those early seas
In search of what I meant to be my home—
For I'm the one who left dark Ireland's shore,
And Poland's plain, and England's grassy lea,
And torn from Black Africa's strand I came
To build a "homeland of the free."

The free?

Who said the free? Not me?
Surely not me? The millions on relief today?
The millions shot down when we strike?
The millions who have nothing for our pay?
For all the dreams we've dreamed
And all the songs we've sung
And all the hopes we've held
And all the flags we've hung,
The millions who have nothing for our pay—
Except the dream that's almost dead today.

O, let America be America again—
The land that never has been yet—
And yet must be—the land where *every* man is free.
The land that's mine—the poor man's, Indian's, Negro's,
ME—
Who made America,
Whose sweat and blood, whose faith and pain,
Whose hand at the foundry, whose plow in the rain,
Must bring back our mighty dream again.

Sure, call me any ugly name you choose—
The steel of freedom does not stain.
From those who live like leeches on the people's lives,
We must take back our land again,
America!

O, yes,
I say it plain,
America never was America to me,
And yet I swear this oath—
America will be!

Out of the rack and ruin of our gangster death,
The rape and rot of graft, and stealth, and lies,

We, the people, must redeem
The land, the mines, the plants, the rivers,
The mountains and the endless plain—
All, all the stretch of these great green states—
And make America again!

The American Dream

ERIC SEVAREID

"It is Europeans, for the most part, who have constructed these great ships, but without America they have no meaning. These ships are alive with the supreme ecstasy of the modern world, which is the voyage to America. There is no other experience that is remotely comparable to it, in its sense of joy, its exultancy, its drunken and magnificent hope, which believes in the miracle and sees it invariably achieved." So wrote Thomas Wolfe, himself drunk with the grandeurs and grotesqueries of America, in the 1930s.

What was the impulse that pushed and pulled those who came? It was, simply—change, and it is not given to human creatures in the mass to believe that change is going to be for the worse. There had been no change in the Old World; no essential, drastic change in the relations of man to man for centuries. "America," says Eric Hoffer, "is the only new thing in history."

What was the dream? It was rebirth, the eternal, haunting craving of men to be born again, the yearning for the second chance. The New World was the second chance. The most illiterate knew it in their bones, as we would all know the meaning, if, today, a new, rich, habitable planet were discovered within our common means of access. Our past would fade in significance, this life would become our prehistory, nothing more.

That is what happened when the great migration flowed to the West. In the end it was discovered that the Europeans had not brought Europe with them; Europe's history became our prehistory. A rebirth had, indeed, occurred; and no place in the world, not Europe itself, has ever been the same.

There were a thousand varieties of finite dreams within the one encompassing dream. Many of the poor came dreaming to be rich; many of the rich, dreaming to be richer. The energetic came, eager to put their hands to work; the lazy, hoping to live with no work at all. The God-conscious came, expecting to find Him speaking to them directly, the message ungarbled by official interference. The weak were sure they would become strong, the fearful were certain of confidence. Thieves dreamt of easier thieving; roughnecks wanted more room to swagger; the sick sought health; and from the new air and light and waters and herbs and drugs, the ugly would surely be transformed with beauty. And the apostles of brotherhood came, ignoring the teachings of the sages about the dual, good and evil, nature of man, seized with the lofty and ludicrous notion of Jean Jacques Rousseau that civilization had corrupted man, instead of the other way around. And that, restored to a "state of nature," man would be automatically tolerant, loving, and peaceable.

These are among the drives in men that produce revolutions. The migration was revolution. It was not recognized as such except gradually, as time wore on, its fuses were delayed. The first big fuse caught fire with Washington's war against British rule, which was political revolt and a new intellectual synthesis, but which charged the atmosphere with the moral electricity that was to set off a long train of fuses as the migrants increased, pushed over the mountains, scattered far from authority and orthodoxy, made frontier life the typical American life, and put in motion the true social revolution that has never stopped revolving and shows no signs of stopping.

Its coat of arms bore and bears only one word—Freedom. Not the freedom of a region or sect or point of view. Just freedom, the condition in which a man feels like a human being, like himself. It is the purpose, the definition, and consequence of rebirth. It is The Dream.

There are those who say the dream is dead or dying, poisoned by self-interest, rotted by surfeit and indifference, maimed by violence. The great aspiration is ended, they tell us, and America is now only another crowded nation, not even able to maintain order; a Power, but not a society, not a culture. We have gone, almost directly, they would have us believe, from primitiveness to decadence, a far poorer record than that of Rome.

The fireworks of this July 4—which may well illuminate the scene, again, of whole urban blocks consumed by flames, from the Molotov cocktail, not the holiday sparkler—will give further force to this cry of the Cassandras.

But the cry is as old as the nation. It was sounded in Jefferson's time, when the states seemed ready to drift apart; in Lincoln's time, when they split apart; in Roosevelt's time, when, by the millions, husbands shuffled in soup lines; in Truman's time, when the Russians and Chinese were supposedly reordering the earth and Communist traitors were supposedly infesting the Government.

But this is not It—this is not our Armageddon, not the great day of judgment on America. For America is change, and the changes have come, often enough, in convulsive spasms. This country is the most experimental laboratory in human relations for the twentieth century; it is in a sense defining and creating the twentieth century for much of the world.

Unless it is seen in this light, America cannot be understood at all. If many of our contemporary intellectuals, especially those communing with one another in New York City, almost a separate nation in spirit, do not understand it, this is partly because they do not understand themselves. As they attest in innumerable books, they do not know who they are. It may be news to them that the overwhelming majority of Americans *do* know who they are, do *not* feel alienated from their country or their generation.

This is not a "sick society." It is a deeply unsettled and bewildered society, and the reason is not merely the extraordinary changes in this last generation but the speed of these changes. It is the *rate* of change that is new. The life of Americans today resembles that of, say, Grant's time, less than life in Grant's time resembled life in ancient China. The nation is not overpopulated, but the population has shifted out of balance. In the last twenty years alone, eighteen million people, including, of course, the Negroes, have moved into the urban centers. This second industrial-scientific revolution has jammed us together, polluted much of our air and waters, smeared ugliness over much of our countryside, obliged us to work within greater economic units, and increased the tensions of daily living.

Two other revolutions have been taking place in concert with the new industrial-scientific revolution. One is the communications revolution, which brings every social evil, every human tragedy and conflict, immediately and intimately within everyone's ken. The other is the educational revolution, which adds millions every year to the ranks of those moved to add their investigation, articulation, or actions to the processes of problem-solving and problem-creating.

We are not becoming less democratic but more democratic. It is not our individual freedom that is in jeopardy, in the first instance, but our public order. It could be argued that we are moving away from representative government in the direction, at least, of direct democracy, by no means an unmixed blessing. For the immediate future, the problem is not only the indifference or "apathy" of the much-abused middle class or any other group. It is also the problem of too many untrained cooks in the kitchen.

Many current phenomena to the contrary notwithstanding, Americans are the most natural workers-together in the world. We say we live by the system of individual enterprise, while we are the supreme cooperative society. Totalitarian countries say they are cooperative societies, while their regimes must coerce their people to work. It is absurd to believe that the races of men who turned an empty, forbidding continent into the most efficient engine of production and distribution ever seen, who created the first *mass* democracy with essential order and essential freedom, will not solve the problems of crowding, poverty, pollution, and ugliness. The solutions will create new problems, after which there will be new solutions, then new problems, and so our life will go on. Time is life. Were human problems ever totally solved, change would come to a stop, and we would begin to die.

American cynics and Cassandras see neither their own history nor the rest of the world with clarity. Violence? We have *always* had a high tolerance level for violence. Abraham Lincoln worried about what he called "the increasing disregard for law which pervades the country; the growing disposition to substitute the wild and furious passions, in lieu of the sober judgment of courts; and the worse than savage mobs, for the executive ministers of justice."

It is even to be doubted that crime is more prevalent than it was in the nineteenth century. Historian Arthur Schlesinger, Jr., reminds us that a century ago, every tenth person in New York City had a police record.

Alienated and irreverent youth? To a degree, youth is always alienated and to a degree ought to be. More than two thousand years ago, Plato wrote that in a democracy, the father "accustoms himself to become like his child and to fear his sons. . . . The schoolmaster fears and flatters his pupils . . . the young act like their seniors, and compete with them in speech and action, while the old men condescend to the young." This happens because democratic life carries the in-built impulse to wish to please and accommodate to others.

The alarm over drug-taking is also exaggerated. There is far less use of dangerous drugs today than a half century ago, before narcotics control, when about one American in every four hundred was an addict of some harmful drug, ten times the present rate.

Americans, of course, are not spiritually geared to the past but to the future. It is a reflection of what John Steinbeck, speaking of the onpushing, haggard "Okies" in the dust-bowl years, called the "terrible faith," that we are constantly seized with concern for our children more than for ourselves. Yet it is not possible to see our society in perspective without these backward glances to what we once were, with the consequent realization that we are using different scales of measuring well-being today.

At the turn of the century, a newborn could expect to live about to the age of fifty; today, the expectancy is about seventy. Once, a mother had sound reason to fear giving birth; today, death in childbirth is regarded as intolerable. Once, a full high school education was the best achievement of a minority; today, it is the barest minimum for decent employment and self-respect. Once, the timber and mining barons stripped away the forests and topsoil wholesale; today, these companies are confronted by their communities at every other move.

One could cite hundreds of similar examples of how our standards of expectancy have risen, as they should, along with our standard of life. The truth is that we Americans are perfectionists, which simply means that we were not, are not, and never will be satisfied either with the quantities or the qualities in our life.

By the year 2000, we will look back upon these present years not only as one of America's periodic convulsions but as a rather backward period. By then, the typical American family will have an income of around twenty thousand dollars a year or more; the typical American adult will have had at least two years of college, with far broader intellectual and aesthetic horizons. By then, the old urban centers will have been rebuilt, and many millions will live in satellite "new cities," part-urban, part-rural. The incurable diseases like cancer and arthritis will be under far better control.

The present explosion in books, theater, music, and art will have transformed tastes and comprehension to an enormous degree. And already, according to the Englishman C. P. Snow, something like 80 percent of the advanced study of science in the Western world is going on in the United States of America. This is the heart reason for the "brain drain" from abroad to the United States, not merely the higher pay. The facilities, the action, the creative excitement, are increasingly here. None of this guarantees a single new Shakespeare, Rembrandt, Beethoven, or Einstein, because genius is not developed (though even this may occur one day through selective breeding, and cell transplant).

What it does guarantee is a great lifting of the massive center, of the "ordinary" people. This is the premise and the point about America—ours is the first organized dedication to *massive* improvement, to the development of a *mass* culture, the first attempt to educate *everyone* to the limit of his capacities. We have known for a long time that this can be done only through the chemistry of individual freedom. Soviet Russia is just now beginning to discover this for itself. I am unable to understand the thrust of the sufferings and strivings of Western man over the last thousand years save in terms of this kind of achievement.

The popular passion of Americans is not politics, baseball, money, or material things. It is education. Education is now our biggest industry, involving more people even than national defense. The percentage of children in kindergarten has doubled in a rather short period; the percentage of youth in college climbs steeply upward. Today, even a Negro boy in the South has a better statistical chance of getting into college than an English youth. And there are about forty-four million full- and part-time *adult* students pursuing some kind of formalized learning on their own!

Intelligent foreigners nearly everywhere understand the mountainous meaning of all this for the world as well as for America. They know that much of the world will be transformed in the American image, culturally if not politically. They know that struggle is really all over—it is the Western way of living and doing, our way and the way of Europe combined, that the world wants. It is North America and West Europe that make up the "in" world; Russia and China are still the outsiders trying to enter.

Communism already appears irrelevant, essentially passé. The more the Communist regimes educate their people, the more complex their life will become. They will struggle with the complexities the Western world confronts already, and they will discover that authoritarian direction from the top cannot cope with them. Only the essential liberal society can manage twentieth-century life, even in practical terms. They will learn, as we have always known, that the effective, the lasting revolution lies in the West, particularly in America.

Why, then, are we in such a state of uproar in this year of Our Lord, and why is much of the world upset about the America of today? Because, as a philosopher once said, "nothing that is vast enters into the life of mortals without a curse," and America is struggling to rid itself of one old curse and one new one. The old curse is the Negro slavery Europeans fastened upon this land long ago, which continues in a hundred psychological, social, and economic, if not legal, forms. The Negro Passion of today is a revolution within the continuing American revolution, and the one absolute certainty about it is that it is going to succeed, however long and distracting the agony for everyone. It will succeed not only because it has justice with it (justice has been suppressed before) but because there is a deep evangelical streak in the American people, a true collective conscience, and it has been aroused.

Racism exists in almost all societies on this globe, virulently so, incidentally, in Black Africa. It may be that race prejudice—the psychologists' "stranger hatred"—is an instinct tracing from our animal origins, and therefore ineradicable. Yet man is the only animal *aware* of his instincts; the only animal, therefore, capable of controlling, if not eliminating, his instincts. New law, enforced, compels new behavior. Behavior repeated daily comes to seem normal, and attitudes change. Illusions tend to vanish. The idea that a difference in skin color is an essential difference is an illusion. I am struck by an observation of McGeorge Bundy of the Ford Foundation. He said discrimination will end, partly because this college generation regards racial equality as natural, whereas the older generation regards it only as logical.

The twentieth-century war over racial injustice is now in its virulent stages. The nineteenth-century war in its virulent stage lasted four years. This one will last much longer because it is fought on a thousand narrow fronts, like guerrilla war, and because no grand climacteric is possible. But it is not going to "tear this country apart" or "burn America down" or anything of the sort. A tiny percentage of extremists among only 12 percent of the American population can do much, but they cannot do that.

The new curse has come with America's new military power. A form of Parkinson's Law operates here. The greater the power, the more the men who associate with it, extoll it, and find needs, real or sophistical, for its use. The use of available, flexible force becomes easier than hard thought, and the worst aspect of the curse is the gradual, almost unconscious identification of power with virtue. John Adams said, "Power always thinks it has a great soul and vast views beyond the comprehension of the weak."

We have fallen into this trap with the Vietnam intervention. For the first time, we have misused our power on a massive scale. But it does not mean that we are a "Fascist" or aggressive people, any more than the racial mess means that we are a hating or oppressive people. Vietnam is not typical; it is a mistake, now recognized as such by most serious thinkers in this country. If millions of people in Europe (every province of which is soaked in blood) stand aghast at what we have done and reproach us bitterly, one unarticulated reason is that they *expect* the United States to act with humaneness and common sense. They do not shout advice to Russia and China, whatever their misdeeds, for the same reason that the crowd in the bullring does not shout advice to the bull but to the bullfighter.

The reassuring thing is not merely that we will get out of this trap and undo the damage as best we can but that we will do so because our own people demand it, not because the enemy is too strong, not because of foreign criticism. We could, if we would, lay North Vietnam totally waste. The American conscience will not permit it. We may not win a military victory in Vietnam, but we will win a victory in our own soul.

No—the humaneness of the American people is still here. The new problems have piled up too rapidly for our brains and our institutions to cope with at anything like the same rate, but the will for justice is as strong as ever—stronger, in my own belief, because thought and expression are freer today than ever before. This is why the Negro revolution has come now—not because conditions of life became worse, save for some, but because of a climate of free expression. In just such periods of great intellectual freedom have nearly all revolutions been generated.

It is a remarkable fact that great numbers of very ordinary people in distant lands understand all this about America better than some of our own intellectuals. If, by some magic, all barriers to emigration and immigration around the world were lifted tomorrow, by far the single biggest human caravan would start moving in one direction—our way.

One day recently, I asked a Cuban refugee why most Cubans like himself wanted to come to the United States rather than go to Latin American countries with the same language and the same general culture. Was it just the thought of greater economic opportunity?

"No," he said, "many of us would have an easier time, economically, in the Latin country. It's just that we feel better here. We can feel like a human being. There seems to be something universal about this country."

This is living testimony, not abstract argument, from men who know the meaning of America in their bones and marrow. Of course, it is the truth. Of course, the dream lives on.

Let those who wish compare America with Rome. Rome lasted around a thousand years.

Adam

KURT VONNEGUT, JR.

It was midnight in a Chicago lying-in hospital.

"Mr. Sousa," said the nurse, "your wife had a girl. You can see the baby in about twenty minutes."

"I know, I know, I know," said Mr. Sousa, a sullen gorilla, plainly impatient with having a tiresome and familiar routine explained to him. He snapped his fingers. "Girl! Seven, now. Seven girls I got now. A houseful of women. I can beat the stuffings out of ten men my own size. But, what do I get? Girls."

"Mr. Knechtmann," said the nurse to the other man in the room. She pronounced the name, as almost all Americans did, a coloress Netman. "I'm sorry. Still no word on your wife. She is keeping us waiting, isn't she?" She grinned glassily and left.

Sousa turned on Knechtmann. "Some little son of a gun like you, Netman, you want a boy, bing! You got one. Want a football team, bing, bing, bing, eleven, you got it." He stomped out of the room.

The man he left behind, all alone now, was Heinz Knechtmann, a presser in a dry-cleaning plant, a small man with thin wrists and a bad spine that kept him slightly hunched, as though forever weary. His face was long and big-nosed and thin-lipped, but was so overcast with goodhumored humility as to be beautiful. His eyes were large and brown, and deep-set and long-lashed. He was only twenty-two, but seemed and felt much older. He had died a little as each member of his family had been led away and killed by the Nazis, until only in him, at the age of ten, had life and the name of Knechtmann shared a soul. He and his wife, Avchen, had grown up behind barbed wire.

He had been staring at the walls of the waiting room for twelve hours now, since noon, when his wife's labor pains had become regular, the surges of slow rollers coming in from the sea a mile apart, from far, far away. This would be his second child. The last time he had waited, he had waited on a straw tick in a displaced-persons camp in Germany. The child, Karl Knechtmann, named after Heinz's father, had died, and with it, once more, had died the name of one of the finest cellists ever to have lived.

When the numbness of weary wishing lifted momentarily during this second vigil, Heinz's mind was a medley of proud family names, gone, all gone, that could be brought to life again in this new being—if it lived. Peter Knechtmann, the surgeon; Kroll Knechtmann, the botanist; Friederich Knechtmann, the playwright. Dimly recalled uncles. Or if it was a girl, and if it lived, it would be Helga Knechtmann, Heinz's mother, and she would learn to play the harp as Heinz's mother had, and for all Heinz's ugliness, she would be beautiful. The Knechtmann men were all ugly, the Knechtmann women were all lovely as angels, though not all angels. It had always been so—for hundreds and hundreds of years.

"Mr. Netman," said the nurse, "it's a boy, and your wife is fine. She's resting now. You can see her in the morning. You can see the baby in twenty minutes."

Heinz looked up dumbly.

"It weighs five pounds nine ounces." She was gone again, with the same prim smile and officious, squeaking footsteps.

"Knechtmann," murmured Heinz, standing and bowing slightly to the wall. "The name is Knechtmann." He bowed again and gave a smile that was courtly and triumphant. He spoke the name with an exaggerated Old World pronunciation, like a foppish footman announcing the arrival of nobility, a guttural drum roll, unsoftened for American ears, "*KhhhhhhhhhhhhhNECHT! mannnnnnnnnnnn.*"

"Mr. Netman?" A very young doctor with a pink face and closecropped red hair stood in the waiting-room door. There were circles under his eyes, and he spoke through a yawn.

"Dr. Powers!" cried Heinz, clasping the man's right hand between both of his. "Thank God, thank God, thank God, and thank you."

"Um," said Dr. Powers, and he managed to smile wanly.

"There isn't anything wrong, is there?"

"Wrong?" said Powers. "No, no. Everything's fine. If I look down in the mouth, it's because I've been up for thirty-six hours straight." He closed his eyes, and leaned against the doorframe. "No, no trouble with your wife," he said in a faraway voice. "She's made for having babies. Regular pop-up toaster. Like rolling off a log. Schnip-schnap."

"She is?" said Heinz incredulously.

Dr. Powers shook his head, bringing himself back to consciousness. "My mind—conked out completely. Sousa—I got your wife confused with Mrs. Sousa. They finished in a dead heat. Netman, you're Netman. Sorry. Your wife's the one with pelvis trouble."

"Malnutrition as a child," said Heinz.

"Yeah. Well, the baby came normally, but, if you're going to have another one, it'd better be a Caesarean. Just to be on the safe side."

"I can't thank you enough," said Heinz passionately.

Dr. Powers licked his lips, and fought to keep his eyes open. "Uh huh. 'S O.K.," he said thickly. " 'Night. Luck." He shambled out into the corridor.

The nurse stuck her head into the waiting room. "You can see your baby, Mr. Netman."

"Doctor—" said Heinz, hurrying out into the corridor, wanting to shake Powers' hand again so that Powers would know what a magnificent thing he'd done. "It's the most wonderful thing that ever happened." The elevator doors slithered shut between them before Dr. Powers could show a glimmer of response.

"This way," said the nurse. "Turn left at the end of the hall, and you'll find the nursery window there. Write your name on a piece of paper and hold it against the glass."

Heinz made the trip by himself, without seeing another human being until he reached the end. There, on the other side of a large glass panel, he saw a hundred of them cupped in shallow canvas buckets and arranged in a square block of straight ranks and files.

Heinz wrote his name on the back of a laundry slip and pressed it to the window. A fat and placid nurse looked at the paper, not at Heinz's face, and missed seeing his wide smile, missed an urgent invitation to share for a moment his ecstasy.

She grasped one of the buckets and wheeled it before the window. She turned away again, once more missing the smile.

"Hello, hello, hello, little Knechtmann," said Heinz to the red prune on the other side of the glass. His voice echoed down the hard, bare corridor, and came back to him with embarrassing loudness. He blushed and lowered his voice. "Little Peter, little Kroll," he said softly, "little Friederich—and there's Helga in you, too. Little spark of Knechtmann, you little treasure house. Everything is saved in you."

"I'm afraid you'll have to be more quiet," said a nurse, sticking her head out from one of the rooms.

"Sorry," said Heinz. "I'm very sorry." He fell silent, and contented himself with tapping lightly on the window with a fingernail, trying to get the child to look at him. Young Knechtmann would not look, wouldn't share the moment, and after a few minutes the nurse took him away again.

Heinz beamed as he rode on the elevator and as he crossed the hospital lobby, but no one gave him more than a cursory glance. He passed a row of telephone booths and there, in one of the booths with the door open, he saw a soldier with whom he'd shared the waiting room and hour before.

"Yeah, Ma—seven pounds six ounces. Got hair like Buffalo Bill. No, we haven't had time to make up a name for her yet . . . That you, Pa? Yup, mother and daughter doin' fine, just fine. Seven pound six ounces. Nope, no name. . . . That you, Sis? Pretty late for you to be up, ain't it? Doesn't look like anybody yet. Let me talk to Ma again. . . . That you, Ma? Well, I guess that's all the news from Chicago. Now, Mom, Mom, take it easy—don't worry. It's a swell-looking baby, Mom. Just the hair looks like Buffalo Bill, and I said it as a joke, Mom. That's right, seven pounds six ounces. . . ."

There were five other booths, all empty, all open for calls to anyplace on earth. Heinz longed to hurry into one of them breathlessly, and tell the marvelous news. But there was no one to call, no one waiting for the news.

But Heinz still beamed, and he strode across the street and into a quiet tavern there. In the dank twilight there were only two men, tête-à-tête, the bartender and Mr. Sousa.

"Yes sir, what'll it be?"

"I'd like to buy you and Mr. Sousa a drink," said Heinz with a heartiness strange to him. "I'd like the best brandy you've got. My wife just had a baby!"

"That so?" said the bartender with polite interest.

"Five pounds nine ounces," said Heinz.

"Huh," said the bartender. "What do you know."

"Netman," said Sousa, "wha'dja get?"

"Boy," said Heinz proudly.

"Never knew it to fail," said Sousa bitterly. "It's the little guys, all the time the little guys."

"Boy, girl," said Heinz, "it's all the same, just as long as it lives. Over there in the hospital, they're too close to it to see the wonder of it. A miracle over and over again—the world made new."

"Wait'll you've racked up seven, Netman," said Sousa. "*Then* you come back and tell me about the miracle."

"You got seven?" said the bartender. "I'm one up on you. I got eight." He poured three drinks.

"Far as I'm concerned," said Sousa, "you can have the championship."

Heinz lifted his glass. "Here's long life and great skill and much happiness to—to Peter Karl Knechtmann." He breathed quickly, excited by the decision.

"*There's* a handle to take ahold of," said Sousa. "You'd think the kid weighed two hundred pounds."

"Peter is the name of a famous surgeon," said Heinz, "the boy's great-uncle, dead now. Karl was my father's name."

"Here's to Pete K. Netman," said Sousa, with a cursory salute.

"Pete," said the bartender, drinking.

"And here's to *your* little girl—the new one," said Heinz.

Sousa sighed and smiled wearily. "Here's to her. God bless her."

"And now, *I'll* propose a toast," said the bartender, hammering on the bar with his fist. "On your feet, gentlemen. Up, up, everybody up."

Heinz stood, and held his glass high, ready for the next step in camaraderie, a toast to the whole human race, of which the Knechtmanns were still a part.

"Here's to the White Sox!" roared the bartender.

"Minoso, Fox, Mele," said Sousa.

"Fain, Lollar, Rivera!" said the bartender. He turned to Heinz. "Drink up, boy! The White Sox! Don't tell me you're a Cub fan."

"No," said Heinz, disappointed. "No—I don't follow baseball, I'm afraid." The other two men seemed to be sinking away from him. "I haven't been able to think about much but the baby."

The bartender at once turned his full attention to Sousa. "Look," he said intensely, "they take Fain off of first, and put him at third, and give Pierce first. Then move Minoso in from left field to shortstop. See what I'm doing?"

"Yep, yep," said Sousa eagerly.

"And then we take that no-good Carrasquel and . . ."

Heinz was all alone again, with twenty feet of bar between him and the other two men. It might as well have been a continent.

He finished his drink without pleasure, and left quietly.

At the railroad station, where he waited for a local train to take him home to the South Side, Heinz's glow returned again as he saw a co-worker at the dry-cleaning plant walk in with a girl. They were laughing and had their arms around each other's waist.

"Harry," said Heinz, hurrying toward them. "Guess what, Harry. Guess what just happened." He grinned broadly.

Harry, a tall, dapper, snub-nosed young man, looked down at Heinz with mild surprise. "Oh—hello, Heinz. What's up, boy?"

The girl looked on in perplexity, as though asking why they should be accosted at such an odd hour by such an odd person. Heinz avoided her slightly derisive eyes.

"A baby, Harry. My wife just had a boy."

"Oh," said Harry. He extended his hand. "Well, congratulations." The hand was limp. "I think that's swell, Heinz, perfectly swell." He withdrew his hand and waited for Heinz to say something else.

"Yes, yes—just about an hour ago," said Heinz. "Five pounds nine ounces. I've never been happier in my life."

"Well, I think it's perfectly swell, Heinz. You should be happy."

"Yes, indeed," said the girl.

There was a long silence, with all three shifting from one foot to the other.

"Really good news," said Harry at last.

"Yes, well," said Heinz quickly, "well, that's all I had to tell you."

"Thanks," said Harry. "Glad to hear about it."

There was another uneasy silence.

"See you at work," said Heinz, and strode jauntily back to his bench, but with his reddened neck betraying how foolish he felt.

The girl giggled.

Back home in his small apartment, at two in the morning, Heinz talked to himself, to the empty bassinet, and to the bed. He talked in German, a language he had sworn never to use again.

"They don't care," said Heinz. "They're all too busy, busy, busy to notice life, to feel anything about it. A baby is born." He shrugged. "What could be duller? Who would be so stupid as to talk about it, to think there was anything important or interesting about it?"

He opened a window on the summer night, and looked out at the moonlit canyon of gray wooden porches and garbage cans. "There are too many of us, and we are all too far apart," said Heinz. "Another Knechtmann is born, another O'Leary, another Sousa. Who cares? Why should anyone care? What difference does it make? None."

He lay down in his clothes on the unmade bed, and, with a rattling sigh, went to sleep.

He awoke at six, as always. He drank a cup of coffee, and with a wry sense of anonymity, he jostled and was jostled aboard the downtown train. His face showed no emotion. It was like all the other faces, seemingly incapable of surprise or wonder, joy or anger.

He walked across town to the hospital with the same detachment, a gray, uninteresting man, a part of the city.

In the hospital, he was as purposeful and calm as the doctors and nurses bustling about him. When he was led into the ward where Avchen slept behind white screens, he felt only what he had always felt in her presence—love and aching awe and gratitude for her.

"You go ahead and wake her gently, Mr. Netman," said the nurse.

"Avchen—" He touched her on her white-gowned shoulder. "Avchen. Are you all right, Avchen?"

"Mmmmmmmmmm?" murmured Avchen. Her eyes opened to narrow slits. "Heinz. Hello, Heinz."

"Sweetheart, are you all right?"

"Yes, yes," she whispered. "I'm fine. How is the baby, Heinz?"

"Perfect. Perfect, Avchen."

"They couldn't kill us, could they, Heinz?"

"No."

"And here we are, alive as we can be."

"Yes."

"The baby, Heinz—" She opened her dark eyes wide. "It's the most wonderful thing that ever happened, isn't it?"

"Yes," said Heinz.

About the Authors

Sherwood Anderson (1876–1941) was born of lower-class origins in Camden, Ohio. He quit high school before graduation to take on odd jobs. By 1906 he had become president of the mail-order firm United Factories Company, a position which led him to establish his own business in Elyria, Ohio. At the age of thirty-six he suffered a nervous breakdown, rejected his past, and embarked on a writing career.

Essentially a lyrical prose writer, Anderson's interest in fiction was never in plot, but rather in atmosphere, nuance and milieu. He drew upon the people and subjects of his midwestern youth—farmhands, laborers in factories, jockeys and stableboys, county fairs, and the grotesquerie of village life—in order to reveal the essence of human existence. A major theme of his work was the tragicomic nature of death-in-life.

Although *Winesburg, Ohio* is probably his major work, Anderson published other important collections of short stories, including *The Triumph of the Egg, Horses and Men,* and *Death in the Woods.* Responding to an interviewer for the *Paris Review,* William Faulkner summarized Anderson's importance: "He was the father of my generation of American writers and the tradition of American writing which our successors will carry on. He has never received his proper evaluation."

Gwendolyn Brooks (1917–   ) was born in Topeka, Kansas, but has lived all but the first month of life on Chicago's South Side in the black community identified as Bronzeville. After graduation from Wilson Junior College, she worked for several years as a secretary. Brooks has been awarded numerous accolades: two Guggenheim Fellowships, an American Academy of Arts and Letters grant, a Pulitzer Prize, and the Eunice Tietjens Memorial Award given by *Poetry* magazine. In 1968 she succeeded Carl Sandburg as Poet Laureate of Illinois.

Known for her technical versatility, Brooks has mastered conventional forms like the sonnet as well as freer forms, including the blues. Her keen sense of poetic discipline has never diminished her commitment to expressing the black experience in such varied verse collections as *A Street in Bronzeville, Annie Allen, The Bean Eaters,* and *In the Mecca.* As one critic has noted, however, the poems of Brooks are "not merely personal or racial but universal in their implications."

Also a fine prose writer, Brooks has published *Maud Martha,* a novel about a young black girl growing up in Chicago, and *Report from Part One: An Autobiography.*

Willa Cather (1873–1947)—Although born in Virginia, Willa Cather spent her youthful years in Nebraska where she graduated from the state university at Lincoln. Unable to devote herself wholly to a literary career, Cather taught Latin and English in Pittsburgh before serving as managing editor for *McClure's Magazine* in New York.

In her regional fiction Cather dealt with the Nebraska prairies, range lands, and villages of her childhood. Stories written during her literary apprenticeship revealed the aridity and drabness of the frontier. With aesthetic, emotional and intellectual maturity, however, she produced her principal pastoral novels, *O Pioneers!* and *My Ántonia.* These works emphasized the heroism and piety of the pioneers without neglecting their hardships and sacrifices. After the First World War, Cather longed nostalgically for the past when there were still frontiers to conquer. Her published novels from this period included *Death Comes for the Archbishop* and *Shadow on the Rocks.*

Two of the author's most famous short-story collections are *The Troll Garden* and *Obscure Destinies.*

Theodore Dreiser (1871–1945), the twelfth of thirteen children, was born in Terre Haute, Indiana. His father was dogmatic and fanatically religious; his mother was selfless and warm-hearted to her family. Because of severe poverty, the Dreisers moved from Terre Haute to other Indiana towns, including Sullivan, Evansville, and Warsaw. Once he was old enough, the young Dreiser left for Chicago where he worked at a series of menial jobs before becoming a reporter for the *Daily Globe.* He later took newspaper assignments in St. Louis, Toledo, Cleveland, and Pittsburgh, and eventually did freelance and editorial work in New York.

In prose that was loose, expansive, and metaphoric, Dreiser attempted to document natural human emotions. Central in his work were the sense of moral ambiguity and the theme of an individual's compulsive drive for success. His novels also repeated with variations a character's departure from the restrictive homelife in a small town for the promise of independence and acceptance in the city.

Sister Carrie and *An American Tragedy* are among Dreiser's most popular novels. His shorter fiction is collected in *The Best Short Stories of Theodore Dreiser.*

Paul Laurence Dunbar (1872–1906) was born and educated in Dayton, Ohio. He graduated from high school in 1891 and took a job as an elevator operator in a local hotel. In school he exhibited literary potential while in the positions of editor-in-chief for the school newspaper, president of the literary society, and class poet. Dunbar continued to write and subsequently published with borrowed money the volume *Oak and Ivy.* His second collection *Majors and Minors* brought him national prominence, largely because of a favorable review by William Dean Howells, a novelist and critic for *Harper's Weekly.*

Dunbar wrote in both standard literary English and in dialect. Subjects for his verse were drawn from the plantation tradition of the South as well as the problems of black Americans. From the titles of several collections such as *Lyrics of the Lowly Life* and *Lyrics of the Hearthside,* the poet's preference for the lyrical form is evident. Dunbar also wrote a partly autobiographical novel, *The Uncalled,* and a series of stories entitled *Folks from Dixie.*

James T. Farrell (1904–) was born on the near Southwest side of Chicago to a teamster and his wife. At three he was taken to live with his maternal grandparents. Though staying with the Dalys had economic advantages, it exposed Farrell to their family quarrels and led to tensions with his own parents. By his admission, Farrell's youth was one of commonplaceness, formal religious fanaticism, spiritual poverty and an authoritative education in parochial schools.

The creative potential inherent in Farrell's lower-class origin has been basic to his literary career. His native environment profoundly conditioned the character of his insights, subject matter and style. So acutely did Farrell feel his city's influence that he considered Chicagoans to be the best indicators of national attitudes and problems and the city itself to be the most "concentrated social laboratory of American life."

The central novels of Farrell's career include *Young Lonigan, The Young Manhood of Studs Lonigan* and *Judgment Day.* A prolific writer, he has also produced other novels, short stories, essays and criticism.

F. Scott Fitzgerald (1896–1940)—From youth, F. Scott Fitzgerald of St. Paul, Minnesota, wanted to be a writer. At St. Paul Academy, at Newman School in New Jersey, and at Princeton University, his academic record played a secondary role to his fiction writing. Fitzgerald enlisted in the United States Army, where he trained at several bases in the Midwest and South while he worked on a novel. Once discharged from the service, he went to New York and entered an advertising agency as a copy writer. Shortly after the appearance of his novel *This Side of Paradise* Fitzgerald married Zelda Sayre, hoping to fulfill his naive dream of glamorous and lavish existence.

Much of Fitzgerald's literary work has strongly autobiographical aspects. The character of Judy Jones in "Winter Dreams," for example, was patterned directly after Ginerva King, a Chicago heiress with whom Fitzgerald once thought himself in love. The experiences depicted in *The Great Gatsby* represented in some interior emotional sense those of the author himself. He saw himself as Nick Carraway, the fictional narrator who had a sustaining memory of his rootedness in the Midwest. He also perceived himself as Jay Gatsby, the novel's midwestern protagonist, who lived by a sustaining dream of aspiration. His turbulent marriage, marked by recklessness and an element of self-destructiveness, is reflected in his novel *Tender is the Night.*

Fitzgerald's short stories were collected in such volumes as *Tales of the Jazz Age* and *All the Sad Young Men.*

Hamlin Garland (1860–1940)—A fictionalist of local color and social protest, Hamlin Garland was born in Wisconsin and reared there as well as in Iowa and South Dakota. He fled the rural environ at his earliest opportunity, going East to teach private classes in literature and to lecture in and about Boston. While there, he also began a productive and varied literary career.

Garland's reputation has come to rest principally on his early "middle-border" fiction and on his final phase of narrative autobiography. The short stories were collected and published under the titles *Main-Travelled Roads* and *Prairie Folks.* Motivated by a mixture of nostalgia and anger, the author showed farm life as he knew it, dispelling the idyllic notion of the frontier as a land of success and the good life. As his interest in fiction writing waned, Garland again turned to boyhood experiences in the Midwest and produced the autobiographical work *A Son of the Middle Border* in 1917.

Robert Hayden (1913–) was born in Detroit. He graduated from Wayne State University and received his M. A. from the University of Michigan. He has taught at Fisk University and the University of Michigan. Collections of his verse include *A Ballad of Remembrance, Words in the Mourning Time, Night-Blooming Cireus, Heart-Shape in the Dust, Selected Poems,* and *Angle of Ascent.* Among the poet's honors are the Russell Loines Award and the Grand Prix de Poesie of the First World Festival of Negro Arts, Dakar, Senegal. Hayden was appointed poetry consultant to the Library of Congress in 1975 and 1977.

Hayden maintains that there is "no reason why a Negro poet should be limited by 'racial utterance' or to having his writing judged by standards different from those applied to the work of other poets." His masterful handling of traditional stanzaic patterns, irregular rhythms of free verse, and both Latinate and Anglo-Saxon vocabulary supports this notion. Moreover, the universal theme of the tension between the ideal and the real is central to much of his work.

Ernest Hemingway (1899–1961)—The son of a physician and sportsman, Hemingway grew up in the Chicago suburb of Oak Park. His summers were spent at Walloon Lake in northern Michigan, a setting for many of the Nick Adams stories. After graduating from Oak Park High School, he became a newspaper reporter on the *Kansas City Star* before volunteering for service as a Red Cross ambulance driver in Italy. After World War I, he settled in Paris as a foreign correspondent for the *Toronto Star.* He later worked as a war correspondent during the Spanish Civil War and World War II. For his "forceful and style-making mastery of the art of modern narration," he earned the Nobel Prize for literature in 1954.

Hemingway's fiction is to a large degree the fiction of his own experiences. A member of the lost generation which witnessed the collapse of traditional values after World War I, he was preoccupied with the human condition and with influences that might control it. The moral code he adopted was one of endurance, of "grace under pressure." Titles such as *In Our Time* (a short-story collection), *The Sun Also Rises* (a novel), *For Whom the Bell Tolls* (a novel), and *Death in the Afternoon* (a book of nonfiction) emphasized the author's concern with time and the theme of mutability.

Langston Hughes (1902–1967) was born in Joplin, Missouri, and went to school in Lawrence, Kansas; Lincoln, Illinois; and Cleveland, Ohio. He attended Columbia University, worked at odd jobs (including in Paris nightclubs), shipped on freighters to West Africa and Europe, and later graduated from Lincoln University in Pennsylvania. In 1941 Hughes founded the Skyloft Players, a black theatrical group in Chicago. He eventually made his home in New York City, where he was literary mentor to aspiring black writers.

Hughes displayed his talent in practically every genre—the novel (*Not Without Laughter* and *Tambourines to Glory*), the short story (the collection *The Ways of White Folks*), drama (*Mulatto*), autobiography (*The Big Sea*), and poetry (beginning with the volume *The Weary Blues* in 1926). His verse was influenced technically by the rhythms of jazz, and thematically by the social consciousness of midwesterners like Sandburg, Masters, and Lindsay. His most original and popular fiction was the "Simple" sketch, a form which revealed his notion of separate worlds in the United States—the white and the black.

Philip Levine (1928–) a midwesterner by birth, has lived in various places in the United States and abroad before settling in California, where he teaches at Fresno State College. Among his obsessions, the poet has listed "Detroit" (the city of his birth, education, and early factory-work experiences), "the dying of America," and "communion with others." His published several volumes of verse including *On the Edge, Not This Pig, Red Dust,* and *They Feed They Lion.*

"Coming Home," from *They Feed They Lion*, with its economy of language and sensitivity to place, is illustrative of the majority of Levine's work. Specific details of the American scene are conveyed with metaphoric and imagistic daring. A Levine poem also exhibits the author's humane responsiveness to a population trapped and frustrated by a massive industrial system.

(Harry) Sinclair Lewis (1885–1951), the son of a country physician, was born in Sauk Centre, Minnesota. Finding his hometown anticultural and aesthetically depressing, he sought a year's education at Oberlin in Ohio in preparation for Yale University. Upon graduation, Lewis served his literary apprenticeship as a journalist for the Waterloo, Iowa *Courier* and the San Francisco *Evening Bulletin*. He also held a series of editorial positions for various periodicals before establishing his reputation with the novel *Main Street* in 1920.

Lewis was the nation's first recipient of the Nobel Prize for literature, an award given in 1930 for his satiric attacks of America's social excesses. His portrait of the typical turn-of-the-century midwestern village in *Main Street* became a national symbol for the conformity and provincialism which governed small-town life. Similarly, in *Babbitt* he detailed the type of businessman to whom money was the gauge of success, and material consumption a measure of the good life.

A productive writer, Lewis also published twenty-one other novels—including *Arrowsmith*, *Elmer Gantry* and *Dodsworth*—and two collections of short stories.

Abraham Lincoln (1809–1866)—A genuine product of the frontier experience, Abraham Lincoln spent his formative years with his family, trekking westward from Hardin County, Kentucky, to Perry County, Indiana, and then to Macon County, Illinois. Dissatisfied with a farming life, he left for New Salem where he served in the capacities of storekeeper, surveyor, and post-master. Licensed to practice law in 1837, Lincoln moved to Springfield and began his political career in the Illinois legislature. At the age of forty-seven, he joined the Republican Party and later became the sixteenth president of the United States.

Lincoln's reputation as a literary writer was secured with his letters and formal addresses. His dignified poetic prose was influenced by the rhythmical quality of the King James Bible, by the simplicity of his humble frontier beginning, and by the nineteenth century concern for the American ideal. His "Gettysburg Address" is one example of this fusion of influences.

Vachel Lindsay (1879–1931)—Part evangelist and part minstrel, Vachel Lindsay was born in Springfield, Illinois, and educated at home until the age of eleven. Subsequently he attended Springfield public schools, Hiram College in Ohio, the Chicago Institute of Arts, and the New York School of Art. Though studying to be a doctor and then an illustrator, Lindsay spent most of his time writing poetry with sharply defined rhythms. From 1906 to 1920 he toured the United States, reciting his verse in exchange for bread.

Lindsay conceived of reforming American society by improving the individual's relationship to his own village or city. To him, Springfield represented the United States at its best: "I believe profoundly in our agricultural and middle west civilization and think it the natural America, and the America with the oldest and most normal history."

The poet's first book of verse *General William Booth Enters into Heaven and Other Poems* was followed by *The Congo and Other Poems, The Chinese Nightingale and Other Poems,* and *Collected Poems* (a volume accompanied by his own drawings).

Edgar Lee Masters (1869–1950) was born in Kansas and attended the public schools in Petersburg, Illinois. His family moved to Lewistown, Illinois, where he studied law with his father. Upon reaching maturity, he fled his hometown and set up a legal practice in Chicago. From 1892 to 1901 he also wrote and published pamphlets on the Constitution and politics. Masters' interest in law and politics was matched by an interest in poetry. *Spoon River Anthology* and *The New Spoon River* are among his most widely read verse collections.

Writing about his creation of *Spoon River Anthology,* Masters stated that Lewistown furnished him "a key which unlocked the secrets of the world at large." His acid commentaries attacked the sterile small-town life "indigenous to Midwestern soil." Lawyers, editors, bankers, and school superintendents were among his primary negative portrayals. By including idealistic poems like "William and Emily," however, Masters kept the volume from becoming totally a work lamenting the corruption of the village.

Harry Mark Petrakis (1923–) was born in St. Louis and raised in the Greek section of Chicago, where his father was an Orthodox priest. Working at times as a laborer, a steelworker, a real estate salesman, a sales correspondent, and a television scriptwriter, he experienced directly differences in social milieu and urban types. At present, he teaches American literature at Columbia College in Chicago.

Petrakis writes of people who bear the ineradicable imprint of their Greek origin. Their attitudes toward life are influenced more by Greek history, geography, and myth than by day-to-day occurrences. His fiction is permeated with earthiness, humor, and compassion.

Pericles on 31st Street, a book of his short stories, was nominated for the National Book Award in 1965. Other works by Petrakis include *Lion at My Heart, A*

Dream of Kings, In the Land of Morning, The Odyssey of Kostas Volakis, and *A Petrakis Reader.*

Theodore Roethke (1908–1963) was born in Saginaw, Michigan. His youth was spent on the twenty-five-acre nursery owned by his father and uncle. He received his B.A. from the University of Michigan, and attended Michigan Law School and Harvard University before earning his M.A. at Michigan in 1936. His life was that of poet and teacher of English at various colleges and the University of Washington. For his posthumously published volume of verse, *The Far Field,* the author received the National Book Award in 1965.

A confessional poet, Roethke exhibited a willingness to write openly about himself and his family. Drawing upon childhood experiences as a florist's son, he chose greenhouses to symbolize the life processes of growth and development, and shoots, roots, and mosses to represent the submerged self. His lyric "Moss-gathering," for instance, was an overt confession of guilt. The poet also revealed sharp contrasts between the spontaneity of nature and the conformity and sterility of modern institutions, chiefly through imagery.

Among Roethke's publications are *Open House, The Lost Son and Other Poems, Praise to the End!, The Waking, Words for the Wind* and *The Far Field.*

Ole Edvart Rölvaag (1876–1931) was a midwesterner by adoption. He grew up in a Norwegian fishing village, but at the age of twenty emigrated to the United States to work on his uncle's farm in South Dakota. Later he attended St. Olaf College in Minnesota, where he eventually became a professor of Norwegian literature.

Originally written in Norwegian and published in Oslo, Rölvaag's initial novel *Giants in the Earth* provided a literary account of the pioneering venture in the Midwest. Equally important, it offered insights concerning the adaptation of European immigrants to the American environment. The novel's fully realized characterizations and its treatment of setting made it artistically superior to other midwestern farm novels of the time.

Rölvaag's succeeding novels, *Peder Victorious* and *Their Fathers' God,* dealt not with the pioneering experience but with the tensions between generations caused by religious and cultural differences.

Carl Sandburg (1878–1967)—The son of poor Swedish immigrants who settled in Galesburg, Illinois, Carl Sandburg held various short-term jobs as a youth—newsboy, janitor, milkman and dishwasher. Driven by a searching spirit of restlessness, he travelled to the wheat fields of Kansas and to the Rocky Mountains for a time. After serving in the Spanish-American War, Sandburg attended Lombard College. During the years that followed, he became an organizer for the Social Democratic party in Wisconsin, secretary to the mayor of Milwaukee, a journalist with the Chicago *Daily News*, and poet laureate of Illinois. In 1926 he was awarded the Pulitzer Prize for his two-volume biography *Abraham Lincoln: The Prairie Years*.

The America Sandburg knew and wrote about was the Midwest—the industrial life of Chicago, the prairie cornfields and agricultural centers, and "the people." In his use of colloquial language, the poet achieved a sense of actuality. Abandoning conventional rhyme and meter, he learned free-verse techniques which included the grammatical paralleling and counterpointing of phrases and clauses. Sandburg also experimented with adapting the Japanese haiku in poems like "Fog" and "Wistful."

Most of Sandburg's verse is collected in *Complete Poems*. Other major works include his autobiography, *Always the Young Strangers*, as well as the biographies *Abraham Lincoln: The Prairie Years* and *The War Years*.

Eric Sevareid (1912–) was raised in Velva, North Dakota, a wheat-growing township in which his father was the local banker. He received his B.A. degree from the University of Minnesota, worked for the *Minneapolis Star* as a reporter, and later became an editor on the staff of the *New York Herald Tribune*. Since 1939, Sevareid has become internationally recognized as a Columbia Broadcasting System correspondent and analyst of world affairs.

In his correspondence, his reminiscences, and his social commentaries, Sevareid has exhibited two midwestern qualities: Americanism and optimism. His attitude is that of a humanitarian. The autobiographical narratives *Canoeing with the Cree* and *Not So Wild a Dream* and the short radio talks *In One Ear* and *Small Sounds in the Night* are some of his journalistic writings.

William Stafford (1914–), a native of Hutchinson, Kansas, has worked as a laborer in sugar-beet fields, in an oil refinery, and in the United States Forest Service. He received his B.A. and M.A. degrees from the University of Kansas, and his Ph.D. from the University of Iowa. Several of the thirty-five poems he submitted as his doctoral dissertation under the title *Winterward* were later drawn upon in the volumes *West of Your City, Traveling through the Dark*, and *The Rescued Years*. For more than twenty-five years, the poet has also taught at universities in Kansas, Iowa, California, Indiana and Oregon. Stafford served as Consultant in Poetry to the Library of Congress in 1970–71.

Stafford's poetry reveals a primary thematic concern: reconciling the values of his boyhood world in Kansas with the mechanized world which surrounds his adult life. Many of his poems are dominated by a father figure who represents an ardent and sustaining moral influence derived directly from an intimate familiarity with the land and the wilderness. His use of the editorial "we" universalizes his personal experience. In commenting on his imagistic verse, Stafford has said: "Often my poetry is discursive and reminiscent, or at least is that way at one level: it delivers a sense of place and event; it has narrative impulses. Forms are not usually much evident, though tendencies and patterns are occasionally flirted with."

Ruth Suckow (1892–1960), born and reared in Iowa, was the daughter of a Congregational minister. Having watched her father prepare his sermons, she became accustomed to the writing process at an early age. After receiving B.A. and M.A. degrees from the University of Denver, where she served as English department head, Suckow held other positions including that of editorial assistant for *The Midland* magazine.

Suckow showed sensitivity and understanding of her characters, and used a straightforward style distinguished by detactment and almost stark simplicity. A gifted regionalist, she depicted Iowa settings with convincing authenticity. As the author herself pointed out in an essay on midwestern literature, "What we have in the Middle West is a particular way, a fresh way, in which the ancient stream of life manifests itself, colored and shaped by local conditions."

Among Suckow's representative works are the short-story volumes *Iowa Interiors* and *Children and Older People*, and the novels *Country People* and *The Folks*.

Kurt Vonnegut, Jr. (1922–) is the product of a solid middle-class upbringing in Indianapolis, Indiana. He studied at the University of Chicago and graduated from Cornell. Captured by the Germans during the Second World War, he was a prisoner of war and survivor of the fire-bombing of Dresden. Before devoting himself to a literary career in 1949, Vonnegut worked as a public relations executive for the General Electric Company. He has also taught in the Writers' Workship at the University of Iowa and is now at Harvard University.

Vonnegut is a satirist ultimately concerned about the problem of self-definition in an increasingly dehumanized America. His extensive social commentaries include big business, politics, nationalism, war, and the domination of cities by one industry or one group of industries. Not always a conventional writer, he relies on recurrent motifs, thematic episodes, and time fragments when not using a chronological pattern of development in his novels. His short stories, though often in a science fiction mode, are traditional in structure.

Among his published works are *Welcome to the Monkey House; Cat's Gradle; Slaughterhouse-Five; God Bless You, Mr. Rosewater; Breakfast of Champions;* and *Slapstick.*

Marnie Walsh (–) spent her formative years in North Dakota near Sioux land. She received B.A. and M.A. degrees in English and creative writing from the University of New Mexico. Some of her poems have been included in *Dacotah Territory,* a publication of Moorhead State College in Minnesota; others have appeared in the anthology *Voices from Wah' Kon-Tah: Contemporary Poetry of Native Americans.*

Walsh's work is generally narrative and reflects her ethnic heritage. It typifies American Indians whose wisdom is derived from an intimacy with the wilderness, and whose lives are enacted according to the tribal rituals and symbolic patterns that bring them into harmony with the forces of nature. Also adversely affected by a technological society, they are consistently defined in Walsh's verse by the qualities of reticence and estrangement, an insight common to the Indian poems of James Wright and William Stafford as well.

James Wright (1927–), originally from Martins Ferry, Ohio, has studied at Kenyon College, in Vienna as a Fulbright scholar, and at the University of Washington. In 1972 he was awarded the Pulitzer Prize for *Collected Poems* and received the Fellowship of the Academy of American Poets "for distinguished poetic achievement." His poems have appeared in many journals, among them *The New Yorker, Poetry, Harper's* and *Yale Review.* The poet has also held teaching positions in English at the University of Minnesota, at Macalester College, and at Hunter College.

In the finest of Wright's poems like "A Blessing," a pattern of observed images is transformed into a personal and subjective instant of emotion. Often the images are metaphoric and work by means of personification. That the fundamental rhythm is the rhythm of images is also evident in his lyrics. Directness, midwestern regionalism, structural and technical excellence, and the use of colloquial language are other notable aspects in Wright's work.

The poet's most characteristic books of verse include *The Green Wall, Saint Judas, The Branch Will Not Break,* and *Collected Poems.*

Richard Wright (1908–1960), discontented with the poverty and intellectual barrenness of his childhood in Mississippi and Tennessee, went North where he imagined that "life could be lived in dignity." Arriving in Chicago in 1927, he soon encountered loneliness, fear, and suffering among the city's black population. His disillusionment led him to adopt a Marxist point of view from 1932 to 1942. Besides holding membership in the Federal Writers' Project, Wright directed the Federal Negro Theater. His later years were spent in France as an expatriate.

Native Son was Wright's attempt to translate his Chicago experiences into a novel which "would be so hard and deep that [white readers] would have to face it without the consolation of tears." It emphasized black society amid deterministic and materialistic forces of Northern urban surroundings. Like that of other literary naturalists, Wright's prose was sometimes awkward in style, structure, and character portrayal—particularly when depicting American whites.

In addition to *Native Son,* Wright's publications include *Black Boy,* an autobiography of his youth in the South; *Uncle Tom's Cabin* and *Eight Men,* two short-story volumes; and the novels *The Outsider, The Long Dream,* and *Lawd Today.*

(*continued from page iv*)

Copyright 1919 by B. W. Huebsch, Copyright 1947 by Eleanor Copenhaver Anderson. Reprinted by permission of The Viking Press.

CARL SANDBURG, "Chicago." From *Chicago Poems* by Carl Sandburg, copyright 1916 by Holt, Rinehart and Winston, Inc.; copyright 1944 by Carl Sandburg. Reprinted by permission of Harcourt Brace Jovanovich, Inc. "Prayers of Steel." From *Cornhuskers* by Carl Sandburg, copyright 1918 by Holt, Rinehart and Winston, Inc.; copyright 1946 by Carl Sandburg. Reprinted by permission of Harcourt Brace Jovanovich, Inc.

PHILIP LEVINE, "Coming Home." From *They Feed They Lion* by Philip Levine. Copyright © 1972 by Philip Levine. This poem appeared originally in the Hudson Review. Reprinted by permission of Atheneum Publishers.

THEODORE ROETHKE, "Dolor," copyright 1943 by Modern Poetry Association, Inc.; "Highway: Michigan," copyright 1940 by Theodore Roethke; "Moss-Gathering," copyright © 1946 by Editorial Publications, Inc. all from *The Collected Poems of Theodore Roethke*. Used by permission of Doubleday & Company, Inc.

JAMES WRIGHT, "A Blessing." Copyright © 1958, 1961 by James Wright. Reprinted from *Collected Poems* by permission of Wesleyan University Press. "A Blessing" first appeared in *Poetry*.

ERNEST HEMINGWAY, "The Three-Day Blow." Reprinted with the permission of Charles Scribner's Sons from *Short Stories of Ernest Hemingway*. Copyright 1936 by Ernest Hemingway.

MARNIE WALSH, "Thomas Iron-Eyes." From *Voices From Wah'kon-Tah* by Marnie Walsh. Reprinted by permission of International Publishers.

OLE RÖLVAAG, "Home-Founding." Sec. IV (pp. 36–42) in *Giants In The Earth* by O. E. Rölvaag. Copyright, 1927 by Harper & Row, Publishers, Inc.; renewed, 1955 by Jennie Marie Berdahl Rölvaag. By permission of Harper & Row, Publishers, Inc.

HARRY MARK PETRAKIS, "Pericles on 31st Street." From *Pericles on 31st Street* by Harry Mark Petrakis. Reprinted by permission of the author.

JAMES T. FARRELL, "The Fastest Runner on Sixty-First Street." Reprinted from *An American Dream Girl* by James T. Farrell by permission of the publisher, Vanguard Press, Inc. Copyright 1950 by James T. Farrell. Copyright renewed 1977 by James T. Farrell.

PAUL LAURENCE DUNBAR, "We Wear the Mask." Reprinted by permission of Dodd, Mead & Company, Inc. from *The Complete Poems of Paul Laurence Dunbar*.

LANGSTON HUGHES, "I, Too, Sing America." Copyright 1926 by Alfred A. Knopf, Inc. and renewed 1954 by Langston Hughes. Reprinted from *Selected Poems of Langston Hughes*, by Langston Hughes, by permission of Alfred A. Knopf, Inc. "Jazz, Jive, and Jam." Reprinted with permission of Farrar, Straus & Giroux, Inc. from *The Best of Simple* by Langston Hughes. Copyright © 1961 by Langston Hughes. "Jazz, Jive, and Jam" originally appeared in *Simple Stakes A Claim*, copyright 1953, 1954, 1955, 1956, © 1957 by Langston Hughes.

ROBERT HAYDEN, "Frederick Douglass," "Runagate Runagate." From *Angle of Ascent*, New and Selected Poems by Robert Hayden, with the permission of Liveright Publishing Corporation. Copyright © 1975, 1972, 1970, 1966, by Robert Hayden.

WILLA CATHER, "The Sentimentality of William Tavener." From *Willa Cather's Collected Short Fiction*, 1892–1912 (Rev. Ed.) with introduction by Mildred R. Bennett. Edited by Virginia Faulkner by permission of the University of Nebraska Press Copyright © 1965, 1970 by the University of Nebraska Press.

GWENDOLYN BROOKS, "Kitchenette Building." Copyright 1945 by Gwendolyn Brooks

Blakely. "What Shall I Give My Children? Who Are Poor," and "Life for my child is simple and is good." Copyright 1949 by Gwendolyn Brooks Blakely. "The Bean Eaters." Copyright © 1959 by Gwendolyn Brooks. From *The World of Gwendolyn Brooks* by Gwendolyn Brooks. All reprinted by permission of Harper & Row, Publishers, Inc.

F. SCOTT FITZGERALD, "Winter Dreams." Reprinted with the permission of Charles Scribner's Sons from *All The Sad Young Men* by F. Scott Fitzgerald. Copyright 1922 Frances Scott Fitzgerald Lanahan.

JAMES WRIGHT, "Complaint." Copyright © 1958, 1961 by James Wright. Reprinted from *Collected Poems* by permission of Wesleyan University Press.

WILLIAM STAFFORD, "One Home." Copyright © 1960 by William Stafford. "Father's Voice." Copyright © 1967 by William Stafford. From *Stories That Could Be True* (1977) by William Stafford. All reprinted by permission of Harper & Row, Publishers, Inc.

ROBERT HAYDEN, "Those Winter Sundays." From *Angle of Ascent*, New and Selected Poems, by Robert Hayden, with the permission of Liveright Publishing Corporation. Copyright © 1975, 1972, 1970, 1966, by Robert Hayden.

SINCLAIR LEWIS, Chapter One from *Babbitt* by Sinclair Lewis, copyright 1922, by Harcourt Brace Jovanovich, Inc.; renewed, 1950 by Sinclair Lewis. Reprinted by permission of the publishers.

EDGAR LEE MASTERS, "Washington McNeely." From *Spoon River Anthology*, 1931, Macmillan Publishing Co., Inc. Reprinted by permission of Ellen C. Masters.

HAMLIN GARLAND, "The Return of a Private." From *Main Travelled Roads* by Hamlin Garland. Reprinted by permission of New American Library, Inc.

VACHEL LINDSAY, "Flower-Bed Buffaloes." From *Collected Poems* by Vachel Lindsay. Reprinted by permission of Nicholas C. Lindsay on behalf of the Estate of Vachel Lindsay. "Factory Windows Are Always Broken." From *Collected Poems* by Vachel Lindsay. Copyright 1914 by Macmillan Publishing Co., Inc., renewed 1942 by Elizabeth C. Lindsay.

RICHARD WRIGHT, from pp. 14–19 in *Native Son* by Richard Wright. Copyright 1940 by Richard Wright; renewed 1968 by Ellen Wright. Reprinted by permission of Harper & Row, Publishers, Inc.

CARL SANDBURG, "The People Will Live On." From *The People, Yes* by Carl Sandburg, copyright, 1936, by Harcourt Brace Jovanovich, Inc.; copyright, 1964, by Carl Sandburg. Reprinted by permission of the publishers.

LANGSTON HUGHES, "Let America Be America Again." From *A New Song* by Langston Hughes. Reprinted by permission of Harold Ober Associates Incorporated. Copyright 1938 by Langston Hughes. Renewed.

ERIC SEVAREID, "The American Dream." © 1968 by Eric Sevareid. Reprinted by permission of Harold Matson Company.

KURT VONNEGUT, JR., "Adam." Excerpted from the book *Welcome to the Monkey House* by Kurt Vonnegut Jr. Copyright © 1954 by Kurt Vonnegut Jr. Originally published in *Cosmopolitan*. Reprinted by permission of Delacorte Press-Seymour Lawrence.

PICTURE CREDITS

Page 2: George Caleb Bingham, *Fur Traders Descending the Missouri* (The Metropolitan Museum of Art, Morris K. Jesup Fund, 1933)

Page 6: Thomas Hart Benton, *July Hay* (The Metropolitan Museum of Art, George A. Hearn Fund, 1943)

Acknowledgments

Page 25: Tombstones (© 1978 Yvonne Freund)
Page 29: Small Town (Webb Photos, St. Paul, Minnesota. Photo by Ted McDonough)
Page 41: Charles Burchfield, *Winter Twilight*, 1930 (Collection of Whitney Museum of American Art, New York. Photograph Geoffrey Clements, New York)
Page 53: Illinois Farm (© Earth Scenes. Photo by George F. Godfrey)
Page 66: Barn raising on the Rainy River (Collection of Minnesota Historical Society)
Page 73: Mr. Jerns, Dry Valley, Custer County, Nebraska 1886. (Solomon D. Butcher Collection. Nebraska State Historical Society)
Page 112: Grant Wood, *American Gothic*. (Courtesy of The Art Institute of Chicago)
Page 119: Michigan Farmer (Photo Researchers, Inc., New York. Photo by Joe Munroe)
Page 147: Illinois Cornfield in Winter (© Earth Scenes. Photo by George F. Godfrey)
Page 173: Barn and Hay (© 1978 Yvonne Freund)
Page 185: Cheap, Unending Energy—A Windmill (© Earth Scenes. Photo by Leonard Lee Rue III)

Index